Remarks on London: being an exact survey of the cities of London and Westminster, Borough of Southwark, and the suburbs and liberties contiguous to them, ... By W. Stow.

William. Stow

ECCO
PRINT EDITIONS

Remarks on London: being an exact survey of the cities of London and Westminster, Borough of Southwark, and the suburbs and liberties contiguous to them, ... By W. Stow.
Stow, William.
ESTCID: T100354
Reproduction from British Library

London : printed for T. Norris, and H. Tracy, 1722.
[12],176,[4]p. ; 12°

Eighteenth Century
Collections Online
Print Editions

Gale ECCO Print Editions

Relive history with *Eighteenth Century Collections Online*, now available in print for the independent historian and collector. This series includes the most significant English-language and foreign-language works printed in Great Britain during the eighteenth century, and is organized in seven different subject areas including literature and language; medicine, science, and technology; and religion and philosophy. The collection also includes thousands of important works from the Americas.

The eighteenth century has been called "The Age of Enlightenment." It was a period of rapid advance in print culture and publishing, in world exploration, and in the rapid growth of science and technology – all of which had a profound impact on the political and cultural landscape. At the end of the century the American Revolution, French Revolution and Industrial Revolution, perhaps three of the most significant events in modern history, set in motion developments that eventually dominated world political, economic, and social life.

In a groundbreaking effort, Gale initiated a revolution of its own: digitization of epic proportions to preserve these invaluable works in the largest online archive of its kind. Contributions from major world libraries constitute over 175,000 original printed works. Scanned images of the actual pages, rather than transcriptions, recreate the works *as they first appeared.*

Now for the first time, these high-quality digital scans of original works are available via print-on-demand, making them readily accessible to libraries, students, independent scholars, and readers of all ages.

For our initial release we have created seven robust collections to form one the world's most comprehensive catalogs of 18th century works.

Initial Gale ECCO Print Editions collections include:

History and Geography
Rich in titles on English life and social history, this collection spans the world as it was known to eighteenth-century historians and explorers. Titles include a wealth of travel accounts and diaries, histories of nations from throughout the world, and maps and charts of a world that was still being discovered. Students of the War of American Independence will find fascinating accounts from the British side of conflict.

Social Science

Delve into what it was like to live during the eighteenth century by reading the first-hand accounts of everyday people, including city dwellers and farmers, businessmen and bankers, artisans and merchants, artists and their patrons, politicians and their constituents. Original texts make the American, French, and Industrial revolutions vividly contemporary.

Medicine, Science and Technology

Medical theory and practice of the 1700s developed rapidly, as is evidenced by the extensive collection, which includes descriptions of diseases, their conditions, and treatments. Books on science and technology, agriculture, military technology, natural philosophy, even cookbooks, are all contained here.

Literature and Language

Western literary study flows out of eighteenth-century works by Alexander Pope, Daniel Defoe, Henry Fielding, Frances Burney, Denis Diderot, Johann Gottfried Herder, Johann Wolfgang von Goethe, and others. Experience the birth of the modern novel, or compare the development of language using dictionaries and grammar discourses.

Religion and Philosophy

The Age of Enlightenment profoundly enriched religious and philosophical understanding and continues to influence present-day thinking. Works collected here include masterpieces by David Hume, Immanuel Kant, and Jean-Jacques Rousseau, as well as religious sermons and moral debates on the issues of the day, such as the slave trade. The Age of Reason saw conflict between Protestantism and Catholicism transformed into one between faith and logic -- a debate that continues in the twenty-first century.

Law and Reference

This collection reveals the history of English common law and Empire law in a vastly changing world of British expansion. Dominating the legal field is the *Commentaries of the Law of England* by Sir William Blackstone, which first appeared in 1765. Reference works such as almanacs and catalogues continue to educate us by revealing the day-to-day workings of society.

Fine Arts

The eighteenth-century fascination with Greek and Roman antiquity followed the systematic excavation of the ruins at Pompeii and Herculaneum in southern Italy; and after 1750 a neoclassical style dominated all artistic fields. The titles here trace developments in mostly English-language works on painting, sculpture, architecture, music, theater, and other disciplines. Instructional works on musical instruments, catalogs of art objects, comic operas, and more are also included.

The BiblioLife Network

This project was made possible in part by the BiblioLife Network (BLN), a project aimed at addressing some of the huge challenges facing book preservationists around the world. The BLN includes libraries, library networks, archives, subject matter experts, online communities and library service providers. We believe every book ever published should be available as a high-quality print reproduction; printed on-demand anywhere in the world. This insures the ongoing accessibility of the content and helps generate sustainable revenue for the libraries and organizations that work to preserve these important materials.

The following book is in the "public domain" and represents an authentic reproduction of the text as printed by the original publisher. While we have attempted to accurately maintain the integrity of the original work, there are sometimes problems with the original work or the micro-film from which the books were digitized. This can result in minor errors in reproduction. Possible imperfections include missing and blurred pages, poor pictures, markings and other reproduction issues beyond our control. Because this work is culturally important, we have made it available as part of our commitment to protecting, preserving, and promoting the world's literature.

GUIDE TO FOLD-OUTS MAPS and OVERSIZED IMAGES

The book you are reading was digitized from microfilm captured over the past thirty to forty years. Years after the creation of the original microfilm, the book was converted to digital files and made available in an online database.

In an online database, page images do not need to conform to the size restrictions found in a printed book. When converting these images back into a printed bound book, the page sizes are standardized in ways that maintain the detail of the original. For large images, such as fold-out maps, the original page image is split into two or more pages

Guidelines used to determine how to split the page image follows:

• Some images are split vertically; large images require vertical and horizontal splits.
• For horizontal splits, the content is split left to right.
• For vertical splits, the content is split from top to bottom.
• For both vertical and horizontal splits, the image is processed from top left to bottom right.

REMARKS
ON
LONDON;
BEING AN
Exact SURVEY
OF THE

CITIES of *London* and *Weſtminſter*, Borough
of *Southwark*, and the Suburbs and Liberties contiguous
to them, by ſhewing where every Street, Lane, Court,
Alley, Green, Yard, Cloſe, Square, or any other Place,
by what Name ſoever called, is ſituated in the moſt
Famous Metropolis; ſo that Letters from the General
and Penny-Poſt Offices cannot Miſcarry for the future
An Hiſtorical Account of all the Cathedrals, Collegiate
and Parochial Churches, Chapels, and Tabernacles,
within the Bill of Mortality Shewing therein the ſett
Time of publick Prayer, Celebrating the Sacraments,
Morning and Evening Lectures, and Preaching Sermons,
both Ordinary and Extraordinary; with many curious
Obſervations. Places to which Penny-poſt Letters and
Parcels are carried, with Liſts of Fairs and Markets
What places ſends Members to Parliament To what
Inns Flying-Coaches, Stage-Coaches, Waggons and
Carriers come, and the Days they go out; lately col-
lected. Keys, Wharfs and Plying-places on the River
of *Thames.* Inſtructions about the General Poſt-Office
Deſcription of the great and croſs Roads from one City
and eminent Town to another, in *England* and *Wales.* A
perpetual Almanack The Rates of Caochmen, Chairmen, Carmen, and Watermen A perpetaul Tide-Table;
and ſeveral other neceſſary Tables, adapted to Trade
and other Buſineſs.
All Alphabetically digeſted; and verv uſeful for all
'Gentlemen, Ladies, Merchants, Tradeſmen, both in City
and Country The like never before extant.

By *W. STOW.*

LONDON Printed for *T. Norris* at the *Looking glaſs,*
and *H. Tracy* at the *Three Bibles,* on *London-Bridge.* 1722.

The Epistle Dedicatory.

To *his Royal Highness*, G E O R G E, *Prince of* Wales.

S I R,

I Must acknowledge this Survey of the Cities of *London* and *Westminster*, the Borough of *Southwark*, with the Suburbs and Liberties contiguous or adjacent to them, is too mean a Trifle to make a Present of to your most Illustrious Person; but as an indubitable Right of Succession (except an Act of Contingency, which God forbid, should deprive these three Kingdoms of so great a Blessing) will bring these most populous Places under your Dominion, the humble Offering claims your Royal Patronage.

Before the dreadful Conflagration, which in 1666, laid the most famous Metropolis of *Great Britain* in Ashes, the Architecture of its Buildings, both publick and private, were very ordinary and irregular; but the ever-wakeful Eye of Providence, having

A 2 always

always a tender regard of preſerving this
Nation from the Fury of Popery, Slavery,
and arbitrary Power, in ſetting your ſacred
Father on the *Britiſh* Throne, it is my
Preſumption to think, that Fate contriv'd
the Magnificence of this great City by
Fire, for the better Reception of a King,
who may juſtly claim the Title of *Defender*
of the Faith.

In the bleſſed Progeny of you and your
Royal Conſort, will all the Cities in your
Father's Dominions, both here and beyond
Sea, rejoice and be always happy : For
the good Order and Government of this
moſt populous Place, which, *Phœnix* like
is riſen out of its Aſhes, and become again
the chiefeſt *Emporium*, or Town of Trade
in the whole World, was conſpicuous e-
nough to all who eſteem you the Darling
of Mankind, when your Royal Highneſs
was left ſole Regent of the Land ; and at
a Time too, when a vile Rabble attempted (but in vain) to eclipſe the Glory of
glorious *Auguſta* with Anarchy and Con-
fuſion.

But not to be too prolix, vouchſafe
(Great Sir) to permit me, to wiſh You,
your Royal Conſort, and Illuſtrious Iſſue,
long Life, Health and Proſperity, mounted

The *Epiſtle Dedicatory.*

ed by Guardian-Angels above the Reach
of Inconſtancy and Envy; whilſt in the
mean time, I preſume to ſubſcribe my
ſelf,

S I R,

Your Royal Highneſs's

Moſt humbly devoted

to command,

W. Stow.

THE

THE
PREFACE.

WHAT has been so long most earnestly desired by all People of this Nation, for the universal Use of City, Town and Country, in the way of Trade and Business, I may say, if ever any Book yet was Multum in parvo, this small Treatise, for its concise Description of the largest City in Europe, with several other necessary Subjects, may justly challenge the Motto. I have read of some Cities in Asia and Africk, of 70, 80, or 90 Miles in Circumference; but their comparing the Proximity or Closeness of the Buildings in London, and its Suburbs and Liberties, with the great Vacuities of large Courts and Gardens, both behind and betwixt the Houses of what are called Great Cities beyond Sea, it may be said to be the greatest and mostly inhabited City in the World.

Greek and Latin Historians give us most pompous Relations of the vast Extent of Babylon, and other Eastern Cities; and Nineveh, for its Spaciousness, is by way of Excellency, call'd, in Scripture, That great City; but yet London is abundantly larger: For to take the Description of every Place in it, and Places contiguous or adjacent thereto, required some Weeks, whereas Jonah was (without taking Notice how long he might stay in each Street, to preach Repentance to the wicked Ninevites) but three Days in traversing its Bounds: Besides, I must observe, that the Cities of London and Westminster, with their Suburbs and Liberties, and Southwark, cannot be less than 25 Miles in Circumference; which Spot contains about 70,000 Dwelling-Houses, and therefore much larger than Paris, Madrid, Vienna,

The PREFACE.

Vienna, or Conſtantinople ; ſo that there is no Occaſion to fortify it with Stone-Walls, Bulwarks and Towers ; for as its Inhabitants are computed to be about 1,500,000 Souls, among which are above 100,000 Men fit to bear Arms, they are able to give a Field Battle to the greateſt Monarch or Potentate on Earth : Nay, was London now, as Rome and Carthage did before in three Punick Wars, ſtand in Competition with any other City for univerſal Monarchy, or to be Miſtreſs of the whole Globe, the Engliſh would undoubtedly win the glorious Prize, and crown Britannia with freſh Laurels.

As I ſaid above, a great many Days were ſpent to take an exact Survey of this City, and all Places about it, the like whereof was never performed before, in ſhewing where every Street, Lane, Court, Alley, Yard, Green, Cloſe, Square, or any other Place, by what Name ſoever call'd, is ſituated ; for our Maps, or Proſpects of London, Weſtminſter, and Southwark, made more for Ornament than Uſe, do not deſcribe a fourth part of the Places contain'd in 'em . Moreover, was a Map 30 Foot long, and 20 deep to be projected, yet would it not comprehend the whole Town to an exact Scale of Feet ; which is the leaſt Denomination that can well be made uſe of in ſuch Mathematical Deſigns. But ſuppoſe a very large Map could be drawn, ſtill the Inconveniency would be ſuch, that the Inſpector muſt have a magnifying Glaſs to read what he looks for ; and then alſo may be pore long enough before he can find the Place ſought for, without ſuch a Book as this, to direct in what part of the Town it lies : For tho' there be certain Rules in Geography for finding out Cities, Towns, or Villages, tho' a Man was never at 'em, by knowing the Longitudes and Latitudes thereof ; yet in the other-Projection abovementioned, Places cannot be found out, without knowing their Scite by ſuch a Guide or Directory here offer'd you, for Service as well as Pleaſure.

Again, as it is many Years ſince theſe Maps of London were made, they muſt be now moſt imperfect, if we

do

The PREFACE.

do but confider, fuch additional Buildings have been joined to the Suburbs and Liberties of London *and* Weftminfter, *that, put together, are not much inferior to the Circuit of* Canterbury *or* Exeter, Winchefter *or* Carlifle, *nor of any other City in* England *or* Scotland, *fo not deciiher'd in thofe Poliographical Pieces.*

Now in this Book, which every Man of Bufinefs ought to make his Pocket-Companion, there is no Place, great or fmall, in and about the Cities of London *and* Weftminfter, *or the Borough of* Southwark, *which extend themfelves over no fmall Tract of* Middlefex *and* Surry, *even to the Counties of* Kent *and* Effex, *but what are fet fo plain, in demonftrating their Situation by fome Hall, College, School, noted Houfe, or fome other publick Edifice, that a meer Stranger may eafily go to it without afking the way. As, fuppofe a Stranger at* Whitechapel *was to go to* Angel-Court *at* Weftminfter, *but perhaps knows not in what part of the City it lies ; why then looking for the Place in this Book, he finds it is in* Long Ditch ; *and if he is ignorant of that Place alfo, he muft farther fearch this Guide or Directory, which is Alphabetically digefted, which will fhew him it is at* Story's Gate *at* St. James's Park : *Thus one Place directing to another, he finds out that he knows, and fo goes more readily to that where Bufinefs requires his Attendance. But obferve, fome Places are called* Great, *fome* Little, *fome* Old, *and fome* New, *as* Great Tower-Street, Little Tower-Street, Old Bond-Street, New Bond-Street ; *however, I have fometimes omitted Adjectives* Great, *where a Street is univerfally known ; therefore, if you find not the Places you look for under the Head you fearch, have no Regard to the Word* Great, *but have Recourfe to the Street it felf ; as for Example, if you would look for* Great Queen-Street *in* Drury-Lane, *you will not find it under the Letter* G, *but* Q; *and fo of fome few more.*

, *The*

The PREFACE.

There is no Place which (to the beſt of my Knowledge) have eſcap'd; excepting Thorough-fares with no Tenements in them; or here and there a ſmall Ally which has no Name; or ſome backward Place, which now, thro' Time, or other Caſualties, is come to Deſolation, and has at this Day nothing but Ruins, to ſhew it was once the Poſſeſſion of poor Inhabitants.

Alſo the Deſign of this Piece is to ſhew People how to ſpell and write proper their Superſcriptions on Letters; for a bad Hand and wrong Orthography, or falſe Spelling, a Fault too incident to many Men, as well as Women in general, have cauſed the Miſcarriage of many Letters; which is not only a Loſs to the Crown, as the General and Penny poſt Offices are a Branch of the Royal Revenue; but may alſo prove a great Detriment to the Writer, as well as the Perſon wrote to. But yet let a Man write never ſo well, his Letter may miſcarry, by not punctually obſerving in what Part of this Great Town the Place lies in, to which he directs it., for ſome People are ſo ignorant, eſpecially in the Country, as to think London, Weſtminſter, and Southwark, is all London, becauſe contiguous to one another; which is a grand Miſtake; for if you ſhould ſend a Letter to a Friend in King-Street which is in Weſtminſter, but write at the bottom of the Superſcription, London; how ſhould the Poſtman know whether you mean King-ſtreet by Guildhall, King-ſtreet on Great Tower-hill, King-ſtreet in Spittle-Fields, King-ſtreet in Prince's ſtreet near St. Anne's Church, King ſtreet near Golden ſquare, King-ſtreet in Dean-ſtreet by Soho-ſquare, King ſtreet in Covent garden, King-ſtreet by Hay's Court near Newport Market, King-ſtreet in Upper Moor-fields, King-ſtreet by Old-ſtreet Square, King ſtreet by Bloomsbury Square, King-ſtreet by St. James's Square, King ſtreet near the Six Dials, or King ſtreet in the Mint? For many Streets, and other Places, bear one and the ſame Name; but here they are ſet down ſo obvious to every intelligent

Reader,

The PREFACE.

Reader, and to be understood likewise by Persons of the meanest Capacity, that such Mistakes may be easily avoided for the future, by seeing what Places lie properly in London, Westminster, *or* Southwark; *signified or denoted by the Capital Letters* L. S. W. *without regarding the Matter sometimes following them; which is some historical or other remarkable Account of that Place in particular from others.*

So large is the Extent of London, Westminster *and* Southwark, *with their Suburbs and Liberties, that no Coachman nor Porter knows every Place in them; therefore this Book may also be a Guide for them, and prevent as hath been too often done, their losing any more Portmanteaus, Trunks, Boxes, or Parcels. Furthermore, to make it as compleat as may be, for the Usefulness of all Gentlemen, Merchants, Tradesmen, Clapmen, County People, and others in any way of Business, taking into Consideration that it is many Years since a List was perfectly taken of all the Inns to which Flying Coaches, Stage Coaches, Waggons, or Carriers Pack-Horses come to, in or about* London *or* Southwark, *and the Day they set out again; for many of them have removed their Stations within these few Years; I have also been at no small Cost, as well as great Pains, to make a new one. And that it may be serviceable to such who have Business by Water, here is shewed on what Part of the River of* Thames, *from* Mill bank *to* Limehouse-hole *on the North side thereof; and from* Strandgate *to* West-Lane, *on the South side, the principal Keys, Wharfs, and Plying-places, for Bargemen, Lightermen and Watermen, are seated, for the Conveniency of carrying Goods or Passengers, above or below* London Bridge; *with a perpetual Tide Table, whereby People may know when to go by Water to Places situated Eastward or Westward. Besides, that People may not be imposed upon, either by Land or Water, I have here inserted the Rates of* Hackney-Coachmen, Chairmen, and Watermen, *with Directions where to complain against them, upon any just and lawful Occasion.* Again

The PREFACE.

gain, to make it as necessary as possibly can be, for Trade
d Business, you have here an exact Account of all the
st notable Fairs, both fix'd and moveable, kept in every
onth of the Year, in England and Wales. Instruc-
ons about the General-post Letters, whether Domestick
Foreign; with a List of the Post-Towns in South-
itain. A List of the Places to which the six Penny-
st Offices send Letters and Parcels, and how often in
e Day. A List of all the Market-Towns in England
d Wales, with the Days of the Week whereon kept.
List of the Cities, Towns and Boroughs that send
embers to Parliament. A perpetual Almanack, for
ding out Time past, present, and to come. Several
cessary Tables, with the Use of them. And an exact
escription of the great Roads from London to all the
nsiderable Cities and Towns in England and Wales,
gether with the cross Roads from one City or eminent
wn to another, in measured Miles and Furlongs, the
stances thereof being taken from the Standard in
rnhill in London, convenient for all Travellers; to
om I give Notice, That the great Roads commencing
m London, and being carried on to the Extremity
the Kingdom, the farthest Place is only named in the
tle of the Road, notwithstanding that many much more
nsiderable Places are passed through, as in the Road
m London to Berwick, you see Huntington, Gran-
am, Newark, York, Durham, Newcastle, are not
entioned in the Title, tho' in prosecuting the way you
e led through them; and so the same of other Roads
other Places. And where any Abbreviations are used
any part of this Book, that it might not swell to too
g a Bulk for the Pocket, the Explanation of 'em is
ade easie to the meanest Capacity. Moreover, for the
se of Gentlemen, Ladies, and others, whose Circum-
ances have mounted them above the Hurry of Trade and
usiness, and therefore have more Time and Leisure per-
itted 'em for publick Devotion, here is a compleat List
f all the Cathedrals, Churches and Chapels within the

Bill

The PREFACE.

Bill of Mortality, with the set Time of reading therein publick Prayers, receiving the Sacrament, performing Morning and Evening Lectures, and preaching both ordinary and extraordinary Sermons.

But it may be Objected, by Men whose Conceit and Ignorance prompt them to carp at other Mens Works, not mend them, Why I should only place St. Margaret's Parish to the City of Westminster, and not the Parishes of St. Martin in the Fields, St. Clement Danes, St. Mary le Savoy, St. Paul Covent-Garden, St. James and St. Anne, as being in the Liberty thereof: To which I reply, Because Use and Custom having gain'd so far as to ascribe them to London, and the Directions herein being so plain, that any Place in those Parishes may be easily found out, I would not altogether deviate from what has been habitual to the Generality of the common People by long Practice. In fine, I have done my best Endeavours, to make it universally serviceable to Foreigners that can speak or write English, as well as to those of my own Nation: And the Project has been so well approved of by some ingenious Gentlemen of my Acquaintance, who are going to Travel, that they assure me they will set others upon the like Invention of Surveying the Capital Cities of Europe; which will be highly beneficial to Merchants holding a better Correspondence, tho' ever so remote from one another: So if this Piece finds a favourable Acceptance among my Countrymen, it is all the Favour the Author expects for his extream Labour, of traversing 2,175 Streets, Lanes Courts, and other Places; which tracing backwards and forwards, comprehended near 250 Miles; a Preambulation never yet performed by any other Man besides my self, in any Age past, nor this wherein we live.

T H I

THE
Stranger's Guide:
OR,
Traveller's Directory.

A B

Abchurch Lane, by St. Mary Abchurch near Lombard Street, L.

Acorn Alley, in Bishopsgatestreet without, L.

Adam a digging Yard, in Peter Street, W.

Adam and Eve Alley, in Whitechapel, L.

Adam's Court, in Pig Street near Threadneedle Street, L.

Addle Hill, in Thames Street, L.

Addle Street, by Aldermanbury, L. In this Street are built Brewers and Plaisterers Halls.

Ailesbury Street, by Clerkenwell Green, L.

Albemarl Street, in Pickadilly, L. It is built where once stood the House of the Earl of *Clarendon*, heretofore Lord High Chanceller of *England*; and afterwards call'd *Dunkirk* House, upon his advising King *Charles* the second to sell that most important Town to *Lewis* the fourteenth, then King of *France*.

Aldermanbury, by St. Alphage's Church, by London Wall, L.

Aldermary Church Yard, in Bow Lane in Cheapside, L. so called from the Church of St. Mary there.

Aldersgate Street, without Aldersgate, L. Here is the Bishop of *London*'s House, and opposite to it

B   the

the House of *Anthony Asbly Cooper*, Earl of *Shaftsbury* now converted into Tenements. And that part of this Street which reaches from the East End of *Long Lane* to the Bars at the Beginning of *Goswell Street*, was formerly call'd *Pickaxe Street*; but the Name is long since disused.

Aldgatechurch Row, by St. Botolph's Church without Aldgate, L.

Aldgate Street, within Aldgate, L.

Aleloof Street, near Lemon Street in Whitechapel, L.

Alhallows Church Yard, in Gracechurch Street, L.

Alhallows Lane, in Thames Street, L.

Allen Street, by Orange Street near Red Lion Square, L.

Almshouse Yard, at Dormant hill, W.

Almshouse Yard, in the little Ambrey, W.

Amen Corner, by Paternoster Row, L.

Anchor Street, by Spittle Fields, L.

Angel Alley, in Aldersgate Street, L.

Angel Alley, in Bishopgate Street without, L.

Angel Alley, in Leadenhall Street, L.

Angel Alley, in Little Moorfields by Moorfields, L.

Angel Alley, in Ratcliff Highway, L.

Angel Alley, in Shoe Lane, L.

Angel Alley, in Whitechapel, L.

Angel Court, against Colson's Court in Drury Lane, L.

Angel Court, against St. Sepulchres Church, L.

Angel Court, by the Kings Bench Prison, S.

Angel Court, in great King Street by St. James' Square, L

Angel Court, in Long Ditch, W.

Angel Court, in Throgmorton Street, L.

Angel Court, in Windmill Street, L.

Angel Court, near Charing Cross, L.

Angel Street, in St. Martin le Grand, L.

Angel Street, near the Old Bargehouse Stairs, S.

Annifeedclean, in Old Street Road, L. At the end thereof is a Street, containing on one side a Building

ng erected by the Weavers in 1670, for the Poor
f their Company ; and on the other fide are Alms-
oufes founded by Judge *Fuller*, in 1629.

Archer Street, by Windmill Street, L.

Arlington Street, in Pickadilly, L.

Arnold Court, in Barbican, L

Artichoak Alley, in Barnaby Street, S.

Artichoak Alley, in Shoreditch, L.

Artichoak Court, in Whitecrofs Street, L.

Artichoak Hill, in Ratcliff Highway, L. It is
ther wife call'd *Effex Street*.

Artichoak Yard, at Newington Caufeway, S.

Artillery Court, in Prince's Row in Chizel
Street, L.

Artillery Ground, in Tothill Fields, W. Near
which, by Weftminfter Pound, are *Hill's* Alms-
oufes ; the Grey Coat Boys Hofpital ; the Green
Coat Boys Hofpital ; and Mr. *Green's* Bluecoat Boys
Hofpital ; who has alfo built not far from it, the
nest brewhoufe in *Europe*.

Artillery Lane, in Bifhopfgate Street without, L.

Arundel Street, in the Strand, L. Here is a Ply-
ng place for Watermen.

Afhentree Court, in White Fryers, L.

Afpark, by Anchor Street in Spittle Fields, L.

Ave Mary Lane, by Paternofter Row, L.

Auftin Fryers, by Winchefter Street, L.

Axe Alley, in Leadenhall Street, L. It is alfo
alled *Cuckolds Alley*.

Axe and Bottle Yard, on St. Margarets Hill, S.

Axe Yard, in Blackman Street, S.

Axe Yard, in King Street, W.

Ayres Street, at the end of Leather Lane, L.

Ayres Street, in Piccadilly, L.

B A

Bab's Meufe, in Jermyn Street, L.

Back Alley, by Cloth Fair, L.

Back Alley, by Saffronhill, L.

Back Alley, in Back Street in Old Street Square, L. Not far from hence is the Peſt-houſe, ſo called from the Burying Ground thereto belonging, wherein thoſe who died of the dreadful Peſtilence in 1665, were buried : but now it is granted by the City of London to the *French* Refugees, who uſe it for an Hoſpital for the Relief of their Sick.

Back Side of St. Clement, behind St. Clement's Church in the Strand, L. Noted for Piece-Brokers.

Back Lane, beyond Roſemary Lane, L. it reaches from Cable Street to a place in the Fields, called *King David's Fort*.

Backſide of St. Thomas Apoſtle, in Queen Street in Cheapſide, L.

Back Street, by the old Artillery Ground in Horſlydown, S.

Back Street, in Old Street Square, L. It is otherwiſe called *Richmond Street*.

Bag and Bottle Alley, in Whitecroſs Street, L.

Bailey's Alley, near Bull Inn Court in the Strand, L.

Bakers Alley, in King Street, W.

Bakers Row, in Whitechapel, L. Near it are two Schools, erected by Mr. *Ralph Davenant*, Rector of St. Mary Whitechapel, in 1680.

Baldwyn's Court, in Baldwyn's Garden, L.

Baldwyn's Garden, in Leather Lane, L.

Baldwyn's Square, in Baldwyn's Garden, L.

Baldwyn Street, in Old Street, L.

Ball Yard, in Beech Lane, L.

Ball Yard, in Golden Lane, L.

Banbury Court, in Long Acre, L.

Bandyleg Alley, by Fleetditch, L.

Bandyleg Walk, in Queen Street, S.

Bangor Court, in Shoe Lane, L.

Baniſter Alley, againſt St. Giles's Church in the Fields, L.

Bank

Bank End, at the East End of Bankside, S.

Bankside, on the Thames, S. where is a Prison for Debtors, call'd *Clink*.

Baptist Head Court, in Whitecross Street, L.

Barbers Yard, in Brown's lane in Spittle Fields, L.

Barbican, in Aldersgate Street, L.

Barnaby Street, S. a noted place for Hatters.

Barns's Hall, in Upper Shadwell, L.

Barret's Alley, in East Smithfield, L.

Barrow's Alley, in Silver Street by Mugwell Street, L.

Bartholomew Close, in Little Britain, L. It is situated by the Church of St. *Bartholomew* the Great, formerly a Priory, to which King *Henry* the second gave the Privilege of Bartholomew Fair for 14 Days, but within these few Years it is kept only three Days.

Bartholomew Court, in Throgmorton Street, L.

Bartholomew Lane, against the Royal Exchange, L. so called from the Church there of St. *Bartholomew* the little.

Barton Lane, in Tower Street, L.

Bartlet Buildings, against Hatton Garden in Holbourn, L.

Bartlet Court, in Bartlet Buildings, L.

Basinghall Alley, by London Wall, L.

Basinghall Street, L. In this Street are Coopers and Girdlers Halls.

Basing Lane, in Bow lane in Cheapside, L.

Bassishaw Court, by the Church of St. Michael Basshaw in Basinghall Street, L.

Batch's Walk, in Ratcliff Highway, L.

Bate's Street, in Ratcliff Highway, L.

Batersby Court, in King Street, W.

Beaufort Street, in the Strand, L.

Baynard's Castle Wharf, in Thames Street, L. It is where *Baynard's* Castle stood, which was built by a Gentleman named *Baynard*, who came over with

William called (but erroneously) the Conqueror; b
that Family being extinct, in a large Course of tim
it fell to the Crown, and King *Henry* the Eigh
repaired it about the Year 1490. After that t
Lady *Jane Grey*, beheaded on Towerhill, was pr
claim'd, and Queen *Mary* the first was crown
there, *July* 6th, 1553.

Bear Alley, by Fleetditch, L. Near it is a Marke
house for Meal.

Bear Alley, in Bride lane, L.

Bear Alley, on Addlehill.

Bearbinder Lane, near Stocks Market, L.

Bear Court, in lower Moorfields, L.

Bear Key, in Thames Street, L. where a Mark
is kept for all sorts of Corn, on *Mondays, Wednesda*
and *Fridays*.

Bear Street, in Castle Street, by Newport Mar
ket, L.

Bear Yard, by Clare Market, L.

Beauchamp Street, by Brooks Market, L.

Beaufort Street, in the Strand, L. It is buil
where Worcester House formerly stood.

Bedford Buildings, in Bedford Street by Bedfor
Row, L.

Bedford Bury, in Chandos Street, L.

Bedford Court, by Theobalds Court in Theobald
Row, L.

Bedford Court, in Bedford Street by Covent Gar
den, L.

Bedford Row, by Grays Inn, L.

Bedford Street, by Bedford Row, L.

Bedford Street, in Liquorpond Street, L.

Bedford Street, in the Strand ; *vide* Halfmoo
Street in the Strand.

Bedlam Court, in Old Bedlam, L. but more pro
perly called *Bethlehem* Court.

Beech Lane, by Barbican, L.

Beehive Alley, on Snowhill, L.

Bee

Beer Lane, in Thames Street, L.

Bell Alley, in Austin Fryers, L.

Bell Alley, in Cannon Street by Budge Row, L.

Bell Alley, in Goswell Street, L.

Bell Alley, in Grub Street, L.

Bell Alley, in Old Fish Street, L.

Bell Alley, in Thieving lane, W.

Bell Alley, in Wapping, L

Bell Alley, in Whitechapel, L.

Bell Court, in Grays Inn lane, L.

Bell Court, in lower Moorfields, L.

Bell Court, in St. Martin le Grand, L

Bell Lane, by Whiterow in Spittle Fields, L.

Bellsavage Yard, on Ludgatehill, L.

Bell's Rents, in the Mint, S. The *Mint* is a place against the Church of St. *George* the Martyr in *Southwark*, which broken Persons and insolvent Debtors (tho' against an Act of Parliament) do make an *Asylum*, to protect them from Arrests.

Bell Yard, in Fenchurch Street, L.

Bell Yard, in Fleet Street, L.

Bell Yard, in Gracechurch Street, L.

Bell Yard, in Great Carter lane, L.

Bell Yard, in King Street, W.

Bell Yard, on St. Margaret's hill, S.

Bell Wharf, by St. Olave Church in Tooley street, S.

Belton Street, by Brownlow Street in Drury lane, L.

Bembridge Street, near St. Giles's Pound, L.

Benjamin Street, in Swallow Street, L.

Bennet Court, in White Street, S.

Bennet Court, near Marygold Alley in the Strand, L.

Bennet Street, in St. James's Street, L.

Bennet Street, near Christ Church, S. This is a pretty Church, built of Brick, and was consecrated in the Year 1670.

Bennet's

Bennets Yard, in Masham Street, W.

Berkly Street, in Piccadilly. L.

Bernard's-Inn, in middle Holbourn, L.

Berwick Alley, in East Smithfield, L.

Berwick Street, by Knaves Acre, L.

Betts's Rents, in Rosemary lane, L.

Bevers Marks, at the end of Camomile Street, L.

Big Street, in Hayhill Row. L.

Billingsgate, in Thames Street, L. Which (tho' now a Wharf, Dock, or Key, for landing all sorts of Commodities, transported hither by Water) was formerly a Gate or Port, while the antient Walls stood on that side of the City, near the River; first built and named from *Belinus*, an ancient King of *Britain*, about 400 Years before the Incarnation of Christ.

Billiter Lane, in Leadenhall Street, L.

Billiter Square, in Fenchurch Street, L.

Birchin Lane, in Cornhill, L.

Bird and Hand Court, against Mercers Chapel in Cheapside, L.

Birdcage Alley, opposite to the King's Bench Prison, S.

Bird's Gardens, in the Mint, S.

Bishops Court, in Chancery lane, L.

Bishops Court, in Chick lane, L.

Bishops Court, in Coleman Street, L.

Bishops Court, in Old Street, L.

Bishopsgate Street, within the Gate, L.

Bishopsgate Street, without the Gate, L.

Bishopshead Court, in Grays-Inn lane, L.

Bishopshead Court, in little Old Baily, L.

Bishops Rents, in Wapping, L.

Black and White Horse Court, in great Old Baily, L.

Blackbourn Court, in Purport-lane, L.

Blackboy Alley, in Barnaby Street, S.

Blackboy Alley, in Blackman Street, S.

Blackboy Alley, in Chick lane, L.

Blackbull

Blackbull Yard, by Hatton Garden, L.

Black Eagle Street, in Spittle Fields, L. Here is handsome Church for the Use of the French oteftants.

Black Fryers, in Ludgate Street, L.

Blackhorse Court, in Fleet Street, L.

Blackjack Alley, in Eaſt Smithfield, L.

Blackjack Alley, in Old Street, L

Blacklyon Yard, in Whitechapel, L.

Blackman Street, near St George's Church, S.

Blackmoor Street, in Drury lane, L

Black Raven Alley, in Leadenhall Street, L.

Black Raven Alley, in Thames Street, L.

Black Raven Court, in Golden lane, L.

Black Spread Eagle Yard, in Kent Street, S.

Black Swan Alley, in little Carter lane, L.

Black Swan Alley, near the Maze, S.

Blake s Court, in Catherine Street in the Strand, L.

Bleinheim Street, in Oxford Street in Tyburn oad, L.

Block Alley, in Tunball Street, L.

Bloomsbury Market, L. of little or no Accouut.

Bloomsbury Square, near High Holbourn, L. On he Northfide of it ſtands Southampton Houſe.

Bloſſom Street, by Spittle Yard in Spittle Fields, L.

Blow Bladder Street, near Cheapfide Conduit, L.

Blue Anchor Alley, in Broad Street, near Ratcliff ighway, L.

Blue Anchor Alley, in Bunhill lane by Upper Moor-elds, L.

Blue Anchor Alley, in Whitecroſs Street, L.

Blueball Court, in Salisbury Court in Fleetſtreet, L.

Blue Boar Alley, in White Street, S.

Blue Boar Court, in Field lane, L.

Blue Boarhead Yard, in King Street, W.

Blue Court, on Saffronhill L.

Bluegate Street, in Ratcliff Highway, L.

Blue

Blue Maid Alley, on St. Margaret's Hill, S.   Not far from hence is the Marshalsea, which is the County Goal for Surry.

Boarded Alley, against London Wall by Bedlam, L.

Boarded Alley, in Baldwyn's Garden, L.

Boar Alley, in Grub Street, L.

Boarhead Alley, in White Street, S.

Boarhead Court, in the Borough, S.

Boarhead Yard, in Petticoat lane near Whitechapel Bars, L.

Belt and Tun Yard, in Fleet Street, L.

Bolton Street, in Hayhill Row, L.

Bond's Stables, in Fetter lane, L.

Boot Alley, in Kent Street, S.

Booth Street, in Spittle Fields, L.

Borough, S. Here is a Market kept on *Wednesday* and *Saturdays*.

Bofs Alley, against Billingsgate, L.

Bafwell Court, in Cary Street by Lincolns Inn Fields, L.

Botolph Lane, near the Monument, L.

Bottle Alley, in Bishopsgate Street without, L.

Bow Church Yard, in Cheapside, L.

Bow Lane, in Cheapside, L. so called from the Church of St. *Mary le Bow*, adjacent to it.

Bowl Court, in Fleet Street, L.

Bowl Court, in Shoreditch, L.

Bowling Alley, by Tufton Street, W.

Bowling Alley, in Tunball Street, L.

Bowling Alley, in Whitecross Street, L.

Bowl Yard, near Middle Row in St. Giles's Street, L.

Bowman Court, in Gardine's lane in Kingstreet, W.

Bow Street, at the West End of High Holbourn, L.

Bow Street, by Covent Garden, L.

Bow Street, in Kingstreet, W. Vulgarly called *Thieving Lane*.

Boxer

Boxen Court, in Robinhood's Court in Shoe lane, L.

Brackly Street, by Bridgwater Garden, L.

Brand Yard, in the great Minories, L.

Breadstreet Alley, on Breadstreet Hill, L.

Breadstreet Hill, in Thames Street, L.

Bread Street, in Cheapside, L. so called from the Bakers formerly keeping there a Market for Bread.

Bream's Buildings, in Chancery lane, L.

Brewers Street, against Execution-dock at Wapping, L.

Brewers Street, against the Almshouses in St. Giles's, L.

Brewers Street, by John Street near Golden Square, L.

Brewers Street, near Bow Street in High Holbourn, L.

Brewers Yard, in Chick lane, L.

Brewers Yard, in King Street, W.

Brewers Yard, in Shoe lane, L.

Brewers Yard, in the Strand, L.

Brewhouse Yard, by Saffronhill, L.

Brick Court, in College Street, W.

Brick Court, in Sheer lane by Templebar, L.

Brick Court, in the Inner Temple, L.

Brick Lane, in Old Street, L

Brick Lane, in Whitechapel, L.

Bride Court, by Bride lane, L.

Bride Lane, in Fleetstreet, L. Noted for Hatmakers; and is situated at the East End of St. Bride's Church, otherwise called the Church of St. Bridget.

Bridewell Alley, in Long lane, S. so called from a Prison, or House of Correction, there built, for Vagrants, and idle Persons.

Bridewell Precinct, by Fleetditch, L.

Bridgefoot, S. It reaches over two Arches without the Bridgehouse on London Bridge.

Bridgehouse

Bridgehouse Gate Yard, in Tooley Street, S.

Bridges Street, by Catherine Street in the Strand, L. Here is the Theatre Royal, where both Tragedies and Comedies are acted.

Bridgewater Garden, L.

Bridgewater Square, by Barbican, L

Britington Court, in Coleman Street, L.

Broad Alley, in Grub Street, L.

Broad Bridge, by Upper Shadwell, L.

Broad Court, in Shoemaker's Row by Aldgate,

Broad Sanctuary, against Westminster Abby, W,

Broad Street, by Cambridge Street, L.

Broad Street, by Ratcliff Cross, L.

Broad Street, near Threadneedle Street, L. Here is the Pay Office, for the Seamen serving on Board the Royal Navy.

Broadway, by great Tothill Street, W. Here was kept formerly an Hay-Market, but is now discontinued; and near this place, are the *White Horse* and *Black Horse* Inns, for the Entertainment of Man and Horse; there being none in the Parish of St. Margaret at Westminster, for Stage Coaches Waggons, or Carriers.

Broad Yard, in Blackman Street, S.

Broken Cross, by Tothill Street, W. Where is at present, an House, possess'd by a Baker, which is more ancient than any House beside, in *Westminster*, *London*, or *Southwark*; or perhaps in any place in *England*.

Broken Wharf, against St. Mary Somerset's Church in Thames Street, L.

Bromly Street, in High Holbourn, L.

Brook Court, by Strand lane, L.

Brooks Court, in the Great Minories, L,

Brooks Market, by Brook Street. L. Where a Market is kept on *Thursdays* and *Saturdays*.

Brook Street, at the End of Cutthroat lane in Ratcliff Highway, L.

Brook

Brook Street, in Middle Holbourn, **L.**

Brook Street, in New Bond Street, **L.**

Brooks-Wharf, against Bread Street hill in Thames reet, **L.**

Brownlow Street, in Drury lane, **L.** built where a oufe formerly flood belonging to the Duke of nox.

Browns Court, in Bricklane at Whitechapel, **L.**

Browns Gardens, in Monmouth Street, **L.**

Buckeridge Street, in Dyet Street, **L.**

Buckingham Court, near Charing Crofs, **L.** Near is the Admiralty Office, built where Wallingford oufe formerly flood.

Buckingham Street, in York Buildings, **L.**

Bucklersbury, by Cheapfide, **L.**

Buckle Street, by Red Lion Street in White-apel, **L.**

Buckshead Court, in Great Diftaff lane, **L.**

Budge Row, by St. Antholin's Church near Can-n Street, **L.**

Bull and Mouth Street, juft within Alderfgate, **L.** ere is a Quakers Meetinghoufe.

Bull Alley, in Nicholas lane, **L.**

Bullhead Court, in Jewin Street, **L.**

Bullhead Court, in Newgate Street, **L.**

Bull Inn Court, in the Strand, **L.** fo called from ing built where the Bull Inn formerly flood; hich fome Years fince fell down, and kill'd 5 or People in their Beds, befides hurting fome others.

Bull Lane Wharf, near Queenhyth in Thames reet, **L.**

Bullen Rents, in Shoe lane, **L.**

Bulliford Court, in Fenchurch Street, **L.**

Bull Yard, in Gofwell Street, **L.**

Bull Yard, in St. John Street, **L.**

Bunhill Lane in Chizzel Street by upper Moor-lds, **L.** By it, on the Eaft fide, is *Tindal*'s Burial round, for the Interment of Diffenters.

C

Bunhill Row, by Bunhill lane, **L.**

Burleigh Court, in Burleigh Street in the Strand, **L.**

Burleigh Street, at the West End of Exeter Exchange in the Strand, **L.** so call'd from one of the Earl of *Exeter*'s honorary Titles.

Burlington Street, in Swallow Street, **L.**

Burr Street, in East Smithfield, **L.**

Bury Court, in Love lane, by Aldermanbury, **L.**

Bury Street, near Camomile Street by Bishopsgate **L.**

Bury Street, near St. James's Street, **L.**

Bushel Court, in Lothbury, **L.**

Bush Lane, in Cannon Street, **L.** Here is Merchant-Taylors School.

Butcher Row, at the end of Brook Street by Ratcliff Highway, **L.**

Butcher Row, by St. Catharine near the Tower, **L.**

Butcher Row, by the Backside of St. Clement, **L.**

Butchers Alley, in St. John Street, **L.**

Butchers Alley, at Windmill hill, **L.**

Butchers Alley, in little Moorfields by Moorfields, **L.**

C A

Cabbage Lane, in Long lane, **S.**

Cabbage Lane, near Petty France, **W.** It is also call'd Cattle Street.

Cable Street, at the End of Rosemary lane, **L.**

Cambridge Street, by little Windmill Street, **L.**

Camomile Street, within Bishopsgate Street, **L.**

Campion Alley, by Market Street, **W.**

Campion Lane, near Alhallows lane, **L.**

Gam's Court, in Hopton Street, **L.**

Cannon Alley, in St. Pauls Church Yard, **L.**

Cannon Street, by Budge Row, **L.** Here is Londonstone, placed for a Boundary by the ancient Romans or Saxons.

Cannon Street, in the Mint, **S.**

Cannon

Cannon Street, near the new Church by Ratcliff Highway, L.

Carnaby Street, by Great Marlborough Street, L.

Carpenters Alley, in Long lane, L.

Carpenters Court, in Aldermanbury, L.

Carpenters Yard, in Fore Old Jewry, by Aldgate, L.

Carriers Street, in Buckeridge Street in Dyet Street, L.

Carter Yard, in Ratcliff Highway, L.

Carthusian Street, in Aldersgate Street, L. built in 1695 and so called from the Convent of Carthusian Monks residing formerly in the Charter House by it.

Cartridge Street, in Rosemary lane, L. It is also call'd, *Churchhead Street*.

Cartwright Street, by the Broadway, W.

Carters Rents, in Brick lane, L.

Cary Court, near Exeter Exchange in the Strand, L.

Cary Street, by Lincolns Inn Fields, L.

Cary Street, in Foster lane, L.

Castle Alley, at the West end of the Royal Exchange, L.

Castle Alley, in Thames Street, L.

Castle Court, in Birchin lane, L.

Castle Court, in Budge Row, L.

Castle Court, in Castle Street behind Long Acre, L.

Castle Court, in Whitecross Street, L.

Castle Lane, in Castle Street by Redcross Street, S.

Castle Street, behind Long Acre, L.

Castle Street, by Fleetditch, L.

Castle Street, by Redcross Street, S.

Castle Street, by the Meuse, L.

Castle Street, in Ayres Street in Piccadilly, L.

Castle Street, in Duke Street in Bloomsbury, L.

Castle Street, in Spittle Fields, L.

Castle Street, W. *vid.* Cabbage lane, W.

Caftle Yard, in Chick lane, L.

Caftle Yard, in Houndſditch, L.

Caftle Yard, near Staples Inn in Mid Holbourn, L

Cat and Wheel Alley, in Biſhopſgate Street without, L.

Cat and Wheel Alley, in Whitechapel, L.

Cat and Wheel Alley, on Snowhill, L.

Cateaton Street, in King Street by Guildhall, L.

Catherine Street, againſt Somerſet Watergate the Strand, L.

Catshead Court, in Orchard Street, W.

Cavindiſh Court, in Houndſditch, L.

Cecil Street, in the Strand, L. It is built where Salisbury Houſe formerly ſtood.

Chambers Rents, in Barnaby Street, S.

Chamber Street, in Ratcliff Highway, L.

Chancery Lane, in Fleet Street, L. Here is the ſix Clerks Office, and ſeveral other Offices belonging to the Municipal or Common Laws of the Land

Chandlers Rents, by Blackfryers Church, L.

Channel Row, by King Street, W.

Chapel Street, by New Chapel, W. That Chapel is alſo call'd, New Church.

Chapel Street, in Wardour Street, L.

Charing Croſs, by St. Martins lane in the Strand, L. Here is a moſt curious Effigies of King Charles the firſt on Horſeback, erected in Braſs, with martial or warlike Trophies carv'd on the Stone Pedeſtal.

Charity Court, in Alderſgate Street, L.

Charles Court, by Hungerford Market in the Strand, L. Here is a Plyingplace for Watermen.

Charles Square, by Hoxton Square, L.

Charles Street, by Bridgwater Square, L.

Charles Street, by Covent Garden, L.

Charles Street, by St. James's ſquare, L.

Charles Street, in King Street, W.

Charterhouſe Lane, by Smithfield Bars, L.

Charterhouſe

Charterhouse Square, L. so called from the Charterhouse therein ; being a noble Foundation founded by one 'Squire *Sutton*, for the Maintenance of several decay'd Gentlemen, and Education of Youth.

Charterhouse Street, in Long lane, L.

Cheapside, by St. Paul's Churchyard, L.

Checquer Alley, in Bunhill Row by upper Moorfields, L.

Checquer Alley, in Old Bedlam, L.

Checquer Alley, in the Borough, S.

Checquer Alley, in Whitecross Street, L.

Checquer Court, against Northumberland House in the Strand, L. Here many Stage-Coaches may be hired for the Western Parts of *England* ; and the Waters had fresh from *Bath*, and the hot Well at *Bristol*.

Checquer Yard, in Bush lane in Thames Street, L.

Checquer Yard, in Golden lane, L.

Cherry Alley, in Whitecross Street, L.

Cherry Court, in Gardiners lane, W.

Cherry Garden, by Southwark Wall, S.

Cherrytree Alley, in Bunhill lane by Upper Moorfield, L.

Cherrytree Alley, in Golden lane, L.

Cheshire Rents, by Fleet lane, L.

Chichester Rents, in Chancery lane, L.

Chick Lane, near West Smithfield, L. Most of the Inhabitants here, buy and sell old Cloaths.

Chimneysweepers Alley, in Barnaby Street, S.

Chizel Street, by Upper Moorfields, L. Here are some Fletchers, or those who make Bows and Arrows.

Christopher Alley, in Upper Moorfields, L.

Christopher Court, by St. Christopher's Church in Threadneedle Street, L.

Christopher Court, in St. Martin le Grand, L.

Christopher Court, on St. Margaret's Hill, S.

Christ's

Christ's Hospital, by Christ Church in Newgate Street, L. This Hospital, which was formerly a Monastery of the Grey Fryers, was given by King *Edward* the Sixth to the City of *London,* in 1552 for the Education of poor Fatherless Children.

Church Alley, by Five Inkhorn Alley in White-chapel, L.

Church Alley, by the Church in Black Fryers, L.

Church Alley, by the Church of St. Giles in the Fields, L.

Church Alley, by the Church of St. Lawrence Jewry near Guildhall, L.

Church Alley, in Chick lane, L.

Church Alley, in Harp Alley in Shoe lane, L.

Church Alley, in the Strand, L.

Church Court, by St. Thomas's Church, S.

Church Court, by St. James's Church in Jermyn Street, L.

Church Court, in the Strand, L.

Church Entry, in Black Fryers, L.

Churchhead Street, vid. Cartridge Street.

Church Hill, by Blackfryers Church, L.

Church Lane, by St. Mary's Church at White-chapel, L.

Church Lane, by the New Church near Limehouse hole, L.

Church Lane, in Houndsditch, L.

Church Passage, in Piccadilly, L.

Church Street, against St. Anne's Church, L.

Church Street, at the end of Prescod Street, L.

Church Street, in Long Acre, L.

Church Street, near St. Giles's Pound, L.

Church Street, near King Edward's Row by Whitechapel, L.

Churchyard Alley, in Fetter lane, L.

Cinnamon Street, by Wapping Dock, L.

Clare Market, L. It is commonly call'd New Market ; and it's kept on *Wednesdays* and *Saturdays.*

Clare Street, by Clare Market, L. Clarges

Claiges Street, in Hayhill Row, L. Built *Anno* 1714.

Clark's Alley, in Camomile Street by Bishopsgate, L.

Cleaveland Court, by St. James's Palace, L. fo call'd from the late Dutchess of *Cleaveland's* House.

Clement's Court, in Milk Street, L.

Clement's Inn, at the Backside of St. Clement, L.

Clement's Lane, by the Backside of St. Clement's Church, L. Here is an ancient well of very wholsome Water, call'd Clement's Well.

Clement's Lane, in Cannon Street, L.

Clerkenwell Close, by Clerkenwell Green, L. Near it is a Bridewell for the Correction of Vagrants, idle People, Strumpets, and sturdy Beggars.

Clerkenwell Green, L. It is by the Church of St. James, and near it is New Prison, a Jayl for Thieves, and other Offenders. And it is called Clerkenwell from an old Well, rising out of the West End of the Green, call'd Clerk's Well; where the Parish Clerks of London assembled yearly, to act some historical Part of the Scripture before much People.

Clifford's Inn, by St. Dunstan's Church in Fleet Street, L. Here is kept the Office for issuing out Writs for the Marshalsea Court in Southwark.

Clifford's Street, in New Bond Street, L.

Cloak Lane, in Queen Street in Cheapside, L.

Cloth Fair, in West Smithfield, L. Noted for the Sale of Cloth, Druggets, and other Woollen Manufactures.

Club Row, in Spittlefields, L.

Cob's Court, in Blackfryers, L.

Cock Alley, at Norton Faldgate, L.

Cock Alley, by Fleet lane, L.

Cock Alley, by St. John Street, L.

Cock Alley, in East Smithfield, L.

Cock Alley, in Shoreditch, L.

Cock Alley, in Whitecross Street, L.

Cock Alley, in Whitecrofs Street by Cripplegate, L.

Cock Alley, in Whitechapel, L.

Cock and Hoop Court, in Houndfditch, L.

Cock Court, in St. Martin le Grand, L.

Cock Court, on Ludgatehill, L.

Cock Court, on Snowhill, L.

Cock Hill, by Ratcliff Highway, L.

Cock Lane, near Weft Smithfield, L.

Cockpit, againft the Privy Garden, W. It is part of the Royal Palace of Whitehall, ftanding in a Street fituated betwixt two Gateways ; the one fronting Chairingcrofs, and the other Weftminfter Abby. Here the Principal Secretaries of State generally keep their Offices.

Cockpit Alley, in Drury lane, L.

Cockpit Court, in Dean ftreet by Soho fquare, L.

Cock Row, in Spittlefields. L.

Cockshead Court, in Golden lane, L.

Codpiece Court, in Petty France, W.

Codpiece Row, by Hockly in the Hole, L.

Coffin Alley, by Cowcrofs, L.

Colchefter Street, in Church lane by Whitechapel, L.

Cold Harbour, in Thames ftreet, L. Here is Watermens Hall.

Coleman Street, near London Wall, L Adorn'd with a Church dedicated to St. Stephen.

Cole's Alley, in Whitechapel, L.

Cole Yard, in Drury lane, L.

College Court, by Stable Yard, W.

College Hill, in Cloak lane by Queen ftreet in Cheapfide, L So called from the Collegiate Church of St. Spirit and St. Mary, heretofore founded there by Sir Richard Whitington, thrice Lord Mayor of London, about the Year 1400 ; afterwards call'd Whitington's College ; but it was fuppref'd by Edward the Sixth.

College Street, by Mill Bank, W.

College

College Street, by the Marſh, S. Here is a Plying place for Watermen on the River of Thames, called *King's Arms Stairs*.

College Yard, near St. Margaret's Hill, S.

Collingwood Street, in the Maze, S.

Colſon's Court, in Drury lane, L.

Comber's Alley, in Blackman ſtreet, S.

Comber's Court, in Blackman ſtreet, S.

Come again Row, near Whitechapel, L.

Compton Street, by Newport Market, L.

Compton Street, in Goſwell ſtreet, L.

Conduit Street, in Long Acre, L.

Conduit Street, in New Bond ſtreet, L.

Coney Court, in Grays Inn, L.

Cock's Court, in Cary ſtreet near Lincolns Inn Fields, L.

Cooly's Lane, in Brook ſtreet near Ratcliff Highway, L.

Cooper's Alley, in Whitechapel, L.

Cooper's Rents, in Eaſt Smithfield, L.

Corbet Court, in Browns lane in Spittlefields, L.

Corbet Court, in Gracechurch ſtreet, L.

Cork Street, near Old Bond ſtreet, L.

Cornhill, L. ſo called from a Market of Corn kept here in ancient Times.

Covent Garden, L A Square adorn'd with lofty Piazza's under ſtately Houſes on the North and Eaſt Sides; and a Church dedicated to St. *Paul*, on the Weſt

Covent Garden Market, by Southampton ſtreet in the Strand, L. Where Herbs, Flowers, Fruits, and other things pertaining to Gardens, are ſold on *Tueſdays*, *Thurſdays*, and *Saturdays*.

Coventry Street, by the Hay Market, L.

Court Street, in Whitechapel, L. It is near Whitechapel Goal, where Debtors are confin'd up in very ſmall Actions.

Cow Croſs, by Smithfield Bars, L.

Cow

Cow Lane, by Weſt Smithfield, L. A Place n̄ ted for Coachmakers and Harneſsmakers.

Coxon's Court, by Dorſet ſtreet in Shoreditch, L

Cozen Lane, at Dowgate Wharf in Thames ſtreet L. Here is Mr. *John Pool*'s Brew houſe, where the beſt Malt Liquors of all ſorts, (as eſteem'd Gentlemen skilled therein) are brewed.

Cradle Court, in Redcroſs ſtreet, L.

Crags Court, near Charing Croſs, L

Cranborn Alley, in Leiceſterfields, L. Inhabit moſtly by ſhoemakers.

Crane Court, in Alderſgate ſtreet, L.

Crane Court, in Fleet ſtreet, L.

Crane Court, in Old Cnange, L.

Crane Court, on Lambeth-hill, L.

Creechurch Alley, by St. Catharine Creechurch Leadenhall ſtreet, L.

Creechurch Lane, in Leadenhall Street, L.

Creed Lane, in Ludgate ſtreet, L.

Criplegate Street, L. Here is an old Conduit.

Crooked Lane, on New Fiſh ſtreet, L. Here moſt Haberdaſhers of ſmall Wares, and Bird-Cag makers.

Crooked Lane, in the Mint, S.

Crophall Court, in Throgmorton ſtreet, L.

Crosby's Square, in Biſhopſgate ſtreet within, L

Crofsdagger Court, in Grub ſtreet, L.

Crofskey Alley, againſt St. Antholin's Church Watling ſtreet, L.

Crofskey Alley, by London Wall, L.

Crofskey Alley, in Blackman ſtreet, S.

Crofskey Alley, in Whitecroſs ſtreet, L.

Crofskey Court, by Cowcroſs, L

Crofskey Court, in Chick lane, L.

Crofskey Court, in Grub ſtreet, L.

Crofs Lane, in Parker's Lane, L.

Crofs Street, in Eſſex ſtreet, L.

Crofs Street, in Hatton Garden, L.

Cr

Cross Street, in King Street by Golden Square, L.

Croud Alley, in middle Moorfields, L.

Crouderswell Alley, in Jewen Street, L. so called from a Well, the Water whereof is accounted good for sore Eyes.

Crow Alley, in Whitecrofs Street, L.

Crown Alley, in Bridewell Precinct by Fleet-ditch, L.

Crown Alley, in the Great Minories, L.

Crown Alley, in Whitecrofs Street, L.

Crown Alley, in White Street, S.

Crown and Hoop Court, in Whitecrofs Street, L.

Crown and Sheer Alley, in Rosemary lane, L.

Crown Court, against Laurence Lane in Cheapside, L.

Crown Court, in Broad Street, L.

Crown Court, in Butcher Row by Templebar, L.

Crown Court, in Chancery lane, L.

Crown Court, in Chick lane, L.

Crown Court, in Dean Street by Soho Square, L.

Crown Court, in Golden lane, L.

Crown Court, in Grub Street, L.

Crown Court, in Long Walk, L.

Crown Court, in King Street, W.

Crown Court, in Little Moorfields, L.

Crown Court, in Thieving lane, W.

Crown Court, in Pallmall, L.

Crown Court, in Pultney Street, L. Built Anno 708.

Crown Court, in Purpoot lane, L.

Crown Court, in Ruffel Street in Drury lane, L.

Crown Court, in Trinity lane near Cheapside, L.

Crown Court, in Warwick lane, L.

Crucifix Lane, in Barnaby Street, S.

Cruddle Court, in Fore Street by Moorfields, L.

Crutched Fryers, on Great Towerhill, L. Here kept the Navy Office.

Cuckolds Alley, vid. Axe Alley.

Cuckolds Row, vid. *Keeland Row*.

Cullum Street, by Fenchurch Street, L.

Cupid's Alley, in Golden lane, L.

Curl Court, near Denmark Court in the Strand, L.

Cursitors Alley, in Chancery lane, L.

Cushion Court, in Pig Street near Threadneedle Street, L.

Customhouse, in Thames Street, L. Situated by a fine Key ; and the King's Warehouses are adjoining to it.

Cutthroat Lane, in Ratcliff Highway, L. .

Cuttings Abby, in New North Street, by Red Lion Square, L.

D A

Darby Court, in Channel Row, W.

Darby Street, in Rosemary lane, L.

Dartmouth Street, by Queen Street, W.

Dart's Alley, in Whitechapel, L.

Dawson's Alley, in St. Martin's lane in the Strand, L.

Dead Garden, in East Smithfield, L.

Deans Alley, in Coleman Street, L.

Deans Court, in Deans Street, by Red Lion Square, L.

Deans Court, in Deans Street, by Soho Square, L.

Deans Court, in St. Martin le Grand, L.

Deans Court, in St. Paul's Churchyard, L. Here is the Office for entring and searching of Wills.

Dean Street, by Red Lion Square, L.

Dean Street, by Soho Square, L.

Dean Street, in Fetter lane, L.

Deans Yard, W. It is on the Southwest side of St. Peter's Cathedral ; otherwise called, Westminster Abby ; where our British Kings and Queens are crowned ; and have their Royal Sepulchres when Deceased.

Delab

Delahay Street, by Duke Street, W.

Denmark Court, in the Strand, L. Part of this court, next to Exeter Street, was formerly called Exeter Court, but by pulling down a Wall which parted them, they promiscuously bear the Name of Denmark Court.

Denmark Street, in Ratcliff Highway, L.

Denmark Street, near the Church of St. Giles in the Fields, L.

Denzil Street, vid. Peter Street in Stanhope Street.

Devereaux Court, by Essex Street in the Strand, L.

Devonshire Square, in Devonshire Street without Bishopsgate, L.

Devonshire Street, by Queen's Square, near Great Ormond Street, L.

Devonshire Street, without Bishopsgate, L.

Drake Street, in New Tothill Street, W.

Dice Key, near Billinsgate, L.

Dick's Shore, in Forestreet at Limehouse, L. A-int it is a Plying-place for Watermen.

Dirty Lane, behind the Mint, S.

Dirty Lane, by Old Palace Yard, W. At the south end of this Lane, by College Street, is Lindy House, possess'd now by the Earl of Abingdon.

Dirty Lane, in Long Acre, L.

Distaff Lane, in Friday Street, L.

Dob's Court, in Swithin lane, L.

Dock Head, S.

Dockside Alley, at the Hermitage, L.

Doctors Commons, in Great Knight Rider Street, This is a sort of an Inn only for Civilians, and others who study the Canon and Civil Laws.

Dodington Street, by Brooks Market, L.

Dog Alley, by the Bowling Alley, W.

Dog and Bear Yard, in Horslydown, S.

Dog Lane, in Fivefoot lane, S.

Dog's Head and Porridge Pot Court, in Whitecross street, L.

D   Dogwell

Dogwell Court, in Whitefryers, L.

Dog Yard, in College Street, W.

Dolphin Court, on Ludgatehill, L.

Dolphin Yard, in Blackman Street, S.

Doolittle Alley, in little Carter lane, L.

Dormant Hill, by Chapel Street, W.

Dorset Court, in Channel Row, W.

Dorset Street, by St. Leonard's Church in Shoreditch L.

Dorset Street, in Spittlefields, L.

Dove Court, in Old Jewry, L.

Dove Court, on Old Fishstreet Hill, L.

Dove Street, in Piccadilly, L.

Dowgate Hill, L. Here are the Skinners and Tallow-Chandlers Halls.

Downing Street, in King Street, W.

Dowse Key, near Billinsgate, L.

Drake Street, by Red Lion Square, L.

Drapers Court, in Lothbury, L.

Drapers Court, in Princes Street, near Stock Market, L.

Drews Court, in Peter Street, W.

Drout Alley, at Norton Faldgate, L.

Drum Alley, against the Playhouse in Drury lane, L

Drum Alley, in Whitechapel, L.

Drury Dane, near the new Church in the Stand, L

Duck Court, in Castle Street in Holbourn, L.

Duck Lane, in West Smithfield, L. Here are many Bookbinders.

Duck Lane, near Old Pye Street, W.

Duckfoot Lane, in Thames Street, L.

Dukes Court, in St. Martins lane in the Strand, L

Dukes Court, in the little Ambrey, W.

Dukes Place, near Aldgate, L. So called from Dwellinghouse here in which *Thomas*, Duke of *Norfolk*, liv'd, in the Time of *Henry* the Eighth. And the Jews had here a Synagogue, which is now useless, since their building a new one near within these few Years.

Du

Duke Street, by Charles Street, W. Here is a chapel for the Service of the Church of England, taken out of the House of the Lord Chancellor *Jones*, whose Memory still stinks in the Nostrils of all good Men, for his most bloody and inhuman cruelties acted in the West of England, in the reign of King *James* the Second.

Duke Street, by Lincolns Inn Fields, L.

Duke Street, in Artillery lane, in Bishopsgate street without, L,

Duke Street, in Great King Street, by St. James's square, L.

Duke Street, in York Buildings in the Strand, L.

Duke Street, near Montague House, L,

Duke Street, near Queen Street, S.

Duffin's Court, in King Street, W.

Dunstan's Hill, by St. Dunstan's Church in the East, L.

Dunstan's Square, in Whitechapel, L.

Dunning's Alley, in Bishopsgate Street without, L.

Durham Yard, by the New Exchange in the Strand, L. It is built where formerly stood *Durham* House, belonging to the Bishops of that See

Durham Yard, in Chick lane, L.

Dutchy Lane, near Somerset House in the Strand, So called as being in the Dutchy Liberty belonging to the County Palatine of *Lancaster*.

Dutchy Street, by Bloomsbury Market, L.

Dyers Court, in Aldermanbury, L.

Dyot Street, in St. Giles's Street, L.

E A

Eagle and Child Alley, by Fleetditch, L.

Eagle and Child Court, by the Church of St. Giles in the Fields, L.

Eagle Court, by Catherine Street in the Strand, L.

Eagle Street, by Red Lion Square, L.

Eagle

Eagle Street, by Piccadilly, L.

Earls Court, in Drury lane, L.

Earl Street, by the Six Dials, L. It bears th same Name to another Street opposite to it there.

Eastharding Street, by little New Street, near Fetter lane, L.

East Lane, at Southwark Wall, S. Against it a Plying-place for Watermen.

East Smithfield, L.

East Street, in New North Street, by Red Lion Square, L.

East Street, in Spittlefields Market, L.

Edmunds Court, in Princes Street by St. Anne Church L.

Edwards Street, in Berwick Street, L.

Elbow Lane, in Ratcliff Highway, L.

Elbow Lane, in Thames Street, L.

Ely Court, by Hatton Garden, L.

Elm Court, in the Inner Temple, L.

Essex Court, in the Middle Temple, L.

Essex Court, in Whitefryers, L

Essex Street, against St. Clement's Church in th Strand, L. Built where formerly stood the Hou of the Earl of *Essex*, the chief Favourite of Quee *Elizabeth*, who died with Grief a little after h was beheaded.

Essex Street, in Whitefryers, L.

Essex Street, vid. *Artichoak Hill.*

Evans's Court, in Basinghall Street, L.

Ever's Street, by Gravel lane, S.

Exchange Court, behind Exeter Exchange in th Strand, L.

Execution Dock, against Brewers Street at Wap ping, L. So called from Pyrates being hange there till it's high Watermark, when Condemne by an High Court of Admiralty, for Robbing o the high and open Seas.

Exeter Court, the East end of Exeter Exchange the Strand, L.   *Exet*

Exeter Exchange, in the Strand, L.
Exeter Street, by Burleigh Street in the Strand,
L. Built where the Earl of *Exeter's* House stood.

F A

Fair Street, in Horslydown, S.
Falcon Court, in Codpiece Row, by Hockly i' th'
Hole, L.
Falcon Court, in Fleetstreet, L.
Falcon Court, in Long lane, S.
Falcon Court, in Shoe lane, L.
Falcon Court, opposite to the King's Bench Pri-
son, S.
Falconers Alley, in Tunball Street, L.
Falcon Yard, in Tooly Street, S.
Fan Alley, in Goswell Street, L.
Fan Court, in Fenchurch Street, L.
Farmers Street, in Ratcliff Highway, L.
Farthing Alley, near the Maze Pond, S.
Farthing Street, in Spittlefields, L.
Fashion Street, in Spittlefields, L.
Feathers Court, against Craven House in Great
Drury lane, L.
Feathers Court, at Cowcross, L.
Feathers Court, in High Holbourn, L.
Fell Court, in Fell Street by Mugwell Street, L.
Fell Street, in Mugwell Street, L.
Fenchurch Street, L. Near Northumberland House,
here is the Church of St. Catharine Coleman.
Fetter Lane, in Fleetstreet, L.
Field Lane, at Holbourn Hill, L.
Figtree Court, in Barbican, L.
Figtree Court, in the Inner Temple, L.
Finch Lane, by Threadneedle Street, L.
Fishers Alley, in Water lane, L.
Fishers Street, by Red Lion Square, L.
Fishmarket Court, in Bloomsbury Market, L.

Fishmongers Alley, in Redcrols Street, S.

Fish Yard, in St. Margaret's lane, W.

Fitakers Yard, in little Drury lane, L.

Fitch Court, in Noble Street, near Foster lane, L

Firebell Alley, in little Moorfield, L.

Fivefoot Lane, in Barnaby Street, L

Five Inkhorn Court, in Whitechapel, L.

Fleet Ditch, in Fleetstreet, L. It extends fro the River of Thames to Holbourn Bridge, and hat over it three other Bridges; namely, Fleetstre Bridge, Bridewell Bridge, and Fleetlane Bridge aud is now very commodious for importing Coal and other Necessaries, into the City; consisting many large Cellars for that Purpose. The Bridewe by it is for the Correction of Vagabonds and Harlot

Fleet Lane, near the Fleet Prison, L. This is Goal for Debtors, who have the Liberty of Rule, and belongs to the High Court of Chancery an Common Pleas.

Fleetstreet, in Spittlefields, L.

Fleetstreet, within Templebar, L.

Flowerdeluce Alley, in Wheeler Street in Spitth fields, L.

Flowerdeluce Court, by Fetter lane in Fleet street, L.

Flowerdeluce Court, in Hughs Alley in Black fryers, L.

Flowerdeluce Court, In Shoemakers Row in Blad fryers, L.

Flowerdeluce Court, in Tooly Street, S.

Flowerdeluce Court, in Tunball Street, L.

Flowerdeluce Yard in Tunball Street, L.

Flyinghorse Court, in Grub Street, L.

Fore Old Jewry, by Aldgate, L.

Foreside of St. Thomas Apostle, by Queenstreet Cheapside, L.

Fore Street, at Limehouse, L.

Fore Street, by Moorfields, L.

Fore Street, by Spittlefields, **L.**

Forster's Buildings, in Whitecrofs Street, **L.**

Foster Lane, in Cheapfide, **L.** Here are many Silverfmiths.

Fountain Court, by Aldermanbury, **L.**

Fountain Court, by Bread Street in Cheapfide, **L.**

Fountain Court, in Lothbury, **L.**

Fountain Court, in the Strand, **L.**

Fourcrown Court, in Rofemary lane, **L.**

Fourftable Alley, in Clement's lane by Clement's in, **L.**

Fowl Lane, in the Borough, **S.**

Fox Court, in Grays Inn lane, **L.**

Fox's Lane, at the Eaft end of St. Paul's in Upper hadwell, **L**

Fox's Ordinary, in Nicholas lane, **L.**

Francis Court, in St. John's lane, **L.**

Freeman's Court, in Cornhill, **L.**

Freeman's Lane, in Horflydown, **S.**

Freefchool Street, in Horflydown, **S.**

French Alley, in Artillery lane in Bifhopfgate ftreet without, **L.**

French Alley, in Gofwell Street, **L.**

French Court, by the Bars in Bifhopfgateftreet, **L.**

French Ordinary Court, in Crutchedfryers, **L.**

Friday Street, in Cheapfide, **L.**

Froggets Alley, in Thieving lane, **W.**

Fryers Street, in Shoemakers Row, in Blackfryers, **L.**

Fryingpan Alley, in the Borough, **S.**

Fryingpan Alley, in Tooly Street, **S.** Oppofite to is a Plying place for Watermen, called *Tooly's* ftairs.

Fryingpan Alley, in Tothill Street, **W.**

Fryingpan Alley, in Tunball Street, **L.**

Fryingpan Alley, in Wood Street, **L.**

Fullers Rents, near Grays Inn in High Holbourn, **L.**

Furnival's Inn Court, by Furnival's Inn in Mid Holbourn, **L.**

Furnival's

Furnival's Inn, in Middle Holbourn, L.

Furriers Alley, in Shoe lane, L.

Fyford Lane, by the Church of St. Mary Somerſt in Thames Street, L.

G A

Gardiners Lane, in King Street, W.

Gardiners Lane, in Petty France, W.

Gurland Alley, in Biſhopſgate Street without, L.

Garlick Hill in Thames Street, L. So call'd be cauſe there was a Place or Market, where formerl it was landed or fold.

Garter Lane, in Barbican, L.

George Alley, in Shoe lane, L

George Alley, in York Buildings, L.

George Alley, near the King's Bench Priſon, S.

George Alley, on Saffronhill, L.

George and Plough Yard, in the Broadway, W.

George Court, againſt the Herald's Office at Paul. Chain, L.

George Court, in St. John's lane, L

George Lane, near the Monument, L.

George Street, in Foſter lane, L.

George Street, in Pallmall, L. Built *Anno* 1668.

George Street, in the Mint, S.

George Street, in York Buildings, L.

George Yard, in Biſhopſgate Street without, L.

George Yard, in Coleman Street, L.

George Yard, in Field lane, L.

George Yard, in Kent Street, S.

George Yard, in Kingſtreet, W. So call'd (I ſup poſe) from an ancient Inn therein, bearing the Sign of St. George killing (if it is not a Fiction) Dragon.

George Yard, in Lombard Street, L.

George Yard, in Shoreditch, L.

George Yard, in Whitechapel, L.

George

33

George *Yard*, in Whitecrofs Street, L.
George *Yard*, on Great Towerhill, L.
George *Yard*, on Saffronhill, L.
Gerard *Street*, by Newport Market, L.
German *Yard*, near St. Mary Overy's Church, S.
Gibsons *Court*, in Marybone Street, L.
Gilbert *Street*, near Montague Houfe, L.
Giltfpur *Street*, by Great Old Baily, L.
Glafshoufe *Alley*, in Whitefryers in Fleetftreet, L.
Glafshoufe *Field*, by Cockhill at Ratcliff, L.
Glaffenbury *Court*, in Rofe Street near Covent
aiden, L.
Glafshoufe *Street*, in Swallow Street, L.
Glafshoufe *Yard*, by the Bars in Aldersgate
treet, L.
Glafshoufe *Yard*, in Blackfryers, L.
Glean *Alley*, in Tooly Street, S.
Globe *Court*, in Shoe lane, L.
Glocefter *Street*, by Red Lion Square, L.
Gloverhall *Court*, in Beech lane, L.
Goat *Alley*, in Upper Ground, S.
Goat *Yard*, in Horflydown, S.
Goat *Yard*, in Whitecrofs Street, L.
Goddards *Rents*, by Wheeler Street in Spittle-
lds, L.
Godfrey *Court*, in Milkftreet, L.
Golden *Lane*, at the end of Barbican, L.
Golden *Square*, L.
Goldfmiths *Street*, in Wood Street, L.
Goodchilds *Alley*, near Market Street, W.
Goodmans *Fields*, by Whitechapel, L
Goodmans *Yard*, in the Great Minories, L.
Goofe *Alley*, by Fleetditch, L
Goofetree *Yard* in Peter Street, W.
Gofwell *Street*, without Aldersgate Bars, L.
Goulftons *Square*, in Whitechapel, L.
Gracechurch *Street*, by Cornhill, L. fo called from
Grafs Market formerly kept there, L.

Gracious

Gracious Alley, in Wellclose, L.

Grafton Street, near Newport Market, L.

Grange Court, in Cary ſtreet, by Lincolns Inn Fields, L. ſo called from the Grange Inn adjacent to it ; and kept at preſent by one *John Banfield.*

Grange Road, by King John's Court, S.

Grange Walk, in King John's Court, S.

Graſhoppers Alley, in Whitecroſs ſtreet, L.

Gravel Lane, by Falcon Stairs, S.

Gravel Lane, in Houndſditch, L.

Grays Inn, in Holbourn, L. It is one of the Inns of Court.

Grays Inn Lane, in High Holbourn, L.

Grays Inn Paſſage, by Red Lion Square, L.

Great Ambrey, near Tothill ſtreet, L.

Great Bell Yard, in Coleman ſtreet, L.

Great Carter Lane, by Puddledock hill, L.

Great Chapel Street, W.

Great Eaſtcheap, near Fiſhſtreet Hill, by the Monument, L.

Great George Street, by Hanover Square, L.

Great Gloceſter Court, in Whitecroſs Street, L.

Great King Street, by St. James's Square, L.

Great Kirby Street, by Hatton Garden, L.

Great Lamb Alley, in Blackman ſtreet, L.

Great Marlborough Street, L.

Great Minories, by Towerhill, L. Moſtly occupied by Gunſmiths.

Great Old Bailey, L. Here is Juſtice Hall, where Criminals are Tryed every Seſſions for Capital Crimes, and other Miſdemeanors.

Great Rider Street, in Bury ſtreet, near St. James Street, L.

Great St. Andrew's Street, at the Six Dials, L.

Great St. Anne's Lane, W.

Great St. Helen's, by the Church of St. Mary Axe, L.

Gr

Great Stone Stairs, in Broad Street by Ratcliff Cross, L. Againſt this Place is an old Free School.

Great Street, near Brooks Market, L.

Great Tothill Street, W. At the Eaſt end hereof a very ancient Gatehouſe built of Stone, whither both Debtors and Felons are committed; and here are the Swan and two Necks and Fleece Inns, for the Entertainment of Man and Horſe.

Great Towerhill, L. Here is an ancient Arſenal, ſaid to be built by *Julius Cæſar*, before the Birth of Chriſt. And on this Hill, Peers of the Realm are uſually beheaded, for High Treaſon, and other Crimes.

Great Tower Street, near the Tower, L.

Great Turnſtile, in High Holbourn, L. Inhabited moſtly by Milliners and Shoemakers.

Greek Street, by Soho Square, L.

Green Arbour Court, in little Moorfield, L.

Green Arbour Court, in little Old Baily, L.

Greens Alley, in the Broad Sanctury by St. Margaret's Church, W.

Green Bank, in Tooly Street, S.

Green Dragon Court, at New Crane by Wapping, L.

Green Dragon Court, in the Broadway, W.

Greennutſiers Lane, in Cannon Street, L.

Green Street, in Caſtle Street by Newport Market, L.

Green Street, by Theobalds Row, L.

Green Wall, by Chriſt Church, S.

Green Yard, in Horſlydown, S.

Green Yard, in Tooly Street, S.

Green Yard, in Upper Ground, S.

Gregory Court, in High Holbourn, L.

Grey Eagle Street, in Spittlefields, L.

Grey Fryers, in Newgate Street, L. ſo called from ſonaſtery of Grey Fryers founded herein in 1325, but afterwards it was converted into an Hoſpital poor Fatherleſs Children, by King *Edward* 6th.

Greyhound

Greyhound Court, in Chick lane, L.

Greyhound Court, in Milford lane, L.

Greyhound Lane, at Whitechapel, L.

Greyhound Yard, in Upper Ground, S.

Grey's Ynd, in Brand's Yard in the Great Mino ries, L.

Griffins Yard, in Blackman Street, L.

Grocers Alley, in the Poultry, L. In Grocers Hal here is kept the Bank of England.

Grub Street, by Market Street, W.

Grub Street, in Chizel Street, L. Tho' it go by the Name down into Forestreet by lower Moor field, yet it is not properly Grub Street any farth than the Post and Chain ; and the other part of in the Freedom or Liberty of the City, is G*Street*.

Guildhall Yard, by Guildhall, L. This Hall wa first built by Sir *Thomas Knolles*, Lord Mayor London, in the 12th Year of King *Henry* the fourth *Anno* 1411; but after the Fire of London, it wa built more magnificently, and adorned with ic Hangings, lively Effigies of Kings and Queens many of the Nobility, Ministers of State, Judge the Statues of the famous Giants *Gogmagog* and Co *rineus*, and several Trophies taken from the *French* at the bloody Battle of *Ramillies*.

Gun Alley, in Barnaby Street, S.

Gun Alley, in Wellclose, L.

Gunpowder Alley, in Shoe Lane, L.

Gun Ynd, in Bishopsgatestreet without, L.

Gun land, in Honndsditch, L.

Gun Yard, near St. Mary Overy's Church, S.

Gutter Lane, in Cheapside, L.

H A

Haberdashers Square, in Grub Street, L.

Halfmoon Alley, in Bishopsgatestreet without, L

Halfmo

Halfmoon Alley, in Foster lane, L.

Halfmoon Alley, in little Moorfield, by Moor-fields, L.

Halfmoon Alley, in Purpool lane, L.

Halfmoon Court, without Ludgate, L.

Halfmoon Street, in Petty France in lower Moor-field, L.

Halfmoon Street, in the Strand, L. so called from the Halfmoon Tavern at the Corner of it; but its present Name is Bedford Street.

Halfpav'd Court, in Salisbury Court in Fleet-street, L.

Halfpenny Alley, by London Street, S.

Hand Alley, in Bishopsgatestreet without, L.

Hand Alley, opposite almost to Great Turnstile, L.

Hand and Crown Alley, at Cowcross, L.

Hand and Pen Alley, on Great Towerhill, L.

Handcock's Yard, in Water lane, L.

Hand Court, near Dowgate Wharf, in Thames street, L.

Hanging Sword Alley, in Water lane, L.

Hanging Sword Alley, on Ludgatehill, L.

Hanging Sword Court, in Fleetstreet, L.

Hanover Court, in Butler's Alley in Grub Street, L.

Hanover Court, in Houndsditch, L.

Hanover Square, L.

Hanover Street, by Hanover Square, L.

Hanover Street, in Long Acre, L.

Hanover Yard, by St. Giles's Pound, L.

Hare Court, in Hare Street in Brick lane, L.

Hare Street, in Brick lane in Whitechapel, L.

Harp Alley, in Shoe lane, L. A noted Place for brokers, selling and buying old Houshold Goods.

Harp Court, in Black Horse Court in Fleetstreet, L.

Harp Lane, in Thames Street, L.

Harris's Alley, in Brook Street near Ratcliff High-way, L.

Harrow Alley, at Whitechapel, L.

E

Harrow Alley, in Old Street, L.

Harrow Court, by Fleet lane, L.

Hart Alley, in Grub Street, L.

Hartshorn Lane, in the Strand, L.

Hart Street, by James's Street near Covent Garden, L.

Hart Street, by the New Church near Bloomsbury, L.

Hart Street, in Crutched Fryers, L.

Hart Street, just within Cripplegate, L. The North side of this Street contains, for the most part, Almshouses.

Hastings Rents, by Saffronhill, L.

Hat and Tun Yard, in little Kirby Street, L.

Hatfield Street, in Golwell Street, L.

Hatton Court, in Threadneedle Street, L.

Hatton Garden, in Holbourn, L. It was built out of the Lord *Hatton's* House, and also a Chapel on the East side of it; but never consecrated.

Hatton Wall, by Hatton Garden, L.

Haydon Yard Court, in the little Minories, L.

Haydon Yard, in the Great Minories, L.

Hayhill Row, near Hyde Park, L.

Hay Market, in Piccadilly, L. Here is a fine Theatre where Opera's are acted.

Hanns's Court, in Swallow Street, L.

Hays's Court, by Newport Market, L.

Heart Row Street, just without Newgate, L. So called because it represents the Shape of an human Heart.

Hedge Lane, near Charing Crols, L.

Helmet Court, against London Wall, by Bishopgate, L.

Helmet Court, against London Wall, by Coleman Street, L.

Helmet Court, in Thames Street, L.

Helmet Row, in Old Street, L. It is a pretty Pile of Houses, built *Anno* 1719.

Hem

Hemlock Court, by Ship Yard in the Strand, L.

Hemming's Row, against St. Martin's private churchyard, in St. Martin's lane in the Strand, L.

Hen and Chickens Court, in Fleetstreet, L.

Henneage Lane, by the Jews new Synagogue, L. is otherwise called, *Lousie Lane*.

Henrietta Street, by Covent Garden, L.

Henry Street, by Old Street Square, L.

Hercules Pillars Alley, in Fleetstreet, L.

Hermitage, at Wapping, L.

Hewits Court, near Church Court in the Strand, L.

Hickman's Folly, in Mill Street, S.

High Holbourn, L. It extends from Holbourn Bars St. Giles's Street, L.

High Street, vid. *St. Giles's Street.* – –

High Street, near King Edward's Row, by Whitechapel, L

Hind Court, in Fleetstreet, L.

Hitchers Yard, in Petty France, W.

Hockly i' th' Hole, near Hatton Wall, L. Noted r Bull and Bear-baiting, and Gladiators fighting izes there.

Hockenhall's Court, in Black Eagle Street in Spitefields.

Hockster's Alley, in Tyburn Road, L.

Hog Lane, in Shoreditch, L.

Hog Lane, near Denmark Street, L. It is also ll d Ground Street.

Hog Yard, by Tothill Fields, W. In this Yard e Almshouses, founded by Dame *Dacres*, a Lady Honour to Queen *Elizabeth*; and in the above-id Fields, is a Bridewell for the Correction of idy Rogues and Strumpets

Hog Yard, in Blackman Street, S.

Hole in the Wall Yard, near Bloomsbury Mar-t, L.

Holbourn Hill, L. It extends from Snowhill to itton Garden; and on the North side of it is an

House

Houfe belonging to the Bifhops of *Ely*, almoft op
pofite to St. Andrew's Church.

Halfords Alley, in Drury lane, L.

Holland Street, in Blackfryers, L.

Holland Street, in Wardour Street, L.

Hollis Street, by Clare Market, L.

Holloway Court, in Nevils Court, in Rofema
lane, L.

Holloway Lane, in Shoreditch, L.

Hollybufh Court, on the Backfide of St. Clement's

Holman Alley, in Bunhill Row, L

Holywell Street by St. Leonards Church in Sho
ditch, L

Holywell Street, by the Backfide of St. Cleme
in the Strand, L.

Honey Lane, in Cheapfide, L.

Honey Lane Market, in Honey lane, L. A Mar
is kept here on *Tuefdays*, *Thurfdays* and *Saturdays.*

Honeyfuckle Court, in Grub Street, L.

Hookers Court, in Nicholas lane, L.

Hoop Alley, in Old Street, L.

Hoopers Square, by Rupert Street near Whi
chapel, L.

Hopton Street, near Berwick Street, L.

Horn Alley, in Alderfgateftreet, L.

Horn Court, in Peter Street near Tothill Fields.

Horns Yard, in Kent Street, S.

Horfefhoe Alley, at Whitechapel,

Horfefhoe Alley, in Bunhill Field by upper Mo
field, L.

Horfefhoe Alley, in Cock lane by Weft Smi
field, L.

Horfefhoe Alley, in Gardiners lane in Kingftreet,

Horfefhoe Alley, in middle Moorfield, L.

Horfefhoe Alley in Pety France, W

Horfefhoe Alley, on the Bankfide, S,

Horfefhoe Court, in Clements lane by Cleme
Inn, L,

Horseshoe Court, in Old Street, L.
Horslydown Backstreet, S.
Horslydown, by Tooly Street, S.
Horslydown Forestreet, S.
Horslydown Lane, S
Hosier Lane, in West Smithfield, L.
Houghton Street, by Clare Market, L.
Houndsditch, without Bishop'gate, L.
Howard Street, in Norfolk Street in the Strand, L.
Howfords Court, in Nicholas lane, L
Hoxton Market Place, near Oldstreet Road, L.
ut no Market (tho' it is called so) is kept here
present
Hudsons Court, on Great Towerhill, L.
Hugging Lane, by the Church of St. Michael
Queenhith in Thames Street, L.
Hughs's Alley, in Blackfryers, L.
Hungerford Market, in the Strand, L. The Market is kept here on *Wednesdays* and *Saturdays,* and ere is a Plying-place for Watermen. 'Tis built
here formerly stood an House belonging to a
night of that Name.
Hunt's Court, in Castle Street near Newport Market, L.
Hyde Street, near Bow Street by Broad St.
iles's, L.

J A

Jack Adams's Alley, by Saffronhill, L.
Jackson's Alley, in little Russel Street, in Drury
ne, L.
Jackson's Court, by Ireland Yard in Blackfryers, L.
Jacob's Alley, in Golwell Street, L.
Jacob's Street, in Mill Street, S.
James Street, by Golden Square, L.
James Street, by Petty France, W. At the end
hereof the Viscount *Stafford,* who was beheaded

on Towerhill, in the Reign of King *Charles* the Second, had an House, now not much minded by the Family; and *John Sheffield*, late Duke of *Buckingham*, another, fronting also St. James's Park.

James Street, in Covent Garden, L.

James Street, in the Hay Market, L.

James Street, in Pitfield Street by Hoxton Mad Place, L.

Idle Lane, in Great Tower Street, L.

Jermyn Street, near St. James's Market, L.

Jerusalem Alley, near the Monument, L.

Jerusalem Court, in St. John's Square by St. John Lane, L.

Jewen Street, in Aldersgate Street, L.

Ingram Court, in Fenchurch Street, L.

John's Hill, in Ratcliff Highway, L.

Johnson's Court, in Fleetstreet, L.

John Street, by Golden Square, L.

John Street, in Long Ditch, W.

Joyners Street, in Tooly Street, S.

Ireland Yard, by Fryers Street in Blackfryers, L.

Irish Alley, at Whitechapel, L.

Ironmonger Lane, in Cheapside, L.

Ironmonger Row, in Old Street, L. A pretty Parcel of Houses, built *Anno* 1715.

Ivy Lane, in Paternoster Row.

K E

Keeland Row, at the end of Shoreditch, L. This is also called, *Cuckolds Row*.

Kent Street, S. At the end of it is a Bridge which divides the County of *Kent* from the County of *Surry*. On one side hereof, towards Southwark is a Chapel with Almshouses, built by *Martin Bond* Esq; which are now called the *Lock*, and is a sort of Hospital converted to the Use of Persons infected with the French Pox.

Killigrew

Killigrew Court, in Scotland Yard at White-chapel, L.

King David's Lane, in Ratcliff Highway, L.

King Edward's Row, near Whitechapel, L.

King Edward's Street, at Wapping, L.

King Edward's Street, by Fleetditch, L.

King John's Court, in Barnaby Street, S. It is seated near the Church of St. Mary Magdalen Bermondsey; and by the Stone Walls and Gateways still remaining there, it seems to be a Place of great antiquity.

King John's Court, in Holloway lane in Shoreditch, L. It is an old Piece of Building, but does not shew so much Antiquity as to be built in his reign

King's Arms Court, on Ludgate Hill, L.

King's Arms Yard, in Coleman Street, L.

King's Arms Yard, in Shoreditch, L.

King's Bench Alley, near St. George's Church, S. 'Tis so called from the King's Bench Prison by it, where are Criminals as well as Debtors; who, for Money, may have Privilege of the Marshal to walk at in the Rules thereabouts.

King's Court, in Russel Street in Drury lane, L.

King's Gate Street, in High Holbourn, L. So called from a Fivebar Gate fix'd there when a Field, thro' which our Kings were wont to pass, when they went to Newmarket.

King's Head Alley, in the Maze, S.

King's Head Court, against Vinegar Yard in Drury lane, L

King's Head Court, in Beech lane, L.

King's Head Court, in Golden lane, L.

King's Head Court, in Gutter lane in Cheapside, L.

King's Head Court, in little Carter lane, L.

King's Head Court, in Middle Holbourn, L.

King's Head Court, in Shoe lane, L.

King's Head Court, in St. Martin le Grand, L.

King's

King's Head Court, in Whitecrofs Street, L.
King's Head Court, in Woodftreet, L.
King's Head Yard, in Shoreditch, L.
King's Head Yard, in Tooly ſtreet, L.
King's Square, by Greek Street, L. It is otherwiſe called *Soho Square*, where the Duke of *Monmouth* was building a fine Houſe, before he was beheaded, but never finiſh'd it.
King Street, by Bloomsbury Square, L.
King Street, by Hays's Court near the Hay Market, L.
King Street, by Old Street Square, in Old Street, L.
King Street, by St. James's Square, L.
King Street, in Cheapſide, L.
King Street, in Covent Garden, L.
King Street, in Dean Street, by Soho Square, L.
King Street, in Princes Street, near St. Ann Church in Sono, L.
King Street, in Spittlefields, L.
King Street, in the Mint, S.
King Street, in Upper Moorfield, L.
King Street, near Golden Square, L. Here the Duke of *Argyle* hath a pretty Houſe.
King Street, near the Six Dials, L.
King Street, on Great Towerhill, L.
King Street, W. Here is the *George Inn*, where is good Entertainment for Man and Horſe.
Knaves Acre, L.
Knight Rider Street, L.
Knight's Court, on the Backſide of St. Clements by the Strand, L.

L A

Labour in vain Alley, on St. Margarets Hill, L.
Labour in vain Court, on Old Fiſhſtreet Hill, L.
Labour in vain Hill, L. The ſame as *Old Fiſhſtreet Hill*.

Labour in vain Street, at lower Shadwell, L.

Ladies Alley, in Kingſtreet, W.

Lad Lane, againſt St. Michael's Church in Wood ſtreet, L.

Lamb Alley, in Biſhopſgateſtreet without, L.

Lamb Alley, in Mugwell Street, L. Here is a Chapel, called Lamb's Chapel.

Lamb Court, by Clerkenwell, L.

Lambeth Hill, in Thames Street, L.

Lamb's Conduit Paſſage, by Red Lion Square, L.

Lamb Street, by Spittlefields, L.

Lancaſter Court, in New Bond Street, L.

Lancaſter Court, near St. Martin's lane in the Strand, L.

Langley Street, in Long Acre, L.

Lant's Court, in Orange Street, L.

Laſt Alley, at Cow Croſs, L.

Laundry Court, in Maſham Street, W.

Laurence Lane, by St. Giles's Pound, L.

Laurence Lane, in Cheapſide, L.

Laurence Poultney Lane, in Cannon Street, L.

Leadenhall Market, in Leadenhall Street, L. Where the greateſt and fineſt Market in *Europe* is kept (as one may ſay) every Day in the Week, except *Sundays*.

Leadenhall Street, L. Here are the Houſes of the India and African Companies.

Leather Lane, in Middle Holbourn, L.

Lee's Rents, in Purpool lane, L.

Lee Street, by Red Lion Square, L.

Leg Alley, in Long Acre, L.

Leiceſter Fields, L. So called from the Earl of Leiceſter's Houſe, where the Prince of *Wales*, at preſent, keeps his Court, when in Town.

Leiceſter Street, by little Grays Inn lane, L.

Leiceſter Street, in Swallow Street, L.

Lemon Street, near Whitechapel, L.

Leyden

Leyden Street, in Fox lane at Upper Shadwell, L.

Lichfield Street, near the Six Dials, L.

Lillypot Street, by Foster lane, L.

Limehouse Causeway, near Limehouse Hole, L.

Limehouse Corner, near Limehouse Hole, L.

Limehouse Hole, L.

Lincolns Inn Fields, by Lincolns Inn, L. The West side of it, where the Duke of *Newcastle* has a fine House, is called *Arch Row* ; the South side of it, where the Earl of *Cardigan* has a pretty House, is called *Portugal Row* ; and the North side is called *Holbourn Row*.

Lincolns Inn, in Chancery lane, L. It is one of the four Inns of Court ; and here the Stamp Office is kept.

Lincolns Inn Square, in Lincolns Inn, L. Otherwise call'd *Serle's Court*.

Liquor Pond Street, in Grays Inn lane, L.

Little Ambrey, near Deans Yard, W.

Little Bell Yard, in Coleman Street, L.

Little Bridges Street, in Great Bridges Street, L.

Little Britain, in Aldersgatestreet, L.

Little Carter Lane, by Great Carter lane, L.

Little Cary Street, by Lincolns Inn Fields, L.

Little Catherine Street, in great Catherine Street in the Strand, L.

Little Chapel Street, by New Chapel, W.

Little Distaff Lane, against Cordwainers Hall, L.

Little Drury Lane, against the New Church in the Strand, L. At the North end of it a May-pole lately stood, put up by a Farrier, to commemorate his Daughter's good Fortune of arriving to the Dignity of Dutchess of *Albemarle*, by being married to General *Monk* when he was but a private Gentleman.

Little Eastcheap, against Great Eastcheap, L.

Little Friday Street, in Great Friday Street, L.

Little George Street, in Spittlefields, L.

Little

Little Glocester Street, in Whitecrofs Street, L.

Little Grays Inn Lane, in Great Grays Inn lane, L.

Little Germyn Street, in St. James's Street, L.

Little King street, in St. James's Street, by St. James's Palace, L.

Little Kirby Street, in Hatton Garden, L.

Little Knight Rider Street, by Great Knight Rider Street, L.

Little Lamb Alley, in Blackman Street, S.

Little Love Lane, by St. Alban's Church in Woodstreet, L.

Little Marlborough Street, in Kingstreet by Golden Square, L.

Little Minories, in the Great Minories, L.

Little Moorfield, by Moorfields, L.

Little Newport Street, by Newport Street in St. Martin's lane, L.

Little New Street, near Fetter lane, L.

Little Old Baily, by Great Old Baily, L.

Little Ormond Street, by St. George's Chapel, L.

Little Queen Street, by Great Queen street in Cheapside, L.

Little Queen Street, opposite to Kingstreet in High Holbourn, L.

Little Rider Street, in St. James's Square, L.

Little Ruffel Street, in Drury lane, L.

Little Ruffel street, near Montague House, L.

Little Sanctuary, in Kingstreet, W. Here is the ancient Three Tun Tavern, kept at prefent by Mr. Leech the Quaker.

Little Sheer Lane, against Lincolns Inn Square, L.

Little St. Andrew's street, by the Six Dials, L.

Little St. Anne's Lane, W.

Little St. Helen, within Bishopsgate, L.

Little St. Martin's Lane, at North end of Great St. Martin's Lane in the Strand, L.

Little Suffolk street, near the Hay Market, L.

Little

Little Swallow street, in Great Swallow street, L

Little Swan Alley, in Gofwell street, L.

Little Tothill street, W. Here is a fine Brick Church on the Weft fide of it, call'd *New Chapel* having the pleafanteft Church Yard all about London and Weftminfter.

Little Towerhill, L. Near which is the Victualling Office, for furnifhing his Majefty's Navy with Provifions.

Little Tower street, by Great Tower street, L.

Little Trinity Lane, in Thames street L.

Little Turnftile, in High Holbourn, L.

Little Winchefter street, at London Wall, L.

Little Windmill street, by the Hay Market, L.

Lombard Court, near the Six Dials, L.

Lombard street, by Stocks Market, L. Noted for Bankers and Goldfmiths.

Lombard street, by Well ftreet near Whitechapel, L

Lombard street, in the Mint, S.

Lombard street, in Whitefryers, L.

London Bridge, L. It contains 19 Arches of Stone over the River of *Thames*, whereon are two Rows of Houfes, furnifhed with moft forts of Commodities, a Draw-Bridge, and Bridge-Gate, on which Traytors Heads are fometimes placed upon Poles It was 33 Years a building, and is not to be paralliz'd in the whole World.

Londonhoufe Yard, in St. Paul's Church Yard, L

London street, in Mill street, S.

London Wall, between Cripplegate and Moorgate, L.

London Wall, between Moorgate and Bifhopgate, L.

Long Acre, in Drury lane, L. Here is a fine Bagnio

Long Alley, in Long lane in Shoreditch, L.

Long Cellar Yard, in Eaft Smithfield, L.

Long Ditch, by Story's Gate at St. James Park, W.

Lo

Long *Lane*, by White ſtreet, S.

Long *Lane*, in Shoreditch, L.

Long *Lane*, in Weſt Smithfield, L. A Place no-
d for buying and ſelling old Cloaths.

Long *Walk*, by St. Bartholomew's Hoſpital, L.

Long *Walk*, in King John's Court, S.

Loom *Alley*, in Old Bedlam, L.

Lothbury, by Coleman Street, L.

Love *Lane*, by Aldermanbury, L.

Love *Lane*, in Thames Street, L.

Love *Lane*, near the Gatehouſe, W.

Louſe *Hall*, by Fan Alley in Goſwell Street, L.
ut it is at that End of Fan Alley going towards
idgewater Gardens.

Louſie *Lane*, vid. *Henneage Row*.

Lowen's *Rents*, in Petty France, W.

Lower *Court*, in the little Minories, L.

Lower *Gun Alley*, in Upper Gun Alley at Wap-
ng, L.

Lower *Moorfield*, at Moorgate, L. Noted for
edlam, or its fine Hoſpital for Lunaticks.

Lower *Shadwell*, L.

Loyd's *Court*, by the Church of St. Giles in the
elds, L.

Loyl *Street*, in Princes Street near St. Anne's
hurch in Soho, L.

Ludgate *Hill*, L. Here is a Goal called Ludgate,
here none but Freemen, or Citizens of London,
e confin'd for Debt.

Ludgate *Street*, near Fleetditch, L. Chiefly in-
bited, as well as Ludgate Hill, by Mercers.

Lumley *Court*, againſt Salisbury Street in the
rand, L.

Luckins's *Corner*, by Mill Street, S.

Luterners *Lane*, in Drury lane, L. It is common-
call'd *Newtners Lane*, but the Wickedneſs of its
habitants having gain'd (as well as ſome other
aces by it) the Name of *Little Sodom*, they have

F

given

given it the nice Name of *Charles Street*, as a Stone shews on the West end of it.

Luteners Street, in High Holbourn, L. It formerly went in next Holbourn, by a Gateway, over which was a School, where the learned Mr. *William Banks* taught the Hebrew, Greek and Latin Tongues.

Lydiclark Yard, in Gravel lane, L.

Lyme Street, by St. Dionis Back Church, L. Here is a pretty Hall belonging to the Pewterers Company

Lyon's Inn, in Holywell Street, S.

M A

Maddox Street, by Hanover Square, L.

Magpye Alley, in Aldersgatestreet, L.

Magpye Alley, in Bishopsgatestreet without, L.

Magpye Alley, in Crutched Fryers, L.

Magpye Alley, in Fenchurch Street, L.

Magpye Alley, in Fetter lane, L.

Magpye Alley, in Grays Inn lane, L.

Maidenhead Court, in Aldersgatestreet, L.

Maidenhead Court, in Chizel Street by Upper Moorfield, L.

Maidenhead Court, in Church lane at Whitechapel, L.

Maidenhead Court, in Grub Street, L.

Maidenhead Court, in Halfmoon Alley in little Moorfield, L.

Maidenhead Court, in Wapping, L.

Maidenhead Street, in Dyot Street, L.

Maiden Lane, by College Hill, near Cheapside, L.

Maiden Lane, by Goldsmiths Hall, L.

Maiden Lane, by Shandos Street, L.

Maid lane, S.

Manchester Court, in Channel Row, W.

Mannors Street, by St. Giles's Pound, L.

Mansfield Street, by Prescod Street, L.

Margu

Margates Court, against St. James's Church in
iccadilly, L.

Market lane, near St. James's Market, L.

Market Street, by the Horse Ferry, W.

Mark lane, by Fenchurch Street, L. Its right
ame is *Mart lane*, from a Mart, or Fair, formerly
ept in it.

Marlborough Court, by Berwick Street, L.

Marsh, by Strandgate, in the Parish of St. Mary
Lambeth, S. It extends from Strandgate, or
andgate, to College Street.

Martlet Court, in Bow Street by Covent Garden, L.

Marybone Street, by Warwick Street near Picca-
illy, L.

Marygold Alley, near Burleigh Street in the Strand,
. It was in Old Times called the *Py'd Fryers*,
om some Religious Order, perhaps, that had a
onvent there.

Marygold Street, by West lane at Southwark
Vall, S.

Masham Street, W.

Mason's Alley, in Basinghall Street, L.

Masters's Alley, at Mill Bank, W.

Mayfair Row, behind Hayhill Row, L. Here
as formerly a Fair kept in the Month of *May*, but
hath been put down for some Years, upon Ac-
unt of a Constable being kill'd there, in the Ex-
ution of his Office, by one *Cook*, a Butcher; for
hich Murder he was hang'd at Tyburn, in 1703.

Maypole Alley, in Wich Street, L.

Maypole Alley, on St. Margaret's Hill, S.

Maze Court, at the end of the Maze, S.

Maze, in Tooly Street, S. Here are many Hat-
akers.

Maze Pond, in the Maze, S.

Medes Court, in Old Bond Street, L.

Mercers Court, in Great Tower Street, L.

Mercers Street, in Long Acre, L.

F 2

Merchants

Merchants lane, in Thames Street, L.

Meuse, by Charing Crofs in the Strand, L. H
the K.ng's Coaches and Horfes are kept.

Middle Holbourn, L. It reaches from Hatt
Garden to Holbourn Bars, L.

● *Middle Moorfield*, by Moorgate, L. At the Sou
Corner of it is fixed on a Stone faften'd in t
Ground, an Iron Sun Dial, with this Infcriptn
thereon : This Dial was placed here as a Bound
of the Parifh of St. *Stephen Coleman Street*, in t
memorable Year 1706, and in the 5th Year of t
glorious Reign of our moft gracious Sovereig
whom God long preferve.

Middle Row, at the end of Monmouth Street,

Middle Row, by Holbourn Bars, L. They
moft Perriwig-makers who live here.

Middlefex Court, in Drury lane, L.

Middle Shadwell, by Barns's Hill in Upper Sh
well, L.

Middle Street, by Cloth Fair, L.

Mifoot Alley, by Dormant Hill, W. It is
called *Brack Alley*.

Miless lane, near Fifhmongers Hall in Than
Street, L.

Milford lane, in the Strand, L.

Milk Alley, by St. Anne's Church, L.

Milk Alley, in Peter Street by Stanhope Street,

Milk Alley, in Wapping, L.

Milk Street, in Cheapfide, L.

Mill Bank, by the Thames fide, W. Here
Ferry, which wafts over Coaches, Horfes and f
fengers, to Lambeth.

Mill lane, in Tooly Street, S.

Mill Mount, by Gofwell Street, L.

Mill Street, by Dockhead, S.

Mill Street, in Conduit Street near Piccadilly,

Mill Yard, in Rofemary lane, L.

Minc

Mincing lane, in Fenchurch Street, **L.** Here is he Clothiers Hall.

Mint Street, in the Mint, **S.**

Mitre Alley, in St. John Street, **L.**

Mitre Court, by Friday Street, **L.**

Mitre Court, in Fleetstreet, **L.**

Mitre Court, in Shoemakers Row, just within Aldgate, **L.**

Monmouth Court, by little Turnstile in Holbourn, **L.**

Monmouth Court, in Monmouth Street, **L.**

Monmouth Street, near the Six Dials, **L.** It is mostly inhabited by Salesmen and Brokers.

Montague Court, in Little Britain, **L.**

Montague Street, in Spittlefields, **L.**

Monument Yard, on Fishstreet Hill, **L.** So called rom a Stone Pillar of a most stupendious Height rected there, to perpetuate the Remembrance of hat most dreadful Conflagration which burnt down he City of London in 1666.

Moor's Alley, at Norton Faldgate, **L.**

Moor's Alley, in Kingstreet, **W.**

Moor's Court, on Old Fishstreet Hill, **L.**

Moor's lane, in Forestreet by Moorfields, **L.**

Moor Street, near Compton Street in Soho, **L.**

Morgan s lane, in Tooly Street, **S.**

Morle's Court, in Forestreet by Moorfields, **L.**

Moscovy Court, on Great Towerhill, **L.**

Moses and Aaron Alley, in Whitechapel, **L.**

Moses's Alley, by Smock Alley in Spittlefields, **L.**

Mouse Alley, in East Smithfield, **L.**

Much Court, near Schoolhouse lane in Broad Street, by Ratcliff Highway, **L.**

Muggarts Court, in Milkstreet, **L.**

Mugwell Street, by Silver Street, **L.**

Mutton Court, in Maiden lane, by Goldsmiths Hall, **L.**

Mutton lane, near Clerkenwell Green, **L.**

Nags

N A

Nags Head Alley, on St. Margarets Hill, S.

Nags Head Court, by the Monument on Fishstre Hill, L.

Nags Head Court, in Gracechurch street, L.

Nags Head Court, on Snowhill, L.

Narrow Wall, by the Thames side, L. It extend from College Street to Cupid's Bridge, and thenc to Angel Street.

Naylors Yard, in Queen Street by the Six Dials,

Neat Houses, a little beyond the Earl of *Petc borough*'s House at Mill Bank, W. They are a fe scattering Houses on the Thames Side in Toth Fields, inhabited mostly by Gardiners.

Neckinger, by Southwark Wall, S.

Nelsons Court, in Drury lane, L.

Neptune Street, in Ratcliff Highway, L.

Nettleton Court, in Aldersgate Street, L.

Nevils Alley, in Fetter lane, L.

Nevils Court, in Rosemary lane, L.

New Bond Street, by Old Bond Street, L.

Newcastle Court, in Butcher Row by Templ Bar, L.

New Court, in Cary Street, L. Before *Dan Burges*, the Presbyterian Parson, had a Meetin house built here, it was called *Rogue lane*; havin been in old Times (as Tradition goes) a Place. fc the Execution of Malefactors.

New Court, in little New Street near Fett lane, L.

New Court, in the Middle Temple, L.

New Court, in Throgmorton Street, L.

New Crane, by Wapping, L.

New Exchange, in the Strand, L. It was nam Great Britains *Burse*, by King *James* the first.

New Fishstreet, by Great Eastcheap, L.

New Fishstreet Hill, by the Monument, L.

Newgate Market, in Newgate Street, L. The Market is kept on *Tuesdays, Thursdays* and *Saturdays.*

Newgate Street, L. It was formerly called *Chamberlain Gate* ; and the Place of Confinement over it, the County Goal for Malefactors, and such Debtors who are arrested by the Officers under the Sheriff of *Middlesex.*

New George Street, in Spittlefields, L.

New Gravel lane, in Ratcliff Highway, L.

Newington Causeway, by Blackman Street, S.

New Inn, in Wich Street in Drury lane, L.

New Inn Yard, in Shoreditch, L.

New Leg Court, in Peter Street, W.

Newman's Court, in Cornhill, L.

Newmarket Street, at the end of Old Gravel lane by Wapping, L.

New Middle Row, in Goswell Street, L. Built anno 1692.

New Northstreet, by Red Lion Square, L.

New Ormond Street, by Great Ormond Street, L.

New Packthread Alley, in Grange Road, S.

New Palace Yard, W. Here is the largest Hall in Europe, in which are kept the High Court of Chancery, and the Courts of King's Bench, Common Pleas, and Exchequer. Here is also a Plying-place for Watermen, called Westminster Bridge.

Newport Court, by little Newport Street, L.

Newport Market, L. Built where the Earl of Newport's House formerly stood ; and its Market Days are on *Wednesdays* and *Saturdays.*

Newport Street, in St. Martin's lane in the Strand, L.

New Pye Street, by Orchard Street, W.

New Queen Street, in Oxford Street in Tyburn Road, L.

New Red Lion Court, in Cursitors Alley, L.

New Rents, in St. Martin le Grand, L.

New

New Street, in St. Martins lane in the Strand, L.

New Street, by Cam's Court in Hopton Street, L.

New Street, by Cloth Fair, **L.**

New Street, by Old Street Square, **L.**

New Street, by Shoe lane, **L.** Noted for Cutlers

New Street, by the Maze, S.

New Street, in lower Shadwell, **L.**

New Street, in Pig Street by Threadneedle street, L.

New Street Square, near Fetter lane, **L.**

New Way, near Maze Pond, S.

New Yard, by Holbourn Bars, L.

Nicholas Court, in Rosemary lane, **L.**

Nicholas lane, in Cannon Street, **L.**

Nichol Newstreet, in Spittlefields, **L.**

Nichol Street, in Spittlefields, **L.**

Nightingale lane, by Forestreet at Limehouse, L.

Nightingale lane, in East Smithfield, **L.**

Nippards Court, in Baldwyn's Garden, **L.**

Noah's Ark Alley, in Forestreet at Limehouse, L.

Noble Street, by Foster lane, **L.**

Noble Street, in Goswell Street, **L.**

Norfolk Street, in the Strand, **L.** Built where the Duke of *Norfolk's* House formerly stood.

Norris Street, by St. James's Market, **L.**

North Street, by Red Lion Square, **L.**

North Street, by Spittlefields Market, **L.**

Northumberland Alley, in Fenchurch Street, L.

Northumberland Court, by Northumberland House in the Strand, **L.**

Northumberland Court, in Old Southampton Buildings in High Holbourn, **L.** It is also called *King's Head Court*, from an adjacent Tavern bearing the Sign of King *Henry* the Eighth.

Norton Faldgate, by Bishopsgatestreet, **L.**

Nottingham Street, by Plumstreet Square, **L.**

Norwich Court, by the Maypole in East Smithfield, **L.**

Of

O A

Oar Street, in Gravel lane, S.

Oatmeal Yard, in Crucifix lane, S.

Oat Street, in Noble Street near Foster lane, L.

Off Alley, in York Buildings, L.

Old Artillery Ground, in Spittlefields, L.

Old Bedlam, in lower Moorfield, L. Its right Name is *Bethlehem*.

Old Bond Street, in Piccadilly, L.

Old Change, near Watling Street, L.

Old Fishstreet Hill, by Nicholas Church, L.

Old Fishstreet, L.

Old Gravel lane, in Ratcliff Highway, L.

Old Jewry Court, by the Church of St. Olave Jewry in Old Jewry, L.

Old Jewry, in Cheapside, L. Several Places in London have the Denomination of *Jewry*, from some few Jews who dwelt thereabout in former Times; but now they are exceedingly more increased both in Number and Wealth, than heretofore, when they were banished, taxed, and punished by King *Edward* the First, and others.

Old Packthread Alley, in Grange Road, S.

Old Palace Yard, W. Here is the Parliament House, in which the Lords Spiritual and Temporal sit; and St. Stephen's Chapel is the Place the Commons meet to do Business. Here is also a Plying-place for Watermen.

Old Pye Street, by Duck lane, W.

Old Street, L.

Old Street Square, in Old Street, L. But its right Name is St. *Bartholomew Square*, as belonging to St. Bartholomew's Hospital.

Old Southampton Buildings, in High Holbourn, L.

Old Swan lane, in Thames street, L. Here is a Plying-place for Watermen.

Oliver's

Oliver's Alley, near Lumly Court in the Strand,

Oliver's Court, in the Bowling Alley, W.

Orange Court, in Orange ſtreet, L.

Orange Street, by Red Lion Square, L.

Orange Street, in Caſtle Street by the Meuſe, Built where the Duke of *Monmouth* (that was beheaded) had an Houſe, called *Monmouth's Stables.*

Orchard Street, W.

Ormond Street, by Queen's Square, L. Here is ſtately Stone Houſe, belonging to 'Squire *Herbert* called Lord *Powis*; and behind it is a Well, whoſe Water is reckon'd Medicinal for ſore Eyes.

Oxendon ſtreet, near the Hay Market, L.

Oxford Court, by St. Swithin's Church in Cannon Street, L.

Oxford Square, in Tyburn Road, L. This Road is ſo called from a Gallows having 3 Poſts ſupporting 3 Beams triangular-wiſe, for the Execution of Malefactors.

Oxford ſtreet, by St. Giles's Pound, L. It extends to the new Buildings on both ſides the Road.

P A

Packers Court, in Coleman Street, L.

Pallmall, by St. James's Houſe, L.

Pallmall Court, in Pallmall, L.

Palſgrave Court, near Temple Bar in the Strand, L.

Pancras lane, by little Queen ſtreet near Cheapſide, L. So called from the Church of St. Pancras in it.

Pannier Alley, in Paternoſter Row, L.

- *Panton ſtreet*, by Leiceſter Fields, L.

Paris Garden, by Gravel lane, S. Here was formerly much Bearbaiting, and other the like Sports, which are now uſed at *Hockly i' th' Hole*; alſo here was lately a cucking Stool, hanging over a large Pond, for the ducking of ſcolding Women; but it now down.   And here is a Plying-place for Wa-men

Parish ftreet, in Horflydown, S.

Parkers lane, in Drury lane, L.

Parkers Rents, in Whitecrofs ftreet, L.

Park Place, by the ftone Steps in St. James's ſtreet, L.

Park Profpect, in Queen ſtreet, L.

Park ftreet, by Cartwright ſtreet, W.

Parfons Court, in Bride lane, L.

Parmers Yard, in Shoreditch, L.

Paternofter Row, by Cheapfide Conduit, L.

Paternofter Row, fronting the New Church in Spittlefields, L.

Patricks Court, in Houndfditch, L.

Pav'd Alley, againſt Bridewell Bridge, L.

Pav'd Alley, in King John's Court by Holloway Lane in Shoreditch, L.

Pav'd Alley, in St. James's Market, L.

Pav'd Alley, in Whitefryers, L.

Pav'd Court, in Fullers Rents, L.

Paviours Court, in Grub ftreet, L.

Paulin ftreet, in Hanover Square, L.

Paul's Alley, in Alderfgateftreet, L.   Here is a Prefbyterian Meetinghoufe.

Paul's Alley, in Chizel Street, L.

Paul's Alley, in St. Paul's Churchyard, L.

Paul's Chain, by St. Paul's Churchyard, L.   Here kept the Herald's Office, belonging to the Earl Marfhal of England.

Paul's Court, in Fenchurch ftreet, L.

Paul's Court, in Whitefryers, L.

Paul's Wharf, againſt St. Bennets Church in Thames ſtreet, L.

Peal's Alley, in Upper Shadwell, L.

Pearl ftreet, in Spittlefields, L.

Pearman's Buildings, in Stable Yard, W.

Pear

Pen ftreet, by Duck lane, W.

Peartree Alley, in Shoreditch, L.

Peartree Court, in Hockly in the Hole, L.

Pedlars ftreet, in new Bond Street, L.

Peel's Alley, in Barnaby ftreet, S.

Pelham ftreet, in Spittlefields, L.

Pennington ftreet, by John's Hill in Ratcliff Highway, L.

Penfioners Alley, by Kingftreet, W.

Pepper Alley, near the Bridgefoot, L. Where a Plying-place for Watermen.

Pepper ftreet, near Duke ftreet, S.

Perkins s Rents, by New Pye Street, W.

Perkins's Rents, in Leather lane, L.

Perriwinckle ftreet, by Ratcliff Square, L.

Pefcod Alley, in St. John ftreet, L.

Peter Alley, by St. Peter's Church in Cornhill, L.

Peterborough Court, in Fleetftreet, L.

Peterborough Court, in Little Britain, L.

Peter Hill, in Thames ftreet, L. Here are are Almhoufes for 6 poor Widows, built by Dan Smith, Embroiderer to Queen *Elizabeth*, in the Year 1564; and left to the Governors of Chrift Hofpital; but being burnt down in 1666, the were rebuilt by Sir *Thomas Fitch*, Knight.

Peter lane, by Hicks's Hall, L.

Peter's Court, in Wheelbarrow Alley in Rofema lane, L.

Peter Street, by Berwick ftreet, L.

Peter ftreet, by Bow ftreet at the End of High Holbourn, L.

Peter ftreet, by Smith's Street, W.

Peter ftreet, in Stanhope ftreet, L.

Peter ftreet, in Tunball ftreet, L.

Peter ftreet, near Tothill Fields, L.

Petticoat lane, in Whitechapel, L.

Petty France, by the Broadway, W.

Petty France, in lower Moorfield, L.

Ph

Philip lane, near Sion College, L.

Phillips Court, in Grub street, L.

Philpot lane, near little Eastcheap, L.

Phœnix Alley, in Hart street, near Covent Garden, L.

Phœnix Court, in Newgate street, L.

Phœnix street, in Plumtree street, by St. Giles's church in the Fields, L.

Piccadilly, by the Hay Market, L.

Pickaxe street, vid. Aldersgatestreet.

Pig street, by Broad street, L.

Pilkington Court, in Little Britain, L.

Pine Alley, in the Broadway, W.

Pipemakers Alley, in Great St. Anne's lane, W.

Pinnershall Court, in Broadstreet, L. So called from the Hall of that Company built there; and used by the Presbyterians for a Meetinghouse.

Pissing Alley, against Surry street in the Strand, L.

Pissing Alley, in Bread street, L.

Pitfield street, near Hoxton Square, L. At the north end of this Street is a stately Hospital, built on 48 Pillars of Stone, Anno 1692, at the Charge of Robert Ake, Esq; whose Effigies is placed over the middle of it, with an Inscription on it thus: The Worshipful Company of Haberdashers built this pursuant to the Gift and Trust of Robert Aske, Esq, a late worthy Member of it, for the Relief of Members, and for the Education of 20 Boys, Sons of deceased Freemen of the Company.

Playhouse Yard, in Whitecross street, L.

Plough Alley, in Barnaby street, S.

Plough Court, in Grays Inn lane, L.

Ploughman's Rents, in Tunball street, L.

Plough street, in Whitechapel, L.

Plough Yard, in Fetter lane, L.

Plumtree Court, on Holbourn Hill, L.

Plumtree Square, in Plumtree street, L.

Plumtree street, in St. Giles's, L.

G

Plympton

Plympton Court, in Forestreet, by Moorfields, L

Poland street, by Broad Street near Cambrid Street, L.

Poppins Alley, in Fleetstreet, L.

Puppit Court, in Shoe lane, L.

Porridgepot Alley, in Alderlgate-street, L.

Porte's Block, in St. John's Street, L.

Porter street, near Newport Market, L.

Portugal Street, by Lincolns Inn Fields, L. He is a New Theatre or Playhouse.

Postern by Aldermanbury, L. There is anoth short Street by it, on the lane side of the wa which also goes through London Wall, in For street, called *Postern.*

Postern, by Great Towerhill, L.

Poultry Alley, going into the Poultry Compter,

Poultry, in Cheapside, L. Here is a Prison ca led the *Poultry Compter,* where both Debtors a Criminals are confined.

Powder'd Beef Court, in Cabbage lane, W.

Prescod street, in Lemon Street, near Whit chapel, L.

Preston's Yard, in the Great Minories, L.

Price's Court, in Gravel lane, L.

Prichard's Alley, in Barnaby Street, S.

Primrose Alley, in Bishopsgatestreet without, L

Primrose Alley, near St. Mary Overy's Church,

Prince's Court, in Drury lane, L.

Prince's Court, in Long Ditch, L.

Prince's Court, in Lothbury, L.

Prince's Court, on little Towerhill, L.

Prince's Row, by Chapel Street near Upper Moo field, L. It is a pretty Row of Houses, new built on the South side of the Artillery Ground.

Prince's street, by Hanover Square, L.

Prince's street, by Red Lion Square, L.

Prince's street, by St. Anne's Church, L.

Prince's street, in Barbican, L.

Prince's street, in Drury lane, L.

Prince's street, near Stocks Market, L.

Printinghouse street, in Blackfryers, L.

Printinghouse Yard, in Blackfryers, L. Here is the King's Printinghouse, where Bibles, Common Prayer Books, Proclamations, Acts of Parliament, and other Things, are printed by his Majesty's Authority.

Prior Alley, in Thames street, L.

Prior Lane, in Thames street, L.

Providence Court, in Peter street W.

Pumpkin's Court, in Old Baily, L.

Pudding Lane, near Monument Yard, L. Here, at Baker's House, began the most dreadful Fire of London, betwixt 11 and 12 o' th' Clock on Saturday Night, the 2d of September, 1666.

Puddle Dock, at the bottom of Puddledock Hill, L.

Puddledock Hill, at the West end of Thames street, L.

Pump Alley, in Gardiners lane in Kingstreet, W.

Pump Alley, in Perkins's Rents by New Pye street, W.

Pump Alley, near Ewers's Street in Gravel lane, L.

Pump Court, in the Middle Temple, L.

Pump Court, in White Hart Street in Catherine street in the Strand, L.

Pump Yard, in the Great Minories, L.

Pye Corner, by West Smithfield, L. A noted place for Cooks.

Q U

Quaker Street, in Spittlefields, L.

Queen's Arms Alley, in Shoreditch, L.

Queens Alley, in Upper Ground, S.

Queens Court, in Kingstreet in Covent Garden, L.

Queen's Head Alley, against London Wall by Bishopsgate, L.

Queen's Head Alley, at Wapping, L.

Queen's Head Alley, in Paternoster Row, L.

Queen's Head Court, in Great Windmill Street,

Queenhyth, in Thames Street, L. It is also call the Queen's Bank, because it was an Haven transporting Goods, for the proper Use of the a cient Queens of England ; and at this Day, c Western Barges bring vast Quantities of Corn, the Subsistence of this most populous City.

Queen's Square, by Great Ormond Street, L.

Queen's Square, by Petty France, W. Here i pretty Chapel, wherein the Service of the Chur of England is celebrated.

Queen's square, in Bartholomew Close, L.

Queen street, at the Six Dials, L.

Queen street, behind Forestreet at Limehouse, L

Queen street, by Ewer's Street, S.

Queen street, in Dean Street by Soho Square, L

Queen street, in Drury lane, L.

Queen street, in Greek Street by Soho Square, L

Queen street, in Long Ditch, W.

Queen street, in Rosemary lane, L.

Queen street, in the Mint, S.

Queen street, in Windmill Street, L.

Queen street, near Montague House, L.

Queen street, opposite to Kingstreet in Chea side, L.

Quick Apple Alley, in Bishopsgatestreet without, L

R A

Racket Court, in Fleetstreet, L.

Rag Alley, in Golden lane, L.

Ragged Staff Alley, in Drury lane, L.

Ram Alley, in Fleetstreet, L.

Ratcliff Cross, by Forestreet at Limehouse, L Here is a good Plying-place for Watermen.

Ratcliff Highway, L.

Ratcl.

Ratcliff Square, near Ratcliff Highway, L.
Ratcliff street, in Ratcliff Highway, L. Built ano 1653.
Ratlone's Place, in Tyburn Road, L.
Red Bull Alley, in Kent Street, S.
Red cross Alley, in Jewen Street, L.
Red Cross Alley, on St. Margaret's Hill, L.
Red Cross Court, in Great Tower Street, L.
Red Cross street, at the end of Queen Street, S.
Red Cross *street,* by St. Giles's Church without Cripplegate, L.
Red cross street, in East Smithfield, L.
Red Gate Court, in Rosemary lane, L.
Red Hart Court, in Forestreet by Moorfields, L.
Rathbone's Rents, in Vine street by Hatton Wall, L.
Red Lion Alley, at Cow Cross, L.
Red Lion Alley, by London Wall near Bedlam, L.
Red Lion Alley, in Barnaby Street, S.
Red Lion Court, at St. Paul's Chain, L.
Red Lion Court, at Wapping, L.
Red Lion Court, at Windmill Hill, L.
Red Lion Court, in Bennet Street near Christ church, S.
Red Lion Court, in Cock lane by West Smithfield, L.
Red Lion Court, in Drury lane, L. So called from being built on the Ground where the Red Lion Inn formerly stood.
Red Lion Court, in Fleetstreet, L.
Red Lion Court, in Silver Street by Mugwell street, L.
Red Lion Court, in White Hart Street in Catherine Street in the Strand, L. So called from an ordinary formerly kept there, which bore the Sign of the Red Lion.
Red Lion Court, in Holloway lane, L.
Red Lion Market street, in Whitecross Street, L.
Red Lion Square, L.

G 3 *Red*

Red Lion Street, by Clerkenwell, L.

Red Lion street, in High Holbourn, L. It reach from thence to Lamb's Conduit, which former stood in a Field, but now being almost ruinous, 't situated in this Street, and near it is building a ne Cnapel.

Red Lion street, in the Borough, S.

Red Lion street, in Whitechapel, L.

Red Lion Yard, in Barnaby Street, S.

Red Lion Yard, in Houndsditch, L.

Red Rose Alley, in Whitecross Street, L.

Retten's Court, in Fleetstreet, L.

Reyndeer Yard, by White Horse Yard in Dru lane, L.

Richmond street, in Princes Street near St. Anne Church, L.

Richmond street, vid. *Back street*.

Rickman's Rents, by Limehouse Bridge, L.

Rider's Court, by Newport Market, L.

Robinhood's Court, in Fetter lane, L.

Robinhood's Court, in Thames Street, L.

Rood Lane, by St. Margaret Pattons Church, L

Ropemakers Alley, in little Moorfield by Moor fields, L. At the end of this Alley is an House which has the Privilege to keep a Latch, or Door which lets one into *Grub street*, for which the Pa senger is to pay the Tenant thereof one Farthing from which Custom it is called *Farthing Latch*.

Ropemakers Field, by Three Coal Street near Lime house Hole, L.

Rope Walk, in Goswell Street, L. Near it, on the same side of the way, is another Place bearing the same Name.

Rose Alley, in Bishopsgatestreet, L.

Rose Alley, in Hand Alley in Bishopsgatestreet without, L.

Rose Alley, in High Holbourn, L.

Rose Alley, in Maid lane, S.

Rose

Rose Alley, in Thieving lane, W. It was formerly called *Scotch Alley*; but hath obtain'd its
modern Name from the Sign of the Rose, a Victu-
aling House going into it, and kept at present by
e *Thomas Smith*.

Rose Alley, in Tunball Street, L.

Rose and Crown Alley, at Whitechapel, L.

Rose and Crown Alley, in Blackman Street, S.

Rose and Crown Alley, in Tooly Street, S.

Rose and Crown Court, in Foster lane, L.

Rose and Crown Court, in Grays Inn lane, L.

Rose and Crown Court, in Rosemary lane, L.

Rose and Crown Court, in Shoe lane, L.

Rose Court, on Great Towerhill, L.

Rose Lane, in Spittlefields, L.

Rosemarybranch Alley, in Rosemary lane, L.

Rosemary Lane, by Towerhill, L.

Rose street, by Soho Square, L. Built *Anno* 1690.

Rose street, by White Horse Street near Stepney, L.

Rose street, by New Street in Covent Garden, L.

Rose Tard, in Shoreditch, L.

Round Court, in St. Martin le Grand, L.

Round Court, in the Strand, L. Noted for Mercers.

Royal Exchange, in Cornhill, L. First founded,
also Gresham College in Bishopsgatestreet, by Sir
Thomas Gresham, a rich Merchant.

Royal Oak Alley, in Barnaby Street, S.

Royal Oak Court, in Parkers lane in Drury lane, L.

Rufford's Buildings, by Wood's Close, L.

Rupert street, by Edmonds Court near St. Anne's
Church, L.

Russel Court, against St. James's Guard House, L.

Russel Court, in Drury lane, L. Here is a Chapel
belonging to the Church of England.

Russel street, by Bloomsbury Square, L. Here is
a stately House belonging to the Duke of
Montague.

Russel street, by Covent Garden, L.

Rutland Court, in Thames street, L.

Sab-

S A

Salster's Hall, in Ratcliff Highway, L.

Sickvil street, in Piccadilly, L.

Saffron Hill, near Holbourn Hill, L.

Saint Alban street, by Pall mall. L.

Saint Anne's Alley, in St. Annes lane, near Goldsmiths Hall, L.

Saint Anne's Lane, by St. Anne's Church near Goldsmiths Hall, L.

Saint Anne's Lane, within Aldersgate, L.

Saint Bride's Churchyard, in Fleetstreet, L.

Saint Catherine, by the Tower, L. Here are two Plying-places for Watermen, the Stairs at the East end, are called *St. Catherine's*; and those at the West end, *Iron Gate*

Saint Catherine's Court, by the Tower, L. It stands near the Church dedicated to St. *Catherine*.

Saint Clement's Churchyard, in the Strand, L.

Saint Giles's Pound, L. A Row of Houses on each side the way here, leading to Padington.

Saint Giles's street, by St. Giles's Church in the Fields, L. It is commonly called *Broad St. Giles's* and *High street*.

Saint James's Market, L. The Market Days are *Wednesdays* and *Saturdays*.

Saint James's Place, in St. James's Street, L.

Saint James's Square, in Pallmall, L.

Saint James's street, by Pallmall, L. The King's Palace of St. James is here, which has a most pleasant Prospect over St. James's Park.

Saint John's Close, by St. John's lane near Hicks's Hall, L. Here is Ailesbury Chapel, formerly belonging to the Earl of *Ailesbury's* House.

Saint John's Court, in Chick lane, L.

Saint John's Court, in Hart Street near Covent Garden, L. Here is an Anabaptist Meetinghouse.

Sai

Saint John's Court, in St. Martin le Grand, L.

Saint John's Lane, by Hick's Hall, L.

Saint John's ſtreet, in Spitalfields, L.

Saint John's ſtreet, without Weſt Smithfield Bars, . Here is Hicks's Hall, where the Juſtices of the ace hold their Seſſions ; and the Grand Jury ds Bills againſt Criminals to be tryed at Old aily

Saint Margaret's Churchyard, W.

Saint Margaret's Hill, S. Where under a neat azza, with the Effigies of King *Charles* the Se-nd erected over it in Stone, the Aſſizes have been metimes held for the County of *Surry*.

Saint Margaret's lane, W.

Saint Martin le Grand, in Newgate ſtreet, L. It a Precinct excluſive of the City of London ; and e Inhabitants thereof have a Right of polling for rliamentmen for the City of Weſtminſter : For e great Collegiate Church here (which was found- in 1056, by *Ingelricus* and *Emardus*, two Bro- ers, and Couſins to King *Edward* the Confeſſor) ing deſtroyed, was annexed to Weſtminſter Ab- , by King *Henry* the Seventh, *July* 23d, 1502.

Saint Martin's Churchyard, in St Martins lane in e Strand, L.

Saint Martin's Court, in St. Martins lane in the rand, L.

Saint Martin's lane, againſt Northumberland ouſe in the Strand, L. The Church here dedi- ted to St. Martin is pulling down to be rebuilt: the mean time, a Tabernacle by it is built for vine Service.

Saint Martin's Lane, in Cannon ſtreet, L.

Saint Mary Ax, L.

Saint Mary Hill, near Billinſgate, L.

Saint Mary Overy's Churchyard, S.

Saint Mary Overy's Dockhead, S.

Saint Mary Overy's Dock, S.

Saint

Saint Michael's Alley, by St. Michael's Church, Cornhill, L.

Saint Michael's lane, by Crooked lane, L.

Saint Paul's College, in St. Paul's Churchyard, L

Saint Paul's Court, by St. Albans Churchyard, L.

Saint Paul's Churchyard, L. Here is a moſt famous Cathedral, 20 Foot longer than that of S. *Peter* at *Rome*, and ſome Feet wider; at the Weſt end of it is Pauls School, for the Education of Youth; the North ſide is inhabited by Bookſellers and the South by Woollen Drapers, Leather Gilders, and Cane Chairmakers.

Saint Saviours Dock, by Horſlydown, S.

Saint Sepulchres Alley, L.

Saint Thomas Apoſtle, near Tower Royal, L.

Saint Thomas's ſtreet, in Drury lane, L.

Saint Thomas's ſtreet, in the Borough, S. Here for the Cure of ſick and lame Perſons, is erected S. *Thomas's* Hoſpital, having three ſpacious Courts, in the innermoſt of which is ſet up a Stone Effigies of Sir *Robert Clayton*, Knight, who was once Lord Mayor of London, and a great Benefactor to the Place. And near it, is founded by Mr. *Guy*, Bookſeller, another Hoſpital, to which he gave 100,000 Pounds, for the Relief of Perſons turn'd out of other Hoſpitals as incurable.

Salisbury Alley, in Chizel ſtreet by Upper Moorfield, L.

Salisbury Court, in Fleetſtreet, L.

Salisbury Court, in Salisbury ſtreet, by Southwark Wall, S.

Salisbury Lane, by Southwark Wall, S.

Salisbury ſquare, near Fleetſtreet, L.

Salisbury ſtreet, at Southwark Wall, S.

Salisbury ſtreet, in the Strand, L. Here is a good Plying-place for Watermen.

Salpetre Bank, in Roſemary lane, L.

Sal

Savage Gardens, in Crutched Fryers, **L.**

Savoy Alley, in the Savoy in the Strand, **L.**

Savoy, in the Strand, **L.** This Place was once a royal Palace, belonging to the Dukes of *Lancaster*; since then it was converted into an Hospital; afterward King *James* the Second erected here a Seminary containing four Schools, the Scholars whereof are taught by Mr. *Andrew Polton*, Mr. *Thomas* *Parker*, Mr. *Plowden*, and Mr. *Hall*, all of the Society of *Jesus*. The Church here, and at the North whereof the Communion Table stands, is called *St. Mary le Savoy*.

Serving Alley, by St. Mildreds Church in the Poultry **L.**

Schoolhouse Lane, near Cock Hill, **L.**

Scater street, in Spittlefields, **L.** Built *Anno* 1718.

Scotch Alley, vid. *Rose Alley* in Thieving lane.

Scratcher's Wharf, at Mill Bank, **W.**

Scotch Yard, in Whitecross Street, **L.**

Scotland Yard, in Whitehall, **L.** So called from King of Scotland once having Lodgings there.

Scroop's Court, against St. Andrews Church in Holburn, **L.**

Sea Alley, in King street, **W.**

Seacoal Lane, in Fleet lane, **L.**

Seething Lane, in Crutched Fryers, **L.**

Serjeants Inn, in Chancery lane, **L.** Where Judges and Sergeants have Chambers.

Serjeants Inn, in Fleetstreet, **L.** Where Judges and Sergeants have also Chambers.

Searle's Court, vid. *Lincolns Inn square*.

Sermon Lane, in little Carter lane, **L.**

Sevenstar Alley, in Ratcliff Highway, **L.**

Seymour Court, in Shandos street, **L.**

Shackbury's Walk, in Ratcliff Highway, **L.**

Shadwell Dock, **L.**

Shadwell Market, in Upper Shadwell, **L.** Here a Market kept on *Wednesdays* and *Saturdays*.

Shaft

Shaft Alley, by Leadenhall ſtreet, **L.** So called from a long Maypole, or Shaft, which uſed to ſtand, or be ſet np in the Street, before the Church Door, every *May Day*, which was higher than the Steeple. This Cuſtom continued till *May Day* 1517, afterwards called *Evil May Day*, whereon a Mob of Prentices, and others, exaſperated upon ſome Grievances, did much Evil and Miſchief, after which it was never erected, but lay for ſ Years under the Eaves of the Houſes, and at laſt was ſawed in Pieces b-cauſe one Mr. *Stevin* preached againſt it at St. *Paul*'s Church, and laid it was an Idol.

Shandos ſtreet, in Bedford ſtreet by Covent Garden, **L.**

Sharp's Alley, at Norton Faldgate, **L.**

Sharp's Alley, in Tunball ſtreet, **L.**

Shaw's Court, by St. George's Church, **S.**

Sheepshead Alley, near Vintners Hall in Thames ſtreet, **L.**

Sheer Alley, in White ſtreet, **S.**

Sheer Lane, within Temple Bar, **L.**

Shepherds ſtreet, in New Bond ſtreet, **L.**

Sherwood ſtreet, by James Street near Golden Square, **L.**

Ship Alley, in Wellcloſe, by Ratcliff Highway, **L.**

Ship Yard, by Butcher Row near Temple Bar, **L.**

Ship Yard, in Biſhopſgateſtreet without, **L.**

Ship Yard, in Red Croſs ſtreet, **L.**

Shoe Lane, in Fleetſtreet, **L.** Here are many Braziers

Shoemakers Row, in Blackfryers, **L.**

Shoemakers Row, within Aldgate, **L.**

Shoreditch, **L.** So called from *Jane Shore*, a Goldſmith's Wife, who was Concubine to King *Edward* the Fourth; but after his Deceaſe, and Murder of King *Edward* the Fifth, his Son, King *Richard* the Third, ſeized all ſhe was poſſeſſed of, and made

ade her do Penance at Paul's Crofs in London; er which Difgrace, living in extream Poverty e whole Reign of this Ufurper, King *Henry* the eventh, and part of King *Henry* the Eighth's Time, e ended her miferable Life in the Ditch which to us Day goes by her Name.

Shorter's Court, in Throgmorton ftreet, **L.**

Short's Gardens, in Drury lane, **L.**

Shrewsbury Court, in Whitecrofs ftreet, **L.**

Shovel ftreet, by Clare Market, **L.**

Shug Lane, by Piccadilly, **L.**

Shuttle Alley, in Whitechapel, **L.**

Sice Lane, by St. Antholin's Church in Watling reet, **L.**

Sidney Alley, in Prince's ftreet near St. Anne's hurch, **L.**

Silver ftreet, by Golden Square, **L.**

Silver ftreet, by Mugwell ftreet, **L.**

Silver ftreet, in Whitefryers in Fleetftreet, **L.**

Silver ftreet, near Bloomsbury Square, **L.**

Sion College, by London Wall, near Cripple-e, **L.**

Sir William Warren's fquare, by Wapping, **L.**

Six Dials, in Soho, **L.** They are made on an gn Pillar of Stone, erected in a circular Piece of ound, and give Profpect through 7 Streets, which ar but 5 Names, namely, *Great St. Andrew's ftreet*, ttle *St Andrew's ftreet*, *Earl ftreet*, *White Lion* eet, and *Queen ftreet*.

Skinner ftreet, in Bifhopfgateftreet, **L.**

Slap Alley, by Baldwyn's Garden, **L.**

Slaughter's Court, in lower Moorfield, **L.**

Slaughter's Court, in Nevil's Court in Rofemary ne, **L.**

Sleep Alley, in St. John ftreet near Weft Smith-l, **L.**

Stink ftreet, near the Bankfide, **S.**

Smith's Alley, in Barnaby ftreet, **S.**

H

Smith's

Smith's Court, at Holbourn Hill, **L.**

Smith's Head Court, in Great Windmill ſtreet, L

Smith's Rents, on the Bankſide, **S.**

Smith Street, near Maſham ſtreet, **W.**

Stuck Alley, in Spittlefields, **L.**

Snow Hill, near Holbourn Bridge, **L.** Here is neat Stone Conduit.

Snow's Fields, near Maze Pond, **S.**

Soaper's Alley, in Whitecroſs ſtreet, **L.**

Soaper's Row, near Bloomsbury Market, **L.**

Soho Square, vid. *King's Square.*

Somers Hyth, in Thames ſtreet, **L.**

Southampton Court, in Old Southampton Buildings, **L.**

Southampton Court, in Southampton Row, **L.**

Southampton Row, by King's ſtreet in High Hobourn, **L.**

Southampton ſtreet, by Bloomsbury Square, **L.**

Southampton ſtreet, in the Strand, **L.** Built where the Duke of *Bedford*'s Houſe formerly ſtood.

South ſtreet, by Spittlefields Market, **L.**

Southwark Wall, by Mill ſtreet, **S.**

Spicer ſtreet, in Spittlefields, **L.**

Spittlefields Market, **L.** It is kept on *Monday* *Tueſdays*, and *Saturdays*. Moſt of the Inhabitant hereabouts, and among whom are a great many *Frend* People, are Weavers.

Spittle Square, in Spittlefields, **L.**

Spittle ſtreet, in Spittlefields, **L.**

Spittle Yard, in Spittlefields, **L.** Here the Spittle Sermons were wont to be preached in the Eaſte and Whitſon Holidays, before the Lord Mayo and Aldermen of London ; but now at St. Bride' Church.

Spread Eagle Court, in Grays Inn lane, **L.**

Spread Eagle Court, in Threadneedle ſtreet, **L.**

Spring Garden, near Charing Croſs, **L.** Here are the Houſes of the late Dukes of *Northumberland* and

nd that *Norfolk* who was divorced in Parliament
from his Dutchels, for Incontinency with *Germain*..

Spring *street*, in Fox's lane at Upper Shadwell, L.

Spur *Alley*, near Hungerford Market in the Strand L.

Squire *Alley*, in the Great Minories, L.

Stable *Yard*, by College street, W.

Stable *Yard*, by King street, W.

Stable *Yard*, in Blenheim street, L.

Stable *Yard*, in Great Ormond street, L.

Stable *Yard*, in Queen's Square, W.

Stable *Yard*, in St. James's street, L.

Stable *Yard*, in Somerset House in the Strand, L.

Stafford *street*, in Albermarle street, L.

Stanhope *street*, near Clare Market, L.

Staples *Inn*, in Middle Holbourn, L.

Star *Alley*, by London Wall near Bedlam, L.

Star *Alley*, in East Smithfield, L.

Star *Alley*, in Fenchurch street, L.

Star *Alley*, in Thieving lane, W.

Star *Court*, against Sadlers Hall in Cheap-
de, L

Star *Court*, in Butcher Row by Temple Bar, L.

Star *Court*, in Grub street, L.

Star *Court*, near St. Gregory's Church in Old
fish street, L

Star *Yard*, in Blackman street, S.

Stationers *Alley*, in Ludgate street, L. So called
on Stationers Hall being built there; which
Company consists of Stationers, Bookfellers, Print-
rs, and others.

Stephens *Alley*, in King street, W.

Stepney *Causeway*, in Brook street near Ratcliff
highway, L

Steward *street*, in Spittlefields, L.

Steyning *Court*, by Oat street near Foster lane, L.

Stuffs *Alley*, in Duck lane, W.

Still *Alley*, in Bishopfgatestreet without, L.

Still *Alley*, in Houndsditch, L.

Still Yard, by Alhallows Church in Than
street, L.

Still Yard, on Towerhill, L.

Statchbourn's Court, in High Holbourn, L.

Stocks Market, near the Poultry, L. So call
from a Pair of Stocks formerly set up there for p
nishing Offenders. Here Herbs, Flowers, Roo
and other Commodities of Gardiners, are sold
Tuesdays, *Thursdays* and *Saturdays*. And on a lof
Stone Pedestal, the Effigies of King *Charles* the S
cond on Horseback is erected, trampling on an
nemy.

Stone Court, in Aldersgatestreet, L.

Stone Court, in Fetter lane, L.

Stonecutters Alley, in Warwick street near Ch
sing Cross, L.

Stonecutters Court, by Pallmall, L.

Stonecutters street, in Shoe lane, L.

Stony street, near St Mary Overy's Church, S.

Stony lane, against the Maypole in Tooly street,

Stotward's Court, in Mark lane, L.

Strand, L. It reaches from Temple Bar to Ch
sing Cross, and hath two Churches in it, call
St. Clement Danes, and St. George. It is also.
dorn'd with the Royal Palace of *Somerset* House,
the Stable Yard whereof is a great Plying-pla
for Watermen, also *Wimbleton* House, and *North*
berland House; which last belongs to the Duke
Somerset: Also here is a Quakers Meetinghou
betwixt the great and little Savoy Gates, next
which latter dwells Mrs. *Cowper*, who is at prese
the King's Distiller.

Strand lane, against St. George's Church in t
Strand, L.

Stretten street, by Berkley house in Hayb
Row, L.

Stroud's Court, by Holbourn Bars, L.

Strutten Ground, by New Chapel, W.

Suff

Suffolk street, in Thames Street, **L.**
Suffolk Street, in the Mint, **S.**
Suffolk street, near Charing Cross, **L.**
Sugarloaf Court, in Leadenhall street, **L.**
Summer street, by Hockly i' th' Hole, **L.**
Sun Alley, at Cow Cross, **L.**
Sun Alley, in Barnaby street, **L.**
Sun Alley, in Grub street, **L.**
Sun Alley, in St. John's street, **L.**
Sun Alley, in the Maze, **S̃.**
Sun Alley, in Tooly street, **S.**
Sun Court, in Cornhill, **L.**
Sutton's Court, in Bishopsgatestreet, **L.**
Sutton's Court, in Lincolns Inn Fields, **L.**
Swallows Court, in Rosemary lane, **L.**
Swallow street, in Piccadilly, **L.**
Swan Alley, in Coleman street, **L.**
Swan Alley, in East Smithfield, **L.**
Swan Alley, in Goswel street, **L.**
Swan Alley, in the Borough, **S.**
Swan Alley, in Wardour street, **L.**
Swan Alley, in Whitecross street, **L.**
Swan Yard, against Somerset House in the Strand, **L.**
Swan Yard, by Hockly i' th' Hole, **L.**
Swan Yard, in Newgate street, **L.**
Sweeting's Alley, at the East end of the Royal Exchange, **L.**
Swithin's Lane, by St. Swithin's Church in Cannon street, **L.**
Swordbearers Alley, in Chizel street, **L.**
Symonds Inn, in Chancery lane, **L.** Here is kept the Register Office.

T A

Tabernacle Alley, in Fenchurch street, **L.**
Talbot Court, in little Eastcheap, **L.**
Talbot Court, on Fishstreet Hill, **L.**

Tapping's Wharf, opposite to the new Church Mill Bank, **W.**

Tart's Court, in West Smithfield, **L.**

Tavistock Row, by Tavistock Street near Cove Garden, **L.**

Tavistock street, in Southampton street in t Strand, **L.**

Taylors Court, in Bow lane, **L.**

Temple, in Fleetstreet, **L.** It is two famous In of Court, divided into the Inner and Middle Tem ple; in the first of which is an ancient Chapel, th King's Bench, Crown, and Alienation Offices; i the other, a very fine old Hall, and Rookery

Temple Lane, in Fleetstreet, **L.** Here is a gre Plying-place for Watermen.

Temple Street, in Whitefryers, **L.**

Tennis Court, in Middle Row in Holbourn, **L,**

Tenter Alley, in little Moorfield by Moorfields, **L**

Tenter Alley, in the Maze, **S.**

Tenter Ground, in King Street by Upper Moo field, **L.**

Thacker's Court, in Bishopsgatestreet without, **L**

Thackum's Court, in Vine Street by Shand Street, **L.**

Thames Street, **L.** The longest Street in London.

Thatch Alley, in Chick lane, **L.**

Thatch house Alley, near Halfmoon Street in th Strand, **L.**

Thavy's Inn, on Holbourn Hill, **L.**

Theobalds Court, in Theobalds Row, **L.**

Theobalds Row, by Red Lion Square, **L.**

Thieving Lane, in King Steer, **W.** Vid. *Bi Street*, **W.**

Thomas's Rents, in Forestreet at Limehouse, **L.**

Thomas's Street, in Drury lane, **L.**

Thomas's Street, in Whitechapel, **L.**

Thompson's Rent, at London Wall near Bedlam, **L**

Threadneedle Alley, in lower Moorfield, **L.**

Thread

Threadneedle Street, L. Here is kept the Office the Southsea Company.

Three Coal Street, by the new Church near Lime-house, L.

Three Crane Alley, in Thames Street, L. Here is Plying-place for Watermen.

Three Crane Court, in the Borough, S.

Three Crown Alley, in the Minories, L.

Three Crown Alley, in Bride lane, L.

Three Crown Court, in Fore Old Jewry near Aldte within, L.

Three Crown Court, in the Borough, S.

Three Cup Alley, in Shoreditch, L.

Three Dagger Court, in Fore Street by Moor-lds, L.

Three Dove Court, in St. Martin le Grand, L.

Three Falcon street, in Fleetstreet, L.

Three Fox Court, in Long lane, L.

Three Herring Court, in St. Thomas's Street, S.

Three Horseshoe Alley, in Chick lane, L.

Three Horseshoe Court, in Giltspur Street, L.

Three King Alley, in Whitecross Street, L.

Three King Court, in Fleetstreet, L.

Three Leg Alley, in Fetter lane, L. It is also called *Red Lion Passage*, from a paltry Inn there which bears that Sign; and hath a Thorough fair upon sufferance, through the House of one *Samuel Franc-ne*, Victualler, at the Sign of the Horseshoe in West Harding Street.

Three Leg Alley, in Old Bedlam, L.

Three Leg Court, in Whitecross Street, L.

Three Pidgeon Alley, in Barbican, L.

Three Sheer Alley, on Garlick Hill, L.

Three Tun Alley, in Bishopsgatestreet without, L.

Three Tun Alley, near the King's Bench, S.

Three Tun Alley, opposite to London Wall by Bed-lam, L.

Three Tun Court, in Fleet lane, L.

Three

Three Tun Court, in Red Crofs Street, L.

Thrift ftreet, by Soho Square, L.

Throgmorton ftreet, L.   Here the Drapers have very fine Hall.

Tidewaters Court, in the little Minories, L.

Tight's Alley, in Foreftreet at Limehoufe, L.

Tilt Yard, by Whitehall, L.   Here the Foot Guards daily do Duty, as the Life Guards do them at the Horfe Guard.

Titus Court, by Saffronhill, L

Tobacco Roll Court, in Gracechurch ftreet, L.

Tokenhoufe Yard, in Lothbury, L.

Tooly Corner, by Glean Alley in Tooly ftreet, S.

Tooly Gate, in Tooly ftreet, S.

Tooly ftreet, at the Bridgefoot, S.   Here is Goal called the Compter, for the Confinement of Debtors.

Tothill fide, near Petty France, W.

Tower Royal, by St. Antholin's Church in Walling ftreet, L.

Tower ftreet, near Monmouth ftreet, L.

Towhoufe Yard, at Cockhill, L.

Town Ditch, by Little Britain, L.

Trinity Court, in Alderfgateftreet, L.   'Tis near St. *Botolph's* Church without the Gate.

Trinity Lane, in Bow lane in Cheapfide, L. Here the German Proteftants have a Church.

Trotter Alley, in Barnaby Street, S.

Trump Alley, againft Bow lane in Cheapfide, L.

Trump ftreet, in King Street by Cheapfide, L.

Tufton ftreet, on the Weft fide of the newChurch, W

Tun Alley, by Hungerford Market, L.

Tunball ftreet, by Cow Crofs, L.

Turdfbead Alley, in Golden lane, L.

Turn again Lane, by Fleetditch, L.

Turnftile Alley, in Drury lane, L.   It was formerly (when a moft notorious Neft of Strumpets called *Dog and Bitch Yard*.

Turn

Turnwheel Lane, by London Stone in Cannon
ſtreet. L.

Turtle Court, in Barnaby Street, S.

Tweet ſtreet, in Berwick Street, S.

Twelve Bell Alley, in Bow lane in Cheapſide, L.

Twiford Alley, in Petty France, W.

Twiſters Alley, in Bunhill lane, by Upper Moor-
le, L

Two Brewers Yard, in Golden lane, L.

Two Leg Alley, in Old Bedlam. L.

Tyburn Lane, by Hyde Park, L.

Tyger Court, in Whitecroſs Street, L

Tyler ſtreet, by King ſtreet near Golden Square, L.

V A

Valient Soldier Alley, in Barnaby Street, S.

Vere ſtreet, by Clare Market, L.

Villars ſtreet, in York Buildings in the Strand, L.

Vine Court, in Lamb ſtreet L.

Vinegar Yard, in Drury lane, L.

Vine ſtreet, by Hatton Garden, L.

Vine ſtreet, by little Swallow ſtreet, L.

Vine ſtreet, by Shandos Street, L.

Vine ſtreet, in Alderlgateſtreet, L.

Vine ſtreet, in St. Giles's Street, L.

Vine ſtreet, in the Great Minories, L.

Vine ſtreet, near Market Street, W.

Virginia ſtreet, in Ratcliff Highway, L.

Unicorn Alley, in Foreſtreet by Moorfields, L.

Unicorn Alley, in Kent ſtreet, S.

Unicorn Alley, in the Great Minories, L.

Unicorn Yard, in Horſlydown, S.

Union ſtreet, in King Street, W. At the Eaſt
End of it, formerly was a Stone Gatehouſe, where
both Debters and Criminals were kept in Confinement.

Upper End, near Smock Alley in Spittlefields L.

Uppe

Upper Ground, by the Falcon Stairs, S.

Upper Gun Alley, at Wapping, L.

Upper Moorfield, near Moorgate, L.

Upper Shadwell, by Ratcliff Highway, L.

W A

Wallbrook, by Stocks Market, L. Noted for Furriers.

Walker's Court, in Knaves Acre, L.

Walnut Tree Court, in Bishopsgatestreet without, L.

Walnut Tree ſtreet, in Tooly Street, S.

Walton Court, by Holbourn Bars, L.

Walton Court, on Lambeth Hill, L.

Wapping Dock ſtreet, L.

Wapping, L.

Wapping Wall, L. Here is a Plying-place for Watermen, oppoſite to Shackbury's Walk, called King James's Stairs.

Wardour ſtreet, by Tweet Street, L.

Wardrobe Court, in Great Carter lane, L. Hereabout was kept the Great Wardrobe of the Kings of England many Years, in an old Houſe built (but in the great Fire, Anno 1666, burnt down) by Sir John Beauchamp, Son to *Guy de Beauchamp* Earl of *Warwick*; which after the Death of the Founder Anno 1339, was ſold to King *Edward* the Third, and King *Richard* the Third kept his Court here, and ſeveral of the Gentlemen of the Wardrobe dwelt in it.

Ward's Rents, by Saffronhill, L.

Warwick Court, by Grays Inn, L.

Warwick Court, in Warwick lane, L.

Warwick Lane, by Paternoſter Row, L. Here ſtands the College of Phyſicians.

Warwick ſtreet, by Marybone Street, L.

Warwick

Warwick Street, near Charing Crofs, L. Here the utchefs Dowager of *Shrewsbury* has an Houfe.

Warwick Yard, by Bedford Row, L.

Watercock Alley, in Eaft Smithfield, L.

Water Lane, by the Cuftomhoufe, L.

Water Lane, in Blackfryers, L. Here is a Plying-ce for Watermen.

Water Lane, in Fleetftreet, L.

Water Street, by Bridewell Precinct near Fleet-tch, L.

Water Street, near Arundel Street in the Strand, L.

Watkins's Rents, in Barnaby Street, S.

Weavers Lane, in Horflydown, S.

W.y's Square, in Shoredhch, L.

Weedon Street, in Chancery lane, L.

Well Alley, in the Great Minories, L.

Well Alley, in Wapping, L.

Well and Bucket Alley, near Ironmonger Row in a Street, L.

Well and Bucket Court, near Ironmonger Row in d Street, L.

Well Clofe, near Ratcliff Highway, L. Here is hurch built by the Swedes of the Lutheran fuafion.

Well Court, in Bow lane in Cheapfide, L.

Well Street, in Rofemary lane, L.

Well Street, near King Edward's Row by White-pel, L.

Well Yard, by St. Bartholomew's Hofpital in ng Walk, L.

Weftharding Street, in Fetter lane, L.

Weft Lane, by Southwark Wall, S. This Lane ndes Southwark, next the River of Thames, m Rotherhith, vulgarly called Reddrift.

Weftminster Market, W The Market Days here, on *Wednefdays* and *Saturdays*.

Weftmoreland Court, in Bartholomew Clofe, L.

Weft Smithfield, L. Here is St. Bartholomew's

and

Hofpital, founded by *Rayhere*, in the Year 11
and refounded by King *Henry* the Eighth, *h*
1546, for the ufe now of fick and maimed *P*
ple. On *Mondays* and *Fridays* a Market is kept
and about the Rounds, for all forts of live Catt
Again, this Place is noted for having been t
Slaughterhoufe of bloody Queen *Mary*, who c
fed many Chriftians to fuffer Martyrdom here, *a*
in many other places in England.

Weft Street, by Spittlefields Market, L.

Whalebone Court, in Lothbury, L.

Wheatfheaf Alley, in Barnaby Street, L.

Wheelbarrow Alley, in Rofemary lane, L.

W ee'er Street, in Spittlefields, L.

Wheeler's Yard, in the Great Minories, L.

Whetftones Park, by Lincolns Inn Fields, L. 'T
formerly a Receptacle of wanton Does, till in t
Reign of King *Charles* the Second they were rout
out by the Mob; to fupprefs which Riot, t
King's Life Guard were obliged to go in Arms
gainft them.

Whifter's Yard, at Mill Bank, W.

Whittler's Court, in Oxford Court by St. Swit
in's Church in Cannon Street, L.

Whitcomb Court, in Whitcomb ftreet, L.

Whitcomb Street, in Piccadilly, L.

White Bear Alley, in Whitechapel, L.

White Bear Court, in Kent ftreet, S.

Whitechapel Row, by Whitechapel Square, L.

Whitechapel Square, at Whitechapel, L.

Whitechapel, without Aldgate, L.

Whitecock Alley, in Thames ftreet, L.

Whitecrofs Alley, in Middle Moorfield, L.

Whitecrofs ftreet, by St. Giles's Church witho
Cripplegate, L.

Whitecrofs Street, in Foreftreet by Moorfields, L

Whitecrofs Street, in Queen Street, S.

Whitch

Whitefryers Dock, at the end of Water lane in eetstreet, L.

Whitehall, W. It was a Royal Palace, but con-n'd with Fire, excepting the Banquetting-house, the Reign of King *William* the Third.

White Hart Alley, in Long lane, L.

White Hart Court, by St. Botolph's Church with-t Bishopsgate, L.

White Hart Court, in Castle Street near the eute, L

White Hart Court, in Old street, L.

White Hart Court, in Warwick Street by Charing ofs, L.

White Hart Lane, by Queen's Square, W.

White Hart Street, in Catherine street in the and, L.

White Hart Street, in Warwick Street, L.

White Hart Yard, in the Broadway, W.

White Head Court, in Duke's Place, L.

White Hind Court, in Bishopsgatestreet without, L.

White Horse Alley, at Cow Cross, L.

White Horse Alley, in Barnaby Street, S.

White Horse Alley, in Kent Street, S.

White Horse Alley, in Chick lane, L.

White Horse Alley, in St. John's Street by West ithfield, L.

White Horse Court, in the Borough, S.

White Horse Court, on Addle Hill, L.

White Horse Lane, in White Horse Street near tcliff Highway, L.

White Horse Street, near Ratcliff Highway, L.

White Horse Yard, in Drury lane, L. A Place Call for Journeymen Taylors; and takes its me from the Sign of the White Horse, an Ale-se kept by one *Jewkes*.

White Horse Yard, in Kent street, S.

White Horse Yard, in King Street, W.

White Lion Alley, in Birchin lane, L.

I   *White*

White Lion Court, in Barbican, L.
White Lion Court, in Cornhill, L.
White Lion Court, in Fleetftreet, L.
White Lion Street, at the Six Dials, L. It c
ries the fame Name through another Street.
White Lion Street, in Rofemary lane, L
White Rofe Alley, in Whitecrofs Street, L.
White Rofe Court, near St. Stephen's Church
Coleman Street, L.
White Row, by Smock Alley, L.
White's Alley, in Chancery lane, L.
White's Alley, in little Moorfield, L.
White's Alley, in Long Ditch, W.
White's Alley, in Lothbury, L.
White's Alley, near London Wall by Bedlam, I
White Street, in Horflydown, S.
White Street, near Kent Street, S.
White Yard, in Rofemary lane, L.
White Yard, in Whitecrofs Street, L.
White's Ground, in Horflydown, S.
Wich Alley, in Wich Street, L.
Wich Street, in Drury lane, L.
Widegate Street, in Bifhopfgateftreet without,
Wild Court, in Great Wild Street, L. Bu
where Wild Houfe formerly ftood, which was plu
der'd by the Rabble to the Value of 100000 Poun
where a Spanifh Ambaffadour dwelt, a little af
the late King *William* landed at *Torbay*.
Wilderness, in Salisbury Court in Fleetftreet, L
Wild Paffage, in Drury lane, L,
Wild Rents, in Long Lane, S.
Wild Street, by Great Queen Street, L.
Winchefter Clofe, near St. Mary Overy's Church,
Winchefter Court, in Mugwell Street, L.
Winchefter Street, at London Wall by Bedlam,
Winchefter Street, near St. Mary Overy's Church
Winchefter Yard, near St. Mary Overy's Church,
Winckles Court, in Pallmall, L.

Winds

Windmill Alley, on St. Margaret's Hill, S. Not far from it, on the same side of the way, is the Talbot Inn; where Sir *Jeffery Chaucer*, and 29 Pilgrims, lodg'd in their Journey to *Canterbury*, in 1383.

Windmill Hill, by Upper Moorfield, L.

Windmill Street, against the Hay Market, L.

Windsor Court, in Drury lane, L.

Windsor Court, in Mugwell Street, L.

Windsor Court, in the Strand, L.

Wine Court, in Bishopsgatestreet without, L.

Wine Court, in Harp Alley in Shoe lane, L.

Wire Office Court, in Fleetstreet, L.

Wisdom's Alley, near the Horse Ferry, W.

Wiseman's Court, in King street, W.

Wood's Close, near Goswell Street, L.

Wood's Court, at Norton Faldgate, L.

Woodstock Street, by New Bond Street, L.

Wood Street, by Peter Street, W.

Wood Street, in Cheapside, L. Here is a Prison called the Comptor, for the Confinement of debtors and Criminals.

Woolpack Ally, in Houndsditch, L.

Woolsack Alley, by Farthing Alley near Maze Pond, S.

Wooll Staple, in Channel Row, W.

Wormwood Street, by Bishopsgate within, L.

Worsted Street, in Queen Street S.

Wrestlers Alley, against London Wall by Bedlam, L.

Wyeber Alley, on Addle Hill, L.

Y A

Yate's Court, in Clement's lane by Clement's Inn, L.

York Buildings, by the new Exchange in the Strand, L. Built where York House stood; and here is a fine Plying-place for Watermen.

York Street, by Charles Street near Covent Garden, L.

York Street, in Spittlefields, L.

A List

A Lift of all the Cathedrals, Church and Chapels of Eafe within the Bill Mortality, withal fhewing therein fett Times of publick Prayers, receivi the Sacrament, and hearing Serm both Ordinary and Extraordinary.

Note, Pr. fignifies Prayers ; *Sac.* Sacrament; S. Sermon ; and *Lect.* Lecturer.

SAint *Alban*, on the Eaft fide of *Wood Street*, n *Cripplegate*, is a Church of great Antiqu built about the Year 930, and was perhaps t oldeft Workmanfhip of any about *London*, till was burnt in the Year 1666 ; fince which it b been rebuilt, and is the only Church that is ded cated to the Memory of St. *Alban*, the Proto-M tyr of *England*, a Citizen of *Verulam* in *Hertfor fhire*, where he fuffer'd under *Dioclefian*'s Perfecu on, *Anno Domini* 303, from whence it is called S *Alban*'s to this Day, and his Feftival is celebrat on the 17th of *June*. This Parifh contains abo 260 Dwelling Houfes. Morning Pr. are only *Wednefdays, Fridays,* and all Holy Days, at 11 the Clock ; Annual S. upon the firft and thi *Thurfdays* in *Auguft*, at 12.

All Saints, alias *Alhallows Barking,* in *Great To Street* : It is called *Barking* for Diftinction from thers, becaufe it was the Gift of the Abbefs an Convent in *Effex.* This, and 7 other Parifh Chu che

es, are dedicated to all the Saints; whose Anni-
sary Festival was first celebrated at *Rome* about
e Year 608, by Pope *Boniface* the Fourth, on the
st of *November*, and has ever since been kept ho-
. This Parish contains about 400 Houses. Morn-
g Pr. are daily at 8, and Evening at 7; Sac. is
ministred every *Sunday* at 12, after Forenoon Ser-
on; annual S. *November* 10, *Christmas, Lady, Mid-
summer*, and *Michaelmas* Days; and on New Years
ay

All Saints, commonly *Alhallows* in *Breadstreet*, be-
use its in that street, which was called *Breadstreet*, from a Market of Bread, formerly kept there,
here all the Bakers were obliged by an Act, *Anno
mini* 1303, to sell their Bread. This Parish con-
ins about 100 Houses. Morning Pr. are on all
dnesdays and *Fridays*, in *Lent* only, and on all
oly Days in the Year at 11; a Weekly Lect. is
eached here on every *Thursday* Evening at 4, from
Michaelmas to Ladyday, and annual S. on St. *James's*
y, *Jan.* 30. and *Nov.* 5.

All Saints, alias *Alhallows* the Great, near *Still-
rd*, or *Steel Yard*, on the South side of *Thames
eet*. This Parish contains about 200 Dwelling
uses. Morning Pr. on *Wednesdays* and *Fridays*,
d all Holy Days at 11; a Monthly Lect. every
nday Evening at 4, from *Michaelmas* to *Ladyday*;
nual S *Jan.* 30. *May* 29. *Nov.* 5. *Sept.* 2.

All Saints, alias *Alhallows*, at the upper end of
mbard Street, began to be built *Anno* 1494, and
ished in 1526. This Parish consists of about 120
tely Houses. Morning Pr. on *Wednesdays, Fridays*,
d all Holy Days, at 11; Monthly Lect. every
rd *Sunday* at 5 in the Evening, from *Michaelmas*
Ladyday; annual S. on *Good Friday* at 10.

All Saints, alias *Alhallows* on *London Wall*; so
led because it's built upon, or close to the North
all of the City of *London*, near *Bethlehem* Hospi-
I 3   tal;

tal, between *Bishopsgate* and Great *Moorgate*. Th Parish contains about 300 Dwelling Houses. Morn ing Pr. on *Wednesdays*, *Fridays*, and all Holy Day at 11.

All Saints, alias *Alhallows Staining*, on the We side of *Mark Lane*, or *Mart Lane*, from a Mart Fair which was formerly kept in that Lane, a for more Distinction from others, call'd *Stann* that is, *Stain Church*, or *Stone Church*, being t first that was built of Stones, when others we of Timber, about or before the Time of the *No mans* coming hither, the ancient *Saxons* being ve unaccustomed, and little acquainted with Buildi in Stone. This Church is also remarkable for bei the first wherein Queen *Elizabeth* return'd Than to God for her Delivery from Imprisonment in t *Tower*, and her Accession to the Throne. Th Parish contains 100 Houses. Morning Pr. on *We nesdays*, *Fridays*, and all Holy Days, at 11; annu S on St. *Mark's Day*, *May* 29. *Jan.* 30. in t Forenoon at 10.

St. *Alphage*, near to *Sion* College by *Cripplega* dedicated to the Honour of St. *Alphage*, the Arc bishop of *Canterbury*, who was stoned to Death b the *Danes* at *Greenwich*, about the Year 990; so make him amends, his Memory is eterniz'd by C nonization, and his Festival falls on the 19th *April*. This Parish contains 152 Houses. Mor ing Pr. on *Wednesdays*, *Fridays*, all Holy Days, a publick Days through the Year, at 11; extrao dinary Lect. *Jan.* 30. *Mar.* 8. and *Good Friday*, a an annual S. is preached here in Latin, by the Pr sident of *Sion* College, the third *Tuesday* after *Ea* at 11.

St. *Andrew Holbourn*, but antiently called *Ol bourn*, that is to say, *Old Brook*, which runs y from *Holbourn* Bar into *Fleet Ditch* at *Holbou Bridge*. This Parish contains about 3620 Dwelli Houses oufes. Morning Pr. every Day at 6 in Summer ime, and 7 in the Winter, and again at 11; and vening Pr. at 3 constantly. Sac. is administred every *Sunday* in the Year, and several solemn Occaons, after Forenoon Sermon, but upon *Easter Day*, ly at 7 and 12, S. on all publick Days appoint by the Parliament, as *Jan.* 30. *Sept.* 2. *Nov.* 5. d 30. which last is the annual Commemoration of e tutelar Saint or Patron thereof; and Donation on the last *Sunday* in *Easter* Time, and last *Sunday* *Michaelmas* Term in the Forenoon

St. *Andrew Undershaft*, commonly St. *Mary Axe*, the North side of *Leadenhall Street*, so called on a long Maypole, or Shaft, which used to nd, or be set up in the Street, before the Church oor, every *May Day*, which was higher than the eeple, and consequently the Church was under e Shaft. It is also called St. *Mary Axe*, or *Nax*, cause of the Sign of an Axe which did hang over ainst the end thereof; and under this Appellatiit's dedicated to the Honour of the Virgin *Mary*, is the other to the Apostle St. *Andrew*. This Pah contains about 230 fine Houses. Morning Pr. ery Day at 6 in the Summer, and 7 in the Win, and on all Holy Days at 11; Evening Pr. at 6, cept *Sundays*; annual S. on *New Years Day*, third esday in *September*, and first *Monday* of *August*, II.

St. *Andrew Wardrobe*, alias St. *Andrew* by the ueen's Wardrobe, being near *Wardrobe Court*, where e Great Wardrobe of the Kings of *England* was ept these many Years, till the late Fire, in an old ouse. This Parish consists of about 600 Houses. Morning Pr. on *Wednesdays*, *Fridays*, all Holy Days, nd publick Days.

Sts. *Anne* and *Agnes*, on the North side of St. nne's *Lane* within *Aldersgate*, being the first of hose Churches that are dedicated to two conjunct Saints,

Saints, and the firſt of three that are conſecrat
to St. *Anne*, the Mother of the bleſſed Virgin *M*
ry ; but the only Church of the Name of St. *A*
the Virgin and Martyr. It is called St. *Anne in*
Willows, becauſe in old Time Willows grew ther
about. This Pariſh comprehends about 185 Dw
ling Houſes. Morning Pr. *Wedneſdays, Fridays,*
Holy Days, and publick Days, at 11 ; Evening
only on all Lecture Days, which are on every *Su*
day Evening ; and every *Monday* Evening at
alſo a Sermon on the three laſt *Sundays* of the Mon
at 7 in the Morning, after which the Holy Sacr
ment is celebrated , and on all publick Faſ
Thankſgiving Days, and ſome Holy Days.

St. *Anne*, on the Weſt ſide of *Dean Street* by *Sol*
in the Liberty of *Weſtminſter*. It was formerly
Chapel of Eaſe to the Pariſh of St. *Martin in th*
Fields, but was taken out of that, and made a d
ſtinct and proper Pariſh of it ſelf by Act of Parli
ment, in the 30th Year of King *Charles* the Secon
1678 ; and this Church was built for that end, b
Act of Parliament, in the firſt Year of King *Jam*
the Second, and finiſh'd 1686. This Pariſh con
tains 1500 large and ſtately Dwelling Houſes. He
are Pr. four times in the Day, *viz.* at 6 in the Sum
mer, and 7 in the Winter, and 11, and at 4 and
in the Evening through the Year. Sac. is admini
ſter'd once every firſt and third *Sunday* of the Month
and *Good Friday* at 12, but on *Chriſtmas Day, Eaſt*
and *Whit Sundays* at 7 and 12 ; S. on *Aſh Wedneſda*
Good Friday, moſt Holy Days, and all publick Da
appointed by the Government, in the Forenoon.

St. *Anthony*, commonly called St. *Antholin in Wat*
ling Street, is dedicated to the Memory of St. *A*
thony called the Great, a Monk born in *Egypt in*
251, and died 356, aged 105. This Pariſh contain
185 Dwelling Houſes ; Morning Pr. are every Da
at 6 in the Summer, and 7 in the Winter, and o

Holy Days at 11 ; here are Morning Lectures rough the Year, at 6 in the Summer, and 7 in e Winter.

St. *Augustin*, commonly called St. *Austin*, at the d*Change*, near St. *Paul*'s Cathedral, dedicated to . *Austin* the Monk, sent by Pope *Gregory* the reat, about the Year 590, to convert the *Saxons* *England*, then lying in Pagan Darkness ; there- e he is called the *English* Apostle. This Parish ntains about 265 Dwelling Houses. Morning . of *Wednesdays*, *Fridays*, all Holy Days, and pub- k Solemnities, at 11. S. on the 14th of *May* at , on *Lammas* Day at 10, besides Extraordinary es on *Jan.* 30. *Sept.* 2. *Nov.* 5.

Aylesbury Chapel, in St. *John*'s *Close*, near *West* ithfield ; so called, because it belongs now to e Earl of *Aylesbury*, but is indeed the only Re- ques of that famous and religious Priory of St. hn of *Jerusalem*. Morning Pr. on *Wednesdays*, *Fri-* ys, and all Holy Days ; S. on all *Sundays* at 10 the Morning, and 3 and 6 in the Evening.

St. *Bartholomew* the Great, in *Cloth Fair* and *Bar-* olomew *Close* in *West Smithfield*, was at first a Pri- y, founded by *Robert*, Musician or Minstrel to ing *Henry* the First, about the Year 1102. This rish contains about 290 Houses. Morning Pr. ery Day at 11 ; Evening Pr. at 5, only in the last eek of the Month ; S. extraordinary on *Good* iday, *Nov.* 5. and some other publick Occasions, 11.

St. *Bartholomew* the Less, on the East side of the ysters in St. *Bartholomew*'s Hospital, which was at h the Chapel to the Infirmary of the said Hospi- l. This Parish contains about 200 Houses. Morn- g Pr are every Day at 11.

St. *Bartholomew* the Little, at the Upper end of ntholomew *Lane*, near the *Royal Exchange*, is not ery antient, being first built by *Thomas Pyke*, Alder- man,

man, about 1438. This Parish comprehends ab
130 of the beſt Dwelling Houſes in the City. Mo
ing Pr. on *Wedneſdays, Fridays,* all Holy Days,
publick Days, at 11 ; Evening Pr. at 6 through
the Year ; a weekly Lect. every *Tueſday* through
Year, at 4 in the Evening, paid by the Worſhip
Company of *Haberdaſhers.*

Barwick Street Chapel, near *Soho,* is now mad
Chapel of Eaſe, ſince it has been deſerted by
French Refugees, to the Pariſh of St. *James* s Chu
in *Weſtminſter.* Morning Pr. every Day in
Week at 11, Evening Pr. at 5. S. extraordin
every *Chriſtmas Day,* all Thankſgiving Days, a
all publick and ſolemn Faſts.

St. *Benedict,* vulgarly St *Bennet Fink,* in *Thr*
needle Street, near the *Royal Exchange* ; ſo call
from *Robert Fink,* Sen. by whom it was firſt buil
or new built ; but there is no account of it till t
Year 1633. This Pariſh contains about 100 fi
Dwelling Houſes. Morning Pr. are on *Wedneſd*
Fridays, and all Holy days, at 11 only.

St. *Benedict,* vulgarly St. *Bennet Gracechurch,* ne
the *Monument.* It was formerly called St. *Ben*
in *Graſs Church Street,* becauſe of a Graſs or He
Market kept there ; and then it might be, as h
been reported, that there was only one Tavern, o
Inn, one Coffeehouſe, and one Alehouſe in it. Th
Pariſh contains about 110 Houſes. Morning Pr.
Wedneſdays, Fridays, and all Holy Days, at 11 ;
Donation . *Nov* 5. at 10, and *Chriſtmas Day* at 1

St. *Benedict,* vulgarly St. *Bennet,* on St. *Benne*
Hill by St. *Paul's Wharf* in *Thames Street,* whe
Stone and other Materials were landed for the U
of that Cathedral. This Pariſh contains about 2
Dwelling Houſes. Morning Pr. on *Wedneſday*
Fridays, all Holy Days, and publick Days, at 11
and Evening Pr. on all Holy Days and *Saturda*
only at 3.

Blo

Bloomsbury Chapel, made now a Chapel of Eafe (ut not Parochial) to the Parifh of St. *Giles* in (e Fields, near *Montague* Houfe.

St. *Botolph Alderfgate*, fituated on the South fide (Little *Britain*, dedicated to the Memory of St. (tolph, that famous *English Saxon*, who was born (Cornwal about the Time of King *Lucius*. He (lt a Monaftery and Town in *Lincolnfhire*, called (ton, or *Botolph's* Town, to this Day; wrought (ny Miracles, as 'tis reported, and was buried (ere about the Year 689. This Parifh contains about (o Houfes. Morning Pr. every Day at 11, Even- (g Pr. at 3; extraordinary Sermon on *Jan.* firft (nday in *Lent, Good Friday, Rogation Sunday, Tri-* (y *Sunday*, and *Sept.* 5, at 11.

St. *Botolph Aldgate*, fo called as being very near (dgate. This Parifh contains 1000 Dwelling Hou- (s. Morning Pr. conftantly at 11, Evening Pr. at (in the Summer Time, and 8 in the Winter, except (ednefdays, when they are always at 6. Donation (*Jan.* 12. *April* 11. *June* 7. *Sept.* 1. *Ottob.* 3. *Nov.* (. *Dec.* 19.

St. *Botolph Bifhopfgate*, in the Weft fide of *Bifhopf-* (te Street, upon the Bank of the Old *Town Ditch*, (ithout the Walls, but within the Liberties of (ondon. This Parifh contains about 1680 Houfes. (orning Pr every Week day and Holy day at 11, (ening Pr. at 7.

St. *Bridget*, alias St. *Brides*, an antient Church (Bride Lane, near *Fleetftreet*, the Spire of whofe (teeple is 234 Foot high, which is 17 Foot higher (han that of St. *Mary le Bow* in *Cheapfide*, and has (e moft pleafant Ring of 12 Bells about *London*. (contains about 1400 Dwelling Houfes. Morning (r. every Day at 11, and Evening Pr. at 8; an (nnual S. on St. *Bartholomew's* Day, Mufick S. on (. *Cecilia's* Day, and here alfo are preached the (uttle Sermons, on *Monday, Tuefday*, and *Wednefday*, in
Eafter

Eafter Week, before the Lord Mayor and Aldermen
London, the Governors and Children of Chri
Hofpital, by fome eminent Divines chofen
them.

Bridewell Chapel, is an antient, and was forme
a Royal Chapel ; for this fpacious Court was a
tiently the Royal Palace of King *John,* in 12
and other Kings of *England,* where the Parl
ments fate ; and here King *Henry* Eighth m
magnificently entertained the Emperor *Charles* t
Fifth, King of *Spain,* and his own Nephew, A
1522 ; but King *Edward,* the 6th gave it to t
City of *London,* to be an Hofpital, or Workho
for Loyterers and lazy Perfons. This Chapel,
well as that of the *Fleet,* belong to the Verge
the Parifh of St. *Bridget.* Pr. and S. only on S
days, at 10 and 2 of the Clock.

Cafar's Royal and Extraparochial Chapel, in t
Tower of *London,* is fo called from *Julius Cafar,* t
Roman Emperor, who ('tis thought) built t
White Tower, wherein this is. The Records, Rol
and other Writings, are kept on Shelves here
otherwife it is not ufed for divine Worfhip, or a
other Service.

Charterhoufe Chapel, in Charterhoufe Square, n
Weft Smithfield. Morning Pr. every Day at 11 ;
vening Pr. at 5 in the Summer, and 2 in the Wi
ter, befides Pr. and S. every *Sunday* Morning, a
Evening Pr. at 5 conftantly ; and Sac. adminifter
on the firft *Sunday* of every Month.

Chrift's Church in *Newgate Street,* was firft fou
ded, and fo called, by King *Henry* the Eighth,
1546, out of the Ruins of the old Church of S
Ewine in *Newgate Market,* St. *Nicholas* in the Sha
bles, and Part of St. *Sepulchres* within *Newga*
This Parifh contains about 600 Dwelling Houfe
Morning Pr. daily at 11, Evening Pr. at 5 in Su
mer, and 3 in Winter Time ; annual S. on *July*

12 of the Clock, for the Company of *Cordwainers*
Shoemakers.

Christ's Church in *Southwark*, taken out of the
parish of St. *Saviour's*, for a Parish Church for the
liberty of *Paris Garden* there. This Parish contains
about 800 Dwelling Houses Morning Pr. on *Wed-
sdays, Fridays*, and all Holy days; Preparation S.
for the approaching Sac. on the last *Friday* of the
month at 10.

St. *Christopher's* Church in *Threadneedle Street*, near
the *Royal Exchange*, is of no great Antiquity, being
built and finished *Anno* 1462 ; it is also called St.
Christopher le Stocks, because situated near *Stocks
Market*. This Parish contains about 100 fine Dwelling Houses. Pr. are daily at 6 in the Morning and
evening.

St. *Clement Danes* in the *Strand*, is a Church dedi-
ted to *Clement*, Bishop of *Rome*, who was Martyr'd *Anno* 100, and his Day is annually celebrated
v 4 And it's called *Danes*, because in the Days
Canutus, and other *Danish* Kings, it belong'd to
the *Danes*; herein they buried their Dead, and
particularly *Harold*, the eldest Son of *Canutus*, and
Successor, dying at *Oxford*, was buried at *Westminster*, but some few Months afterwards, was taken up, beheaded, and flung into the *Thames*, by
the Order of *Hardicanute*, his half Brother and
successor ; but afterwards taken up again by some
fishermen, and buried here in 1040; wherefore it
must be at least 700 Years old ; but being greatly
decayed, was pulled down *Anno* 1680, and rebuilt
and finished all of Stone, by the Parishioners, in
82. This Parish contains 1730 Dwelling Houses.
Morning Pr. every Day at 11, Evening Pr. at 3
and 8 in the Week Days, and 7 on *Sundays*; Sac.
ministered every *Sunday*; a publick S. extraordi-
ly preached every Holy day, and publick Day
K ap-

appointed by the Government ; monthly Lect. up the firſt *Sunday*, at 5 in the Evening.

St. *Clement*'s Church, in St. *Clement*'s Lane, ne *Great Eaſtcheap*, is probably of no long ſtanding the firſt Account of it being in 1632, when was repair'd by the Pariſhioners. This Pariſh co tains 160 Dwelling Houſes. Morning Pr. only *Wedneſdays*, *Fridays*, and Holy days, at 11, annu S. for, and before the Company of *Clothwoiks* conſtantly in the Months of *January*, *July*, a *September*, in the Forenoon ; but undeterminate to the Day, which depends upon their Pleaſure.

St. *Dionyſe*, or *Dionis*, commonly called *Dio Back* Church, becauſe it ſtands back from the for part of the Street. It is dedicated to St. *Denn* or *Dionyſius*, the *Areopagite*, who ſuffered Marty dom in *France*, by being beheaded under *Deciu Diocleſian*, and therefore he is made the Champio or Patron of that Nation. This Pariſh contai 150 Dwelling Houſes. Morning Pr. daily at 8 Summer, and 9 in Winter ; Evening Pr. at 5 co ſtantly.

Drapers Almshouſes Chapel, in *Blackman Street* St. *George*'s Fields, and belonging to the Pariſh that Name in *Southwaik*, built by *John Walter*, C izen and Draper of *London*, in 1651. Morn Pr. every Day at 8 in the Summer, and 9 in t Winter, except the *Octaves* of *Eaſter*, *Whitſunt* and *Chriſtmas*, and all publick Days and Holy da when the Alms People are obliged to attend divi Service at the Mother Church, and likewiſe eve *Sunday* Forenoon and Afternoon.

Draters Almshouſes Chapel, in the Pariſh of *Mary Newington Butts*, founded by the abovena *John Walter* ; and of the ſame Order in all Thin with that of St. *George*'s Pariſh, above deſcrib

Duke Street Chapel, by *Story*'s Gate in St. *Ja* Park. Morning Pr. daily at 11, and Evening

4. S. both Forenoon and Afternoon, at the u-
al Hours. It was founded by Mr. *Higgins*, and
ivate Subscriptions, in 1709, in the House be-
nging once to Baron *Wem*, or Lord High-Chan-
lor *Jefferies*.

St. *Dunstan* in the East, between *Idle Lane* and
Dunstan's Hill near the *Tower*, an antient Church,
dicated to St. *Dunstan*, Archbishop of *Canterbury*,
rn at *Glassenbury* in *Somersetshire*, about the Year
3. This Parish contains 300 Dwelling Houses.
orning Pr. upon *Wednesdays*, *Fridays*, and Holy
ys, at 11; annual S. on the first *Tuesday* in *Aug.*
12, *Good Friday* at 10, St. *Simon* and *Jude's* day,
. 30. *Sept.* 2. and *Nov.* 5.

St. *Dunstan* at *Stepney*, alias *Stebon Hythe* or *Heath*,
Church probably built before St. *Dunstan* above-
entioned, and dedicated to *All Saints*; but being
uilt or repaired in his Life Time, or a little af-
wards, it was then dedicated to his Memory.
is Parish is of greater Extent than any in the
orld, if that were true, that it extends to the
e of St. *Helen* in the *East Indies*; however it con-
s of about 9000 Dwelling Houses. Morning Pr.
ery Week day at 11; Evening Pr. at 3 in Win-
, and 6 in Summer; Sac. administered every first
d second *Sunday* of the Month at 12.

St. *Dunstan* in the West, near *Chancery Lane* in
eetstreet, so called to distinguish it from that
urch dedicated to the same Saint in the East end
the City of *London*. This Parish contains (in-
ding the Liberty of the *Rolls*, and Precinct of
efyers) 920 Dwelling Houses. Morning Pr.
continually at 7, except Holy days sometimes,
en there is a S. and Pr. at 10; annual S. *July*
at 10, for the Company of *Shoemakers*; Comme-
ration S. *April* 16, besides other Donation S. on
r. 14. *Dec.* 2.

St.

St. *Edmond* the King and Martyr, on the No[r] fide of *Lombard Street*, dedicated to the Me[mory] of St. *Edmond*, King of the *Eaſt Angles*, mart[yred] by the *Danes* at *Edmundsbury* in *Suffolk*, in 879, [a]bout which Time this Church might be found[ed,] while his Name and Death was freſh among [the] *Saxons*, which is celebrated Annually *Nov.* 20. T[his] Pariſh contains about 150 fine Dwelling Hou[ſes.] Morning Pr. daily at 11, and Evening Pr. at 7.

Elyhouſe Chapel, upon *Holbourn Hill*, in the Ho[uſe] belonging to the Biſhops of *Ely* ever ſince the [Year] 1190. When the Biſhop (but at no other ti[me] reſides here, Morning Pr. are every Day at 8, [and] on all *Sundays*, Holy days, and publick Days, [at] 11, Evening Pr. continually at 4; S. every [Sun]day at 11; and Sac. celebrated every firſt *Sunday* [in] the Month.

St. *Ethelburga*, vulgo *Ethelburgh*, on the Eaſt [ſide] of *Biſhopſgateſtreet*, is an old Church dedicated [to] the Memory of *Ethelburga*, Daughter of *Ethelb[ert,]* and Queen to King *Edwine*, both Chriſtian Kin[gs] converted by St. *Auſtin* the Monk, and for her [holy] Life canonized. This Pariſh contains 120 Dwell[ing] Houſes. Morning Pr. on *Wedneſdays*, *Fridays*, [and] all Holy days, at 11, Lect. extraordinary on *[Jan.]* 20. *May* 29. *Sept.* 2. *Nov.* 5. and all other publ[ick] Solemnities.

Fleet Chapel, in the Priſon for Debtors, by *Fl[eet]* *ditch*. Morning Pr. on all ordinary Days at 11, [on] all *Sundays* and Holy days at 10, and 3 in the Ev[en]ing; S. every *Sunday* in the Forenoon; Sac. [the] firſt *Sunday* of every Month, at *Chriſtmas*, *Eaſ[ter,]* *Whitſunday*, and before *Michaelmas Term*.

St. *George*'s Chapel, in *Queen's Square* near [Or]m[o]nd *Street*, built *Anno* 1706. Morning Pr. ev[ery] Day at 11, and 4 in the Evening, Sac. every S[un]d[a]y, *Good Friday*, and *New Years Day*; Lect. ex[tra]ordinary on *Jan.* 30. *Nov.* 5 and all ſolemn D[ays] appointed by the Government.

St. *George* in *Botolph Lane* and *George Lane* near
he Monument ; called alfo St. *George Eaſtchegp*, be-
uſe ſituated therein. This Pariſh contains 100
welling Houſes. Morning Pr. on *Wedneſdays, Fri-
gs*, and all Holy days, at 11.

St. *George* the Martyr in *Southwark*, dedicated to
t. *George*, who was born in *Cappadocia*, killed (as
radition reports) a mighty Dragon in *Africk*,
hereby he reſcued a Virgin who was to be de-
our'd by it, wrought many Miracles, and was at
ſt beheaded under the Emperor *Dioclefian*, in 287
303 , in Commemoration whereof he is annually
lebrated on the 23d of *April*. This Pariſh con-
irs above 800 Dwelling Houſes. Morning Pr. on
idneſdays, *Fridays*, and all Holy days and publick
ays at 10 ; Preparation S. for the approaching Sa-
ament on the third *Sunday* in the Month, at 5 in
e Evening ; S. and Pr. upon *Jan.* 30. *Nov.* 5. *Aſh
dneſday, Good Friday*, and on all State Days,
10.

St. *Giles Cripplegate*, at the lower End of *Red Groſs
et*, built by one *Alfune*, Biſhop of *London*, in
90 or 1102, and dedicated to St. *Giles*, Abbot of
mes near *Roan* in *France*, where this holy Con-
for died about the Year 700, and his Feſtival is
ebrated annually on the firſt of *September*. Herein
a Stone Monument of one *Conſtance Whitney*, ri-
g out of a Coffin, as an Emblem of the Reſurre-
on of the Dead, which ſome falſly take for Mat-
of Fact, in Remembrance of a Gentlewoman, who
e again. This Pariſh contains about 4000 Dwel-
g Houſes. Morning Pr. are only on *Litany Days*,
Wedneſdays, Fridays, and all Holy days, at 11 ;
ening Pr. at 8, excepting *Sunday* Nights ; Lect.
ry *Sunday* Morning at 6 in Summer, 7 in Win-
; a Charity S. on the laſt *Sunday* of every Month,
5 in the Afternoon, and on all State Days.

St.—

St *Giles*'s in the Fields, fituated at the W
end of St. *Giles's High Street*, a very antient Chur
built whereon an Hofpital was founded by Que
Maud or *Matilda*, Wife to King *Henry* the F
about the Year 1100, and at which Holpital
Criminals carried from *London* to be executed
Tyburn, were prefented with a great Bowl of Dr
call'd St. *Giles* s Bowl, to drink at pleafure as th
laft Refrefhment in this Life. This Parifh conta
about 3000 Dwelling Houfes. Morning Pr.
daily at 10, Evening Pr. at 3 ; the Sac. befides
general Seafon, is adminiftered every fecond *Sun*
in the Month after Morning Pr. at 7 ; annua
extraordinary *Jan.* 30. *Nov.* 5. *Chriftmas Day*,
Good Friday, at 10 and 3 ; a Preparation S. for
Sacrament the laft *Sunday* of the Month, and
in the Evening.

Graycoat Hofpital Chapel, in *Tothill Fields*, bu
Anno 1706, for 70 poor Boys and 40 Girls. Mo
ing Pr. at 7, and 6 in the Evening.

Grays Inn Chapel, near *High Holbourn*, belongi
to the Lawyers of that Inn, which was, in the T
of King *Edward* the Third, the Dwelling Houfe
the Lord *Gray* of *Wilton*. Morning Pr. daily
11 ; Evening Pr. at 3 in Winter, and 5 in Summ
but Pr. and S on *Sundays* begin half an hour bef
10 in the Morning, and at 2 in the Afternoo
Sac. adminiftered twice every Term, at the Difc
tion of the Minifter, befides at *Chriftmas*, *Ea*
and *Whitfunday*.

Guildhall Chapel, fronting *Guildhall Yard*, is E
traparochial, and was firft founded *Anno* 1299,
rebuilt in the Eighth Year of King *Henry* the Six
Anno 1429 ; but it is of no Ufe at prefent.

St. *Helen* the Great, in *Bifhopfgateftreet* with
the Gate, dedicated to the Memory of St. *He*
or as it's over the South Door, to St. *Helena*, w
was Mother of *Conftantine* the Great, the firft Ch
ftr

an Emperor, born at *Colchester* in *Essex*; and call'd *eat*, to diftinguifh it from St. *Helen* the Lefs near *creto*; both Parifhes comprehend about 130 Hou-*s*. Morning Pr. on *Wednesdays, Fridays,* and all *oly days* ; weekly Lect. upon every *Tuesday,* at 4 *the* Evening, from *Michaelmas* to *Ladyday.*

Hog Lane Chapel, between *Monmouth Street* and *.Giles,* belonging to Almshoules founded by fe-*ral* Perfons, in the Years 1680, 1683, 1684, 1685, *d* 1686. Morning Pr. every Day at 11 of the *lock*.

Horfe Guard Chapel, by *Whitehall,* for the Ufe of *he Life Guards,* who were firft ordained by *Henry he* Seventh, in 1485, and ever fince kept up by *he* Kings of *England.* Pr. and S. every *Sunday* Morning.

Hoxton Hofpital Chapel, near *Hoxton Square,* *unded* in 1692, by *Robert Aske,* Efq; Alderman *nd Haberdasher* of *London,* who left 30,000 Pounds *r that* Ufe. Morning Pr. daily at 11, and 3 in *he* Evening from *Michaelmas* to *Ladyday,* and at 5 *om Ladyday* to *Michaelmas.* S and Pr. are every *unday* Morning, and in the Afternoon only from *adyday* to *Michaelmas,* but from that to *Ladyday hete* are only Prayers, Sac every laft *Sunday* of the *Month*.

St. *James* at *Clerkenwell,* fituate upon *Clerkenwell heen,* was firft founded by *Jordan Briffet,* in the *ime* of King *Stephen,* and dedicated to St. *James he* Apoftle and Bifhop of *Jerufalem,* where he was *artyred Anno* 62. This Parifh contains about 1200 *foules*. Morning Pr. every Week day and Holy *ay* at 11, and evening Pr. only on *Saturday* at 2, as Preparation for the holy Sabbath ; a monthly *ect.* on the laft *Sunday,* at 5 in the Evening ; a *reparation* S. for the Sacrament, on the laft *Friday f* the Month, at 11 : an Anniverfary S. on St. *ames's* Day.

St

St. *James*'s Chapel, in the Royal Palace of *James*, which had been the Hospital of St. *James* founded before the *Norman* Conquest, by the Citizens of *London*, for 14 leprous Sisters, or devout Maidens, with whom King *Henry* compounded in the 23d Year of his Reign, and thereon built the Mansion house, after the antient Palace of *Westminster* had been destroyed by Fire in 1512. Morning Pr. at 8 and 11, and Evening Pr. at 5, but in his Majesty's Absence only twice, *viz.* at 11 and Sac. is administered (if the King be present) twice every *Sunday*, at 8 and 12; but if otherwise, only at 12 after Sermon: -besides S on all *Sundays* at the usual Hours; extraordinary S. are on *Jan.* 30. *M* 29. *Nov.* 5. and all other publick Solemnities, *Ash Wednesday*, all *Wednesdays* and *Fridays* in Lent, *Good Friday*, *Easter*, *Christmas*, and several other Holy days.

St. *James*, in *Duke's Place* near *Aldgate*, within a Precinct by it self, was built in the 20th Year of the Reign of King *James* the First. This Parish contains about 160 Houses. Morning Pr. on all *Wednesdays*, *Fridays*, and all Holy days, at 11, Sac. administered upon the second *Sunday* of the Month at 12, besides other Occasions.

St. *James* at *Garlick Hyth*, or *Garlick Hive*, in *Thames Street*, was new built by *Richard Rothing*, Sheriff of *London*, in 1326. This Parish contains about 170 Dwelling Houses. Morning Pr. on *Wednesdays*, *Fridays*, and Holy days, at 11.

St. *James* in *Jermyn Street*, was by Act of Parliament taken out of the Parish of St. *Martin* in the Fields, in the first Year of King *James* the Second, 1685. This Parish contains about 3,000 Dwelling Houses. Morning Pr. at 6 in Summer, and 7 in the Winter, and again at 11, and Evening Pr. at 3 and 6, excepting *Saturday* Nights, on *Sunday* Morning at 6 in the Summer, and 7 in the Winter, but at Night

ght only at 5. Sac. administered every second
nday from *Palm Sunday* to *Trinity Sunday*, and on
w Years Day at 12, on *Christmas Day*, *Palm Sunday*,
ster Day, and *Whitsunday*, at 7 and 12. Lect. ex-
ordinary on *Christmas Day*, *New Years Day*, *Jan.*
, *Mar.* 8. *Ash Wednesday*, and every *Thursday* from
ence to *Passion Week*, *Good Friday*, *Nov.* 5. and on
publick Solemnities appointed by the Govern-
ent.

St. *John* of *Jerusalem*, at *Hackney*. Morning Pr. on
ednesdays, *Fridays*, and Holy days at 11, annual S.
Good Friday, *Ascension day*, Day of Queen *Eliza-*
th's Accession to the Throne, and Gun Powder
eason Day at 10.

St. *John* at *Wapping*, in *Wapping Street*, near the
ames, built in 1617. Morning Pr. on all Days
t 8 in Summer, and 9 in Winter; Evening P. at
in Summer, and 3 in Winter; a Monthly Lect.
pon the penult *Sunday*, or last *Sunday* but one.
his Parish contains 1300 Dwelling Houses.

Islington Alms Houses Chapel, founded by the
Lady *Owen* about 1613, near a Place where she had
Providential escape from Death, by an Arrow
not at random in these Fields, which pierced
hrough her Hat; and in Memory whereof are
everal Arrows set upon the Corners and Top of
he Houses. Pr. are every Week day at 11 and 4,
nd *Sunday* at 5.

St. *Katherine Coleman*, in *Fenchurch Street*, is an
ncient Church, founded or repair'd *Anno* 1182.
his Parish contains about 240 Dwelling Houses.
r. are on *Wednesdays*, *Fridays*, and Holy days at 11.

St *Katherine Cree Church*, near the end of *Leaden-*
all Street is dedicated to St. *Katherine*, an holy
irgin of *Alexandria*, murder'd under *Maxentius*
he *Roman* Emperor; and her Day is annually cele-
rated on *November* 25. This Parish contains a-
bout 360 Dwelling Houses. Morning Pr. on *Wed-*
nesdays,

nesdays, *Fridays*, and Holy days at 10 ; Eveni
Pr. only on *Saturdays* at 3 in Winter, and 4 in Su
mer ; Sac. firſt *Sunday* in the Month at 12,
annual Thankſgiving S. on *Octob.* 16, at 10.
Commemoration of Sir *John Gayer*, Knight, w
gave 200 Pounds for this, in Memory of his De
verance from the Paws of a Lion in *Arabia*.

 St *Katherine* by the *Tower*, a Pariſh containi
about 860 Houſes. Morning Pr. are daily at
and S. on *Wedneſdays* and *Fridays* throughe
Lent.

 King Henry's Chapel, adjoyning to the Eaſt e
of *St. Peter's* Abby in *Weſtminſter*, built by Ki
Henry the Seventh, who laid the firſt Stone there
with his own Hands, on the 24th of *Januar*
1502 : This Place of Sepulture for the Kings an
Queens of *England*, is a Piece of moſt admiral
Workmanſhip both within and without, exce
all others of that nature in *Europe*, and theref
is deſervedly called the Wonder of the World
It is uſed for a retiring Place for publick Pr.
the Morning ; or Pr. and S. when the Abby
Repairing or Beautifying.

 King's Bench Chapel, in *Southwark*, belonging
the greateſt Priſon in *England*, for Debtors, Mu
therers, and Traytors, and is extraparochi
Morning Pr every Day at 7 , and S. every *Sund*
in the Forenoon.

 King's Land Chapel, in *Kingſland* Hoſpital, upe
Kingſland Road ; it is an Appendix to St. *Bartlj*
lomew's Hoſpital, for the Cure of 24 infirm Wo
men ; and on the Dial here is this Motto, *Pj*
voluptatem miſericordia. Herein are Pr. and S. ever
Sunday in the Afternoon.

 King Street Chapel, near the middle of *Km*
Street by *Golden Square*, firſt erected all of Wood
and call'd then St. *James's* Tabernacle ; but rebui
all of Brick, and enlarged in 1702. –Morning Pr
            eve

ry *Sunday* and Week day at 6 in the Summer, 7 in the Winter, and again at 11 ; Evening at 3, and 6, except *Saturday* Night. Sac. laſt day in the Month continually at 12 ; S. on ſtmas Day, *Jan.* 30, *Nov.* 5, and all Holy days, emn Faſts, and Thankſgiving Days.

Knights Bridge Chapel, in the Village of *Knights* dge near *Hyde Park* Corner, built on an old de'd and ruin'd Chapel, belonging to an antient ſaken Chapel there, *anno* 1634. Pr. and S. eve-*Sunday*, both Forenoon and Afternoon, at the ual Hours ; and Sac. every firſt *Sunday* of the onth.

Lambeth Chapel, in *Lambeth* Palace, belonging the Archbiſhop of *Canterbury*. Morning Pr. are ly at 7 in Summer, and 8 in the Winter, and 12, Evening Pr. at 2 and 9 continually. Sac. the firſt *Sunday* of the Month , and S. every nday in the Forenoon.

Lamb's Chapel, in *Hart Street*, near *Cripplegate*, ilt by *William Lamb*, one of the Gentlemen of the apel to King *Henry* the Eighth. Morning Pr. *Wedneſdays* and *Fridays* ; but the Sac. is never miniſtered here ; S. before the Company of *Cloth*-kers on *Ladyday*, *Midſummer Day*, *October* 1. St. phen's Day, at 10.

St. Laurence Jewry by *Guildhall*, conſecrated to e Memory of St. *Laurence* a Spaniard, and Arch acon of the Church of *Rome*, who was broiled a Gridiron, under the Emperor *Valerian*, on the th of *Auguſt*, in the Year 260. This Pariſh con-n 230 fine Dwelling Houſes. Morning Pr. on nday, *Wedneſday*, *Thurſday*, and *Saturday*, at 6 d 11, and on *Tueſday* and *Friday* at 10 ; Evening conſtantly at 8, but on *Thurſday* at 3. Sac. firſt nday of the Month at 12, and on all other *Sundays* 6 in the Morning ; a Charity S. every *Sunday* at and weekly Lect. every *Tueſday* and *Friday* at 10, d *Thurſday* at 3. St.

St. *Leonard* in *Shoreditch*, dedicated to St. *Leona* Bishop of *Limoges*, born in *France*, in the Year 5(he died in 570, and his Festival is annually obf ved on the 6th of *November*. This Parish conta 2000 Dwelling Houses. Morning Pr. on *Wednefd(Fridays*, Holy days, and State Days, at 11; L(on the Annunciation and Nativity of the Vir(*Mary*, in the Forenoon; S. upon the Days of *John Baptist*, St. *Michael*, St. *Stephen*, and Purific tion of the blessed Virgin, *Jan.* 30. *May* 29. a the Powderplot Day.

Lincoln. Inn Chapel, in *Chancery Lane*, which (ter many Alterations in 300 Years Time, was (built, finished, and confecrated in 1626. Morni Pr. daily at 5 and 11, and Evening Pr. at 5 throug out the whole Year; Sac. administered once *Christmas, Easter*, on the fecond *Sunday* of *Septemb* and first and last *Sundays* of every Term, after Fo noon Sermon, two S. every *Sunday* at the uf Hours, and a monthly Lect. every first *Wednef* at 10.

Lock Hofpital Chapel, or *Lazar Houfe*, at t lower end of *Kent Street*, and an Appendix of *Bartholomew*'s Hofpital, for the Support and Cure polluted and unclean Men, as that of *Kings L(is* for Women. Here are Pr. every *Sunday*, and once a Month.

London Houfe Chapel, in *Alderfgateftreet*, cal(formerly *Peter Houfe*, was built by *Humphrey Henc man*, Bifhop of that See, in 1675; but in reg(the more common Refidence of this Prelate (been at his Country Seat at *Fulham*, it has not b(much ufed of a long time.

London Workhoufe Chapel, in *Halfmoon Alley Bifhopfgateftreet*, which place was built for the e(ploying and relieving poor idle People, Vagran(and fturdy Beggars in *London*. Morning Pr. eve Day in the Week at 6, and Evening Pr. at 6.

Ludg(

Ludgate Chapel, a Prison ordain'd for Debtors that are Freemen of *London*, in 1379. Morning Pr. only at 10; and S. every *Sunday* in the Evening.

St. *Magnus* by *London Bridge*, dedicated to the Memory of St. *Magnus* or *Magnes*, who suffer'd under the Emperor *Aurelian* in 276, or else to a Person of that Name, who was the famous Apostle or Bishop of the *Orcades*. Morning Pr every *Wednesday* and *Friday* at 11. This Parish contains about 00 Dwelling Houses.

St. *Margaret* in *Lothbury*, a Parish consisting of 00 Dwelling Houses. Pr. are only on *Wednesdays*, Fridays, and all Holy days, at 11.

St. *Margaret Pattons*, or *Pattens*, so called because Pattens used to be sold here. This Parish contains about 160 Dwelling Houses. Morning Pr. on *Wednesdays*, *Fridays*, and all Holy days; an annual S. on the first of *Jan.* and on some publick Days.

St. *Margaret* near *Westminster Abbey*, dedicated to St. *Margaret*, an holy Virgin, who was born, liv'd and buried in *Antioch* in *Syria*, after she was beheaded under *Decius* the Emperor, *Anno* 292, and her Festival is yearly observ'd on the 20th of *July*, was first built on the place where it now stands, by King *Edward* the Confessor, in 1050. This Parish consists of 3039 Dwelling Houses. Here, on *Easter Day*, 1555, *William Flower*, a Priest, wounded another with a Knife, as he was administring the Sacrament, for which his Right Hand was cut off, *April* 14. and for some Errors he was burnt in the Churchyard soon after. Morning Pr. on *Wednesdays*, Fridays, and Holy days, and all publick State Days, at 10; Evening Pr. at 6 in Summer, and 7 in Winter, both Week Days and Sundays; annual S. on *All Saints* at 10; and several occasional Sermons on all publick State Days, and before the honourable House of Commons on *Jan.* 30. *May* 29. and *Nov.* 5. during the Session of Parliament.

L

Marshalsea

Marſhalſea Chapel in *Southwark*, belonging to the
County Goal of *Surry*. Pr. on *Wedneſdays* and *Sa-
turdays* in the Evening at 3, and Pr. and S. every
Sunday Morning at 10.

St. *Martin* in the Fields, in St. *Martin's Lane*,
near *Charing Croſs*, dedicated to St. *Martin*, Confeſſor and Biſhop of *Tours* in *France*, where he died
when 81 Years of Age, in 399 or 404 ; and his
Feſtival, inſtituted by Pope *Martin* the Firſt, upon
Nov. 11. is annually celebrated by this Pariſh, which
contains 3780 Dwelling Houſes. Morning Pr. in
this Church, (which is lately pull'd down to be
rebuilt) were daily at 6 from *Ladyday* to *Michaelmas*,
and 7 from thence to *Ladyday* again, and on *Wedneſdays*, *Fridays*, Holy days, and State days, at 10 ;
Evening Pr. at 6, but on *Saturdays* and Holy days
at 3. Sac. on every firſt *Sunday* of the Month,
Chriſtmas day, *Eaſter day*, and *Whitſunday* twice, *viz.*
at 6 in Summer, and 7 in Winter ; and again at
12 ; but on every *Sunday* of the Month, except
the firſt, *New Years day*, *Good Friday*, and *Aſcenſion
day*, only at 12 ; a Charity S. on every third *Sunday* of the Month at 5 ; and on all publick Solemnities, and other Occaſions, at 10.

St. *Martin Ludgate*, in *Ludgate Street*, was probably founded by King *Cadwallo*, Father to the
great *Cadwallader* ; he was a valiant *Britiſh* King,
who died *Nov.* 20. *Anno* 677, and his Body was
buried in this Church, and his Image of Braſs afterwards placed upon the Gate, for a Terror to the
Saxons. This Pariſh contains 179 fine Dwelling
Houſes. Morning Pr. every Week day and Holy
day at 11, and 6 in the Evening ; annual S. on the
10th or 14th of *Auguſt*, at the Diſcretion of the
Rector, on the Defeat of the invincible Armado in
1588, on the 5th of *Nov.* and 17th of *Nov.*

St. *Martin Outwich* or *Oteſwich*, in *Threadneedle
Street*, ſo called from *Martin*, *Nicholas*, *William*, and
John

John Oteſwich, who were joint Founders hereof, about the Year 1300, and herein buried. This Pariſh contains about 63 Dwelling Houſes. Morning Pr. are on *Wedneſdays, Fridays*, and all Holy days, at 11; Lect. extraordinary on *Jan.* 30. *Sept.* 2. and *Nov.* 5.

St. *Mary Abchurch*, in *Abchurch Lane*, dedicated to the Virgin *Mary*, and called *Abchurch*, or *Upchurch*, becauſe it ſtands upon riſing Ground, or elſe had its Denomination from A, B, C, which the *Romans* ſcatter'd in the four Corners of the Church at the Conſecration of it. This Pariſh contains about 200 Dwelling Houſes. Morning Pr. on *Wedneſdays, Fridays*, and all Holy days, at 11; and *Saturday* Evening only at 4.

St. *Mary Aldermanbury*, in the middle of *Aldermanbury*, ſo called from a *Bury* or Court of Aldermen, held thereabout till the Building of *Guildhall*. This Pariſh conrains about 200 Dwelling Houſes. Morning Pr. on *Wedneſdays, Fridays*, Holy days, and State days, at 11; a Preparation S. for the approaching Sacrament, on the laſt *Wedneſday* of the Month, at 4 in the Evening.

St. *Mary Aldermary* in *Bow Lane*, an antient Foundation erected before the coming in of the *Normans*, and therefore it has been called *Older Mary*, as being the Older Church of St. *Mary* in the City of *London*. This Pariſh conſiſts of above 300 Dwelling Houſes. Morning Pr. on *Wedneſdays, Fridays*, and Holy days, at 11; annual S. on *Candlemas Day* at 6 in the Evening, for, and before the Company of *Cooks*, on the 2d of *Sept.* Charity S. every ſecond and fourth *Sunday* in the Month, at 5 in the Evening.

St. *Mary at Hill*, near *Billingſgate*, ſo called becauſe of the Hill or Aſcent from the River of *Thames*, on which it ſtands. This Pariſh conſiſts of about 220 Houſes. Morning Pr. on *Wedneſdays, Fridays*, and

Holy

Holydays, at 11; Evening Pr. on *Saturdays* & holydays at 3, a weekly Lect. every *Thursd.* in the Year at 10.

St. *Mary* at *Islington*. Morning Pr. on *Wednesdays, Fridays*, and Holy days, at 11; Evening Pr. on *Saturdays* and Holy days at 3, an annual Gift S. on St. *Thomas's* Day at 11.

St. *Mary* at *Lambeth*, or *Lamblive*, or *Lambhith* being a dirty Haven, and is the largest Parish about *London*, as containing 16 Miles and a half in Circumference. Morning Pr. on *Wednesdays, Fridays* and Holy days at half an Hour after 10, and every Day in *Lent* at 11; Evening Pr. only on *Saturday* at 3; Sac. on *Ash Wednesday, Good Friday*, and the first *Sunday* of every Month; S. on *Jan.* 30. *Nov.* 5. A Lect on the first after Quarter Day, at 10.

St. *Mary* le *Bow* in *Cheapside*, so called because it was the first that was built upon Arches or Bows of Stone, in the Reign of *William* the first. This Parish contains 162 Houses. Morning Pr. daily at 8, Evening Pr. at 5; Lect. against Atheism on the first *Monday* of *Jan. Feb. Mar. Apr. May, Sept. Octob. Nov.* Sac. first *Sunday* of every Month at 12, and every Holy day at 8, immediately after Morning Prayers; annual S. before the Society for Reformation of Manners, on the first *Monday* after *Christmas* at 11, and before the Society for the Propagation of the Gospel in Foreign parts, on the third *Friday* of *Feb.* at 11.

St. *Mary* at *Newington Butts*, in *Surry*, so called because Butts or shooting Marks were here formerly, whereat the *Londoners* exercised themselves with Bows and Arrows Morning Pr. on *Wednesday, Fridays, Saturdays*, and Holy days, at 11.

St. *Mary* at *Rotherhith*, or *Hive*, and commonly called *Redriff*, that is, *Red Rose Haven*, in *Surry*, and seated so near the *Thames*, that the Tide came into it on a *Saturday* in 1705, which so sunk the Floor, that it was new levell'd and pav'd soon afterwards.

terwards. Morning Pr. on *Wednesdays*, *Fridays*, Holy-days, and *Saturday* before the Sacrament at 11; Sac. on the second *Sunday* of the Month; a Preparation S. for the Sacrament every *Thursday* before the second *Sunday* of the Month.

St. *Mary le Savoy*, or St. *Mary* in the *Savoy*, or St. *Mary Strand*, so called from Queen *Mary* the First, or an old Chapel there; but at first it was St. *John* in the *Strand*, and was formerly the Chapel Royal for the Kings of *England*; the Altar stands at the North end of it, and the Parish contains about 30 Dwelling Houses. Morning Pr. every Day at 7 in the Summer, and 8 in the Winter; on *Wednesdays*, *Fridays*, and all Holy days at 10; Evening Pr. every Night at 5, except *Saturdays*, when they are constantly at 3; Sac. every first *Sunday* of the Month at 7 and 12; and a preparation S. before the Sacrament, on the last *Sunday* of the Month, at 6 in the Evening.

St. *Mary Magdalen Bermondsey*, in *Barnaby Street*, founded by *Ailewin Child*, Citizen of *London*, in 1081, and dedicated to St. *Mary Magdalen*, Sister to *Lazarus*, that was raised from the Dead, and *Martha*, taking her Sirname from the Castle of *Magdala*, 2 Miles from *Nazareth*, where she lived, but died at *Ephesus*, about the Year 60, and her Festival is celebrated *July* 21. This Parish contains 1500 Dwelling Houses. Morning Pr. every Day in the Week at 11; Sac. (besides the first *Sunday* of the Month at 12) on all Holy days that fall on the first *Sunday* of the Month, and on *Christmas Day*, *Easter Day*, and *Whitsunday*, at 7 and 12; Lect. on the last *Sunday* of every Month at 5; and a anniversary S. on the 18th of *Nov.* at 10, being the Day of the Death of *John Wright*, a Merchant Taylor.

St. *Mary Magdalen*, in *Old Fishstreet*, a Parish containing 400 Dwelling Houses. Morning Pr. on Holy days at 11; Evening Pr. in *Lent* only on *Saturdays* at 3.

L 3

St.

St. *Mary Somerset*, at *Broken Wharf* in *Thames Street*, so nam'd because it is near to *Somer's Hithe*, and his being the Owner of the Ground thereabouts. This Parish contains 150 Dwelling Houses. Morning Pr. are only on Holy days and State days at 11.

St. *Mary Whitechapel*, called of old St. *Mary Matfellon*, from some Person of that Name, or a Malefactor that was punish'd there by a Mob. This Parish contains about 1900 Dwelling Houses. Morning Pr. on *Wednesdays*, *Fridays*, and Holy days, at 11; Evening Pr. only on *Saturdays* at 3; Sac. on every *Sunday* of the Month.

St. *Mary Woollnoth* in *Lombard Street*, so denominated from a Staple of Wooll, or Beam placed near it, on which Wooll was formerly weighed. This Parish contains about 153 Dwelling Houses. Morning Pr. every Day of the Week at 11, and Evening Pr. at 5; a preparation S. for the approaching Sacrament, on the last *Friday* of the Month, at 6 in the Evening.

St. *Matthew Friday street*, in *Cheapside*, dedicated to the Evangelist of that Name, who was the Son of *Alpheus* a Publican. This Parish contains 120 Dwelling Houses. Morning Pr. on *Wednesdays*, *Fridays*, and all Holy days; Sac. twice upon the first *Sunday* of the Month at 6 after Morning Prayer and Sermon; a weekly Lect. every *Sunday* Night at 5.

Mercers Hall Chapel, in *Cheapside*, belonging to the Company of *Mercers*, which is the first of the 12 Companies; for, and before whom, are Pr. and S. every *Sunday* Afternoon, at 3, from the first *Sunday* after *Michaelmas* Term till *Good Friday*, except the second *Sunday* after *Christmas*; and S. on the 30th of *Jan.* 29th of *May*, and *Nov.* the 5th.

St. *Michael Basinghall*, commonly called *Basishaw*, near *Aldarmanbury*, dedicated to the Memory of St. *Michael* the Archangel; he was Captain of those blessed

blessed Angels, whose Victory over the Devil and his Angels is annually commemorated on *September* 29. called St. *Michael and all Angels*, and *Michaelmas*. This Parish contains 150 Houses. Morning Pr. on *Wednesdays, Fridays*, and Holy days, at 11, Evening Pr. every Night at 5; weekly Lect. every *Wednesday* at 5 in the Evening, from *Michaelmas* to *Lady-day*, annual S first for, and before the *Weavers* Company on St. *James's* Day; the second for, and before the *Coopers* Company, on the *Monday* before *Whitsunday*; and third for, and before the *Girdlers* Company, about the 12th of *August*, at 12.

St. *Michael Cornhill*, in *Michael's Alley* in *Cornhill*, which Parish contains 122 Dwelling Houses. Morning Pr. on *Wednesdays, Fridays*, and Holy days, at 11, Lect. on *Sunday* Morning at 6 a Clock.

St. *Michael Crooked Lane*, near *Cannon street*, which Parish consists of 120 Dwelling Houses. Morning Pr. on *Wednesdays, Fridays*, and Holy days at 11.

St. *Michael Queenhyth*, in *Thames street*, which contains about 220 Dwelling Houses. Morning Pr. only on Holy days and publick days at 11; Evening Pr. constantly at 6.

St. *Michael Royal*, on *College Hill*; which Parish contains 200 Dwelling Houses. Morning Pr. on *Wednesdays, Fridays*, and Holy days, at 11, Evening Pr. at 3; an Evening Lect. every *Friday* in the Year at the same Time.

St. *Michael Woodstreet*, near *Cheapside*, memorable for the Interment of the Head of King *James* the Fourth of *Scotland*, who was kill'd at the Battle of *Floddin Field*, on the 9th of *Sept.* 1513. This Parish contains 140 Houses. Morning Pr. on *Wednesdays, Fridays*, and Holy days, at 11; Lect. upon the first *Tuesday* after St. *Catherine's* Day, being the 25th of *Nov.* for and before the Right Worshipful Company of *Haberdashers*, who meet about 12 of the Clock.

St.

St. *Mildred Breadstreet*, dedicated to St. *Mildred* a Virgin, and Daughter of *Ethelbert*, King of *Kent*, or *Merwaldus*, King of the *Mercians* ; she died about 676. This Parish contains 100 Dwelling Houses. Morning Pr. on *Wednesdays, Fridays*, and Holy days, at 11.

St. *Mildred Poultry*, near *Stocks Market*, is a Parish containing above 130 Houses. Morning Pr. on *Wednesdays, Fridays*, and Holy days, at 11 ; annual S. on *Sept.* 2. *Nov.* 5. and 17. *Jan.* 30. *Mar.* 8. *May* 29. Sac. on the ordinary Times.

New Chapel, or *New Church*, in *Chapel Street*, near *Tuttle Fields*, being a Chapel of Ease in the Parish of St. *Margaret Westminster*, but now design'd for a new Church without Reparation or Addition. It is situated near the middle of a large and decent Church Yard, or Burying Ground, and was built and finished in 1636 ; but afterwards it was plundered, and converted into a Stable for Horses, in the Time of the Civil War ; fitter indeed for those innocent Creatures, than the sacrilegious Regicides that put them there ; as they did also spoil the Mother Church ; but after the Restauration of King *Charles* the Second, it was repaired, enlarged, and beautified. Morning Pr. every Day at 9, but on all Holy days, when there is a Sermon, not till 10, Evening Pr. at 5, from *Candlemas* to *Michaelmas*, at 4 from that to *All Saints* Day ; and at 3 from thence to *Candlemas* ; a preparation S. for the approaching Sacrament, on the last *Friday* of the Month, at 3 ; several Charity S. in *Advent*, and other Times of the Year ; on most part of Holy days, and all publick Days appointed by the Government.

Newgate Chapel, where Morning Pr. are on all Holy days at 10, Evening Pr. at 3 ; S. every *Sunday* at 10, and in the Afternoon at 3 ; and during the Eight Sessions in the Year, Prayers are every Day twice, at 10 and 3, and proper penitential S. for
the

the Use of the Condemn'd Persons, on the first *Sunday* after Condemnation, to the last *Sunday* before their Execution or Reprieve; Sac. on *Christmas day*, *Easter day*, and *Whitsunday*, at 12.

St. *Nicholas Coleabby*, or *Cold Abby*, or (by Contraction) *Cold Bay*, because it stood in a cold place upon the Bank of the River *Thames*, by *Cold Harbour*, dedicated to St. *Nicholas*, Bishop of *Myrra* in *Lycia*, where he died in 343, and his Festival is annually celebrated on the 6th of *December*. This Parish contains 130 Houses. Morning Pr. on *Wednesdays*, *Thursdays*, *Fridays*, and Holy days, at 11, or a little before; a weekly Lect. every Day at 11; and a biennial S. falling out once in two Years, upon the first *Thursday* after St. *James*'s day, for, and before the *Bowyers* Company, at 12.

Noble street Chapel, near *Cripplegate* within, where a S. is preached every *Thursday*, at 6 in the Evening; Pr. and S. every *Sunday* at 10 and 5; Sac. on the second *Sunday* of the Month constantly.

St. *Olave, Hart street*, in *Crutched Fryers*, dedicated to St. *Olave* or *Olaus*, a *Danish* King and Martyr. This Parish contains 220 Dwelling Houses. Morning Pr. on *Wednesdays*, *Fridays*, and Holy days, at 11, Evening Pr. at 3, only on *Saturdays* in *Lent*; Sac. every *Sunday* after the first *Thursday* of the Month; quarterly S. on the first *Sunday* after every Quarter Day, at 10.

St. *Olave Jewry*, on the West side of *Old Jewry*, which Parish contains above 100 fine Dwelling Houses. Morning Pr. on *Wednesdays* and *Fridays* at 11, from the first *Wednesday* in *October* till the last in *May*; and a weekly Lect. on every *Wednesday* in the foresaid Time, at 11.

St. *Olave* in *Southwark*, commonly called *Tooly* Church by *Tooly street*, which contains about 200 Dwelling Houses. Morning Pr. on *Wednesdays*, *Fridays*, and Holy days, at 11; Evening Pr. every *Saturday*

turday only at 3 ; an annual S. on the 5th of *Auguſt* at 10.

Palmer's Almshouſes Chapel, near *Tuttle Fields* where Pr. are daily at 11 in the Forenoon.

St. *Paul's* Cathedral, ſituated on the higheſt Ground of the City, was firſt founded about th Year 610, by *Et.elbert* King of *Kent*, and *Segber* King of the *Weſt Saxons*, in a Wood or Grove, wher ſtood formerly a Temple of *Diana*, the Heathen Goddeſs ; which Opinion was farther confirmed i the Time of King *Edward* the Second, about 1310 and 700 Years after the firſt Foundation, whee Workmen digging thereabout, they found above 100 Heads of Oxen, which were the Sacrifices of fered to the foreſaid Goddeſs. After ſeveral Diſa ſters by Fire, it was wholly conſumed in the dread ful Conflagration in 1665 ; however it was quickly began to be rebuilt, and finiſhed within theſe few Years, ſo that it is now the moſt ample and cele brated Piece of Architecture in the whole World and the largeſt Cathedral, being 20 Foot longe than St. *Peter's* at *Rome*. It is dedicated (as before to the Apoſtle *Paul* ; the Hiſtory of whoſe Conver ſion, and Preaching to the *Bereans*, is curiouſly re preſented upon the Weſt Portico ; oppoſite to which in the Church Yard, is erected a moſt magnificent Statue of white Marble, to the Honour of the late Queen *Anne.* Morning Pr. are every Day in the Chapel at 6 in Summer, and 7 in Winter, but in the Choir again at 10, and Evening Pr. conſtantly at 3 ; Sac. every *Sunday* in the Year at 12 ; a S. every *Sunday* at 10, Afternoon at 3 ; and annual ones on *Jan.* 30. *Mar.* 8. *May* 29. *Sept.* 2. *Nov.* 5. and all other publick Solemnities of Thankſgiving or Faſt Days, appointed by the Government.

St. *Paul* at *Shadwell*, built in 1656, contains about 300 Houſes. *Thomas Sumerly*, the firſt Clerk here, enter'd in the Regiſter Book, the Shower of Hail

Stones

Stones that fell thereabouts, *May* 18. 1683, where-of some were three Inches, and some bigger. Morning Pr. on all Week Days at 11 ; Evening Pr. at 5 in Summer, and 3 in Winter.

Pesthouse Chapel, near *Bunhill Fields*, granted by the City of *London* to the French Refugees ; who have Pr. every Day at 11 and 3.

St. *Peter Cornhill*, so called from a Corn Market which has been there time out of Memory. It is a Church of great Antiquity ; for it's probable that it was the first Christian Church in *London*, an Archbishop's See, and the Metropolitan of this Kingdom, so constituted and built by *Lucius*, the first Christian King in the World, in 179. But notwithstanding there are others who apply this Priority and Antiquity to St. *Peter*'s Abby at *Westminster*, or that most antient Building in the *Great Sanctuary*, now called *Beech's Cellars*. This Parish contains about 174 fine Houses. Morning Pr. every Week day at 11, and Evening Pr. at 4 ; Sac. every *Sunday* at 11, after Sermon ; a weekly Lect. every *Thursday* at 11.

St. *Peter*'s Chapel, in St. *Peter*'s Hospital on the Road to *Newington Butts*, founded by Sir *Thomas Hunt* in 1618. Morning Pr. on *Wednesdays*, *Fridays*, and Holy days, at 11.

St. *Peter Poor* in *Broad street*, called *le Poor*, because of a Friary of the *Augustine* Eremites, called also begging or poor Fryers, who came from *Italy* about 1252, and had some Settlement hereabouts. This Parish contains but 140 Dwelling Houses. Morning Pr. on *Wednesdays*, *Fridays*, and Holy days, at 11.

St. *Peter*'s parochial Church, within the Tower of *London*, built when the Tower was erected by *Julius Cæsar*, before the Birth of Christ, or by *William*, erroneously called the Conqueror, in 1078. Morning Pr. on *Wednesdays*, *Fridays*, and Holy days,

at

at 11 ; Sac. on the first *Sunday* of the Month, unless *Chriſtmas day, Eaſter day,* and *Whitſunday,* fall near or upon that Day, then it's omitted, becauſe of the Nearneſs of thoſe ſolemn Feſtivals.

St. *Peter's* Cathedral, or *Weſtminſter Abby,* from its weſterly Situation from *London,* dedicated to St. *Peter* the Apoſtle. It is equal in Antiquity to any Church, abroad or at home, and inferior to none in the World for Stateineſs and other Rarities, being a Piece of admirable Architecture, and moſt rare Workmanſhip both without and within beautified to the Admiration of all Beholders, with the moſt magnificent and curious Tombs of many Kings and Queens, the Nobles and moſt famous Worthies of *England.* King *Lucius* built a Chriſtian Church here, about the Year 170, which was deſtroyed about 130 Years after that, in the Time of *Dioclesian's* grievous Perſecution, whereby Pagan Superſtition ſo much prevailed again, that a Temple to *Apollo* was built upon the Ruins of that. In the Time of *Antoninus Pius* the *Roman* Emperor, a dreadful Earthquake threw down the old *Profanum,* and then this Plot of Ground lying waſte 3 or 400 Years, was over-run with Water, and overgrown with Thorns, and was called by our Anceſtors, the Iſle of *Thorney,* where, upon this Foundation, *Sebert* the firſt Chriſtian King of the *Eaſt Saxons,* about the Year 610, built another Church, which about 659 was deſtroyed by the *Danes.* About the Year 960, King *Edgar* rebuilt it again. Afterwards King *Edward* the Confeſſor founded and enlarged that ſmall decayed Monaſtery, and made it the Repoſitory of the *Regalia* ; but 156 Years after him, King *Henry* the Third took down the old Fabrick, and rebuilt it from the Ground, with that rare Architecture as it now ſtands. Morning Pr. daily at in the Summer, 7 in the Winter ; again on all Week Days at 10, But on all *Sundays* and Holy days at 9 Even-

Evening Pr. at 4, on *Sundays* half an hour after 3 ;
S. on all *Sundays*, Holy days, and publick State
days, *Afh Wednefday*, *Wednefdays* and *Fridays* through
Lent, at 9 ; a publick S. before the Houfe of Lords
on *Jan.* 30? *May* 29. *Nov.* 5. and other folemn Oc-
cafions during the Time of Parliament. But above
all other Solemnities, is that moft celebrated and
auguft Affembly of the Nobility, at the Coronation
of the Kings and Queens of *England*, before whom
is preached an Inauguration Sermon.

Poplar Chapel, erected about the Reftauration of
King *Charles* the Second. Morning Pr. on *Wednef-*
days, Fridays, and Holy days, at 11 ; Sac. every
third *Sunday* at 12.

Poultry Comptor Chapel. Pr. and S. every *Sunday*
Morning at 10.

Queen's Square Chapel, by St. *James's* Park, founded by *Charles Shales*, in 1706. Morning Pr. on
Wednefdays, Fridays, and Holy days, at 11 in Summer, but every Week day in Winter ; Evening Pr.
conftantly at 4 ; Sac. at ufual Times ; S. every
Sunday and publick State days at 11 ; and only Pr.
at 3.

Queen ftreet Chapel, near *Lincolns Inn Fields*.
Morning Pr. at 11, Evening at 4 ; Sac. on the laft
Sunday of the Month ; S. every *Sunday* Forenoon
and Afternoon, at the ufual Hours.

Rolls Chapel in *Chancery Lane*, fo called becaufe
it's a Repofitory now of Charters, Patents, Com-
miffions, and other Matters, made up in Rolls of
Parchment, from the beginning of King *Richard* the
Third, in 1484 ; thofe before that Time are kept
in *Wakefield* Tower, in the Tower of *London* ; but
at firft here was founded by King *Henry* the Third,
in 1233, an Houfe of converted Jews upon a Jew's
Houfe, which had been formerly confifcated to the
Crown. Pr. and S. are every *Sunday* Morning in
TermTime at 10, and only Pr. at 3, and on Holy days at

10 and 3 ; Sac. every second *Sunday* of the 4 Terms on *Christmas day, Easter Sunday,* and *Whitsunday.*

Russel Court Chapel in *Drury Lane,* where are Pr and S. every *Sunday-* twice, at the usual Hours.

St. *Saviour* in *Southwark,* dedicated to our blessed Saviour, commonly called St. *Mary Overy,* or *Overee,* that is, over the River, b-cause before the Building of *London Bridge,* there was a Ferry over the River ; of the Profits whereof, the Ferry Man's Daughter, (called *Mary)* built a Nunnery in this Place. The Parish contains 2500 Houses. Morning Pr. on *Wednesdays, Fridays,* and all Holy days, at 11.

St. *Sepulchres,* or *Holy Sepulchres,* on the North side of *Snowhill,* called so in Commemoration of the holy Sepulchre, or Grave of our blessed Saviour at *Jerusalem* ; or from some Saints and Martyrs who have been buried there. Here rings the funeral Peal, or great passing Bell for the condemn'd Criminals, as they pass therefrom to *Tyburn,* for which Mr. *Robert Dow* gave 50 Pounds. This Parish contains 1760 Dwelling Houses. Morning Pr. daily at 6 in Summer, and 7 in Winter, and on *Wednesdays, Fridays,* and Holy days at 11 ; Evening Pr. constantly at 3 in Summer, 4 in Winter. Sac (besides every first *Sunday* of the Month) on every *Sunday* from *Easter* to *Trinity Sunday,* after Forenoon Sermon ; an annual S. for, and before the *Cordwainers,* in *June* or *July,* at 10, at their Pleasure ; and another before the Promoters, Masters, Mistresses, and Children, of all Charity Schools in and about *London,* on *Thursday* in *Whitsun* Week, at 10.

Sergeants Inn Chapel in *Chancery Lane,* where Pr. and S. are every *Sunday* Forenoon (and Afternoon Pr. only) in *Easter, Trinity,* and *Hilary* Terms, excepting the first *Sundays* ; but in *Michaelmas* Term, Pr. are every *Sunday* twice, and S. only in the Morn-

Morning. Sac. on the second *Sunday* of every Term.

Sergeants Inn Chapel in *Fleetstreet*, was burnt on the 1st of *Jan.* 1702, and rebuilt in 1703. Pr. and S. only on *Sunday* Morning, and only Pr. at 4 in Term time ; Sac. on the last *Sunday* of every Term.

Skinners Almshouses Chapel, upon *Mile-end Green.* Pr. every Day at 11 ; a weekly Lect. every *Thursday* at 3 ; beside the Duty on *Sunday.*

Somerset House Chapel in the *Strand*, in a Royal Palace built by *Edward*, Duke of *Somerset*, Lord Protector of *England*, and Uncle to King *Edward* the Sixth. Morning Pr. daily at 11, and Evening Pr. at 4 ; Sac. every third *Sunday* of the Month ; S. every *Sunday* Morning, but then Pr. are only in the Afternoon.

Spring Garden Chapel, by St. *James's* Park. Pr. and S. only on *Sunday* at 10 and 3 ; *Jan.* 30. *May* 29. *Nov.* 5. but no Sac.

St. *Stephen's* Chapel, within the antient Royal Palace of *Westminster*, built by King *Stephen* about 1141 ; and being appropriated and appointed for the meeting place of the Honourable House of Commons, during the Sessions of Parliament, it is now of no Use, as to divine Service.

St. *Stephen Coleman street*, was first a Jewish Synagogue. This Parish contains 600 fine Houses. Pr. on all Week days at 11, Sac. every *Sunday* at 12 ; annual S. *April* 30. *Nov.* 11.

St. *Stephen* in *Walbrook*, dedicated to the Apostle St. *Stephen.* This Parish contains 110 Houses. Morning Pr. every Day at 11, and Evening Pr. at 4 on *Saturday* through the Fast of *Lent.*

Stratford le Bow, first built by the Inhabitants of *Stratford* or *Oldford*, in 1311, and is called *Stratford Bow*, or by *Bow*, because of the most antient Stone Bridge (the first of Stone in *England*) built of Arches or Bows of Stone, by Queen *Maud* or *Matilda*,

Wife

Wife to King *Henry* the Firſt, about the Year 1100 becauſe ſne was ſomewhat in Danger, as ſhe paſſec over the River *Lea* or *Lane*. Morning Pr. on *Wed neſdays*, *Fridays*, and Holy days, at 11 ; annua Gift S. *Jan.* 30. *Good Friday*, *Aſcenſion Day*, and St *Bartholomew*'s Day.

St. *Swithin* in *Swithin's Lane*, dedicated to St *Swithin*, Biſhop of *Wincheſter*. This Pariſh contains about 140 Dwelling Houſes. Morning Pr. in Week Days at 11, Evening Pr. at 5 ; a weekly Lect. eve ry *Tueſday*, at 5 in the Evening.

Tabernacle in *Petticoat Lane*, where are Pr. and S twice a Day, at the uſual Hours.

Tabernacle in St. *Martin*'s Churchyard, till its Mother Church is rebuilt, with which it is agree-able in the Duty of divine Service.

Tabernacle in *White Lion Yard* in *Spittlefields*, where-in are Morning Pr. on *Wedneſdays*, *Fridays*, and Holy days, at 11, Evening Pr. at 7 in Winter, 8 in Summer.

Temple Church, between the Inner and Middle Temples, where are Morning Pr. daily at 8 in Vo-cation Time, 7 in Term Time, 9 every Holy day ; Evening Pr. conſtantly at 4, except Holy days, when they are at 3.

St. *Thomas*'s Church, by St. *Thomas*'s Hoſpital in the Borough of *Southwark*, dedicated to St. *Thomas* the Apoſtle. This Pariſh contains 300 Houſes. Morning Pr. on *Wedneſdays*, *Fridays*, and Holy days, at 11 ; Sac. every ſecond *Sunday* in the Month, at 12.

St. *Thomas*'s Hoſpital Chapel in *Southwark*, where-in Evening Pr. only are at 3 ; and on *Sunday* Morn-ing Pr. at 9.

Trinity Almshouſes Chapel, upon *Mile-end Green*, wherein are Morning Pr. at 8 on *Sunday* ; and on *Wedneſdays*, *Fridays*, and Holy days, at 11.

Trinity

Trinity Chapel in *Bond street*, near St. *James's*, where are Morning Pr. daily at 11 ; Evening Pr. at 3 ; Sac. every third *Sunday* of the Month at 12 ; S. twice on *Sunday* ; and a weekly Lect. every *Wednesday* at 10.

Trinity in the *Little Minories*, where are Morning Pr. on Holy days, and *Wednesdays* and *Fridays* through *Lent*, at 11 ; Sac. on the first *Sunday* of the Month at 12.

St. *Vedast*, alias *Foster*, in *Foster Lane*, dedicated to St. *Vedast*, Bishop of *Arras*, who died in 570. This Parish contains about 200 fine Dwelling. Houses. Here are Morning Pr. on *Wednesdays*, *Fridays*, and Holy days, at 11 ; Evening Pr. at 6 constantly.

Vintners Almshouses Chapel, at *Mile-end Green*, where Pr. are every *Sunday* Morning at 8 ; and on *Wednesdays*, *Fridays*, and Holy days, at 11.

Whitehall Chapel, kept now in the Banquetting House of that Royal Palace, where are Morning Pr. every *Sunday* at 7, and all *Sundays* and Week Days at 11 ; Evening Pr. every Day at 6 ; Sac. publick every first *Sunday* of the Month at 12, and privately every *Sunday* Morning at 8 ; S. every *Sunday* and Holy day at 11 ; but on *Ash Wednesday*, and every *Wednesday* and *Friday* through *Lent*, at 11, by Preachers extraordinary, appointed by the Lord Chamberlain of the King's Houshold.

Woodstreet Compter Chapel, where Morning Pr. are on *Wednesdays*, *Fridays*, and Holy days, at 11 ; and S. and Pr. at 10 every *Sunday* Morning.

A List

A List of the most notable Fairs, kept in England and Wales, whether fixed or moveable, throughout every Month in the Year; with the Time and Place, when and where held.

January hath 31 Days.
1 at Lanibither
5 Hickford
6 Salisbury
7 Montgomery
13 Derig
18 Grampound
24 Barkltong
25 Bristol
31 Northallerton, on every *Wednesday* from *Christmas* to *June.*

February hath 28 Days.
1 Llangader
2 Bath
6 Stafford for 6 Days
8 Targaron
9 Llandaff
24 Feversham
26 Stafford for Horses
28 Chesterfield
Winterbourn *the second* Thursday *in the Month.* Abingdon *the first* Monday *in clear* Lent. Banbury *the first* Tuesday *in* Lent. Chichester on Ash Wednesday. Foy *on* Shrove Tuesday.

March hath 31 Days.
1 Llangadog
3 Sevenoke
4 Bedford
5 Paranzand
7 Workep
8 Targaron
12 Wrexham
17 Malmsbury
18 Sturbridge
20 Ailesbury
22 Tocester
24 Llannerdenrick
25 Glocester
27 Darby
Oakhampton *the second* Thursday *in* March. Dalton *the* Wednesday *before* Ladyday. Denbigh *the* Monday *before* Ladyday.

April hath 30 Days.
2 Epping
3 Leek
4 Bewdley
5 Wallingford
7 Darby
9 Billingsworth
10 Shipwash
11 War-

11 Warminster
12 Aberforth
13 Orleton
14 Acton
16 Holdzary
21 Riddrewth -
22 Stafford
23 Ipswich
25 Colbrook
26 Tenterden
27 Bosworth
28 Soham

Cricklade *the third* Wednesday *in* April. Yarmouth *the* 3d Thursday *and* Saturday *in* April. Guilford *on* Good friday. Gainsborough *on* Easter Monday. Helston *the* Saturday *before* Palm Sunday. Basingdown *on* Easter Tuesday. Hereford *the* Wednesday *in* Easter Week. Bricklesworth *on* Monday *after* Low Sunday.

May *hath* 31 *Days.*
1 Andover
2 Leominster
3 Oxford
4 Chatham
5 Heytesbury
8 Stratton
9 Tocking
10 Hetherly
11 Dunstable
12 York

13 Albrighton
15 Cambleford
16 Llanganrannog
17 Tallowdown *to the* 25.
19 Rochester
25 Malmsbury
27 Montgomery
29 Cranbrook
31 Pershore

Winterbourn *the second* Thursday *in* May. Chorlebury *the second* Friday *in* May. Hellaton *on* Ascension Day. Apulby *on* Whitmonday. Grayes *on* Whit tuesday *and* Wednesday.

June *hath* 30 *Days.*
1 Chapplefrith
3 Ailesbury
5 Milton
7 Worksop
9 Maidstone
11 Tewkesbury
13 Newton
14 Bangor
15 Devizes
16 Bealth
17 Highamferries.
18 Merchenleth
19 Hereford -
21 Ystradmerick
22 Shrewsbury
23 Armington
24 Lancaster
26 Northop
27 Folkstone

Royston

28 Royston

29 Westminster

Carlisle *the first* Wednesday *in* June. Thorne *the first* Monday *and* Tuesday *in* June. Gilham *on* Trinity Monday.

July *hath* 31 *Days.*

1 Portsmouth

2 Huntington

3 Congerton

4 Chesterfield

5 Burton

6 Havernill

7 Cirencester

9 Ingolstone

10 Foulness

11 Wantage

13 Fotheringhay

15 Greensled

16 Hadden

17 Winchcomb

19 Lynton

20 Uxbridge

21 Bramyard

22 Exeter

23 Carnarvon

25 Bristol

26 Tanhill

27 Canterbury

28 Fairfax

29 Chapelhage

30 Stafford

Bridgnorth *on the* Thursday *before the* 21st *of* July. Cricklade *the first* Wednesday *in* July.

August *hath* 31 *Days.*

1 Banbury

4 Ludlow

6 Peterborough

9 Aberlew

10 Doncaster

11 Alchurch

13 Tewkesbury

15 Cambridge

20 Devizes

24 London, for 3 Days

25 Brecknock

26 Cambleford

28 Daventry

29 Caermarthen

Winterbourn *the* 2 Thursday *in* Augu[f] Wakefield *the* 3*d* Thur[f]day *in* August. Ashfor *the first* Sunday *after* S[t] Bartholomew's day. Da[r]ington *the first* Monda[y] *after* Lammas.

September *hath* 30 *Days*

1 Wilton

2 Epping

3 Wimbourn

4 Oakham

5 Probus

7 Ware

8 Southwark, for a Fortnight

9 Wington

10 Kirton

11 Evesham

12 Enfield

13 Sedwin

14 Aber

14 Abergavenny
15 Cliff
17 Glocefter
18 Llanvelly
20 Ruthin
21 Chefter
22 Darby
23 Pancridge
24 Malton
28 Dolgeth
29 Glaffenbury

Kettering *the* Thurf-day *before* Michaelmas day. Ockington *the firſt* Tuefday *in* September.

October *hath* 31 *Days.*
1 Coxton
2 Salisbury
3 Bautomoor
5 Bofworth
6 Maidftone
7 Chriftchurch
8 Chichefter
10 Shipwafh
11 Wells
12 Llangoweth
13 Bury
13 Winchefter
14 Queencamonel
16 Windfor
17 Malmsbury
18 Faringdon
21 Coventry
23 Frefton
25 Beverly
26 Wehmerly
28 Warwick

29 Albrighton
30 Rofs
31 Stokefley
Southall *the fecond* Wednefday *in* October. Thorne *the fiſt* Monday *and* Tuefday *in* Octo-ber. Ockington *the fiſt* Wednefday *in* October.

November *hath* 30 *Days.*
1 Chard
2 Loughborough
3 Caermarthen
5 Welfhpool
6 Hartford
10 Shaftsbury, for 2 Days
11 Dover
13 Willington
17 Lincoln
19 Horfham
20 Bury
22 Sawthey
23 Froom
24 Coward
25 Lancefton
27 Lawreft
29 Maidenhead

December *hath* 31 *Days.*
4 Atherfton
5 Dolgeth
6 Grantham
7 Sandhurft
8 Leicefter
11 Newport
12 Amesbury
21 Saltwich

22 Llear-

22 Lleardilavar

29 Canterbury

   Banbury *the* Thursday *after St.* Andrew's Day.

Leskard *the* Monday a[
te1 *the 6th of* Decembe[
Kettering *the* Thursd[
before St. Thomas's day.

Of the General Post-Office *in* Lombard Street.

FOR the Advancement of Trade and Commerce [
   well as the Conveniency of all other Busine[
Letters are convey'd to all Parts of *Great Britai[*
and other Places in *Europe*, besides his Majesty[
Plantations in *America* ; and the Conveyance of a[
Domestick Letters is so expeditious, that every 2[
Hours the Post goes 120 Miles ; and in 5 or 6 Da[
an Answer may be had from a place 300 Miles di[
stant from the Writer.

   Besides this very great and convenient Expedi[
tion, the Charge thereof is easie ; for a Letter con[
taining a whole Sheet, is conveyed 80 Miles for 3[
if a double Letter for 6 *d.* one Ounce of Letters f[
10 *d.* ; but if above 80 Miles, a single Letter 4[
it doubled 6 *d.* and an Ounce 14 *d.*

   The Post Days to send Letters from *London* to [
ny part of *England* and *Scotland*, are *Tuesdays*, *Thur[
days*, and *Saturdays* : And the Returns certain o[
Mondays, *Wednesdays* and *Fridays.*

   But to *Wales* and *Ireland*, the Post goes only twi[
a Week ; *viz* on *Tuesdays* and *Saturdays* ; and com[
from *Wales* every *Monday* and *Friday* : but from *Ir[
land* the Return is uncertain, because it (as a[
other foreign Letters do) depends upon Winds.

   When the Court is in the Country, the Post go[
every Day to the place where it resides. The sam[
is with *Kent*, and the usual Stations of the Roy[
Fleet, as the *Downs*, *Spithead*, and other Place[

o which we may fend every Day but *Sunday*; and
om whence we may alfo hear every Day but *Sun-*
y.

For foreign Intelligence in Times of Peace, *Mon-*
ys and *Thurfdays* are the Pofts for *France, Spain,*
nd Italy; and *Tuefdays* and *Fridays* for *Holland, Ger-*
any, Denmark, and *Sweden.*

On *Mondays* and *Fridays*, the Poft goes alfo for
landers, and from thence to *Germany, Denmark*, and
weden.

For the Tranfport of Letters and Pacquets over
a, there are in Time of Peace,

etween *England* and
{
France 3
Spain 2
Flanders 2
Holland 3
Ireland 3
}
Pacquet Boats.

The Pacquet Boats for *France*, go from *Dover* in
nt for *Calais*, 7 Leagues over, on *Tuefdays* and
days in the Evening, if the Wind ferves: For
ain, one goes every Fortnight from *Falmouth* in
rnwal, to *Corunna*, or the *Groyn*: For *Flanders*,
om *Dover* to *Newport*, 20 Leagues over, on *Tuef-*
ys and *Saturdays* in the Evening: For *Holland*,
om *Harwich* in *Effex* to the *Brill*, about 30 Leagues
er, on *Wednefdays* and *Saturdays* in the Evening.
nd for *Ireland*, from *Holyhead* in *Anglefea*, (a *Welfh*
ounty) to *Dublin*, about 20 Leagues over, on
ndays and *Thurfdays.*

Alfo, for the farther Encouragement of Trade and
ommerce, the late Queen *Anne* appointed Boats,
carry Letters and Pacquets from *England* as far as
e *Weft Indies*; which never was done before. One
thefe Boats fets out from the *Thames* on the laft
ufday of the Month, particularly for the Ifles of
badoes, Montferrat, St. Chriftopher, Antegoa, and
maica. The Rate for every Letter is *9d.* a Sheet,
double Letter 18 *d.* a Pacquet weighing an Ounce
r 6 d. and fo in proportion. And

22 Lleardilavar   Leskard *the* Monday
29 Canterbury   te: *the* 6*th of* Decem
   Banbury *the* Thurfday   Kettering *the* Thurf
after St. Andrew's Day.   *before St.* Thomas's da

Of the General Poſt-Office *in* Lomba Street.

FOR the Advancement of Trade and Commerc
well as the Conveniency of all other Buſin
Letters are convey'd to all Parts of *Great Bri*
and other Places in *Europe*, beſides his Majeſ
Plantations in *America*, and the Conveyance of
Domeſtick Letters is ſo expeditious, that every
Hours the Poſt goes 120 Miles ; and in 5 or 6 L
an Anſwer may be had from a place 300 Miles
ſtant from the Writer.

Beſides this very great and convenient Exp
tion, the Charge thereof is eaſie ; for a Letter c
taining a whole Sheet, is conveyed 80 Miles for
if a double Letter for 6 *d.* one Ounce of Letters
10 *d.* ; but if above 80 Miles, a ſingle Letter
it doubled 6 *d.* and an Ounce 14 *d.*

The Poſt Days to ſend Letters from *London* t
ny part of *England* and *Scotland*, are *Tueſdays, T*
days, and *Saturdays* : And the Returns certain
Mondays, Wedneſdays and *Fridays.*

But to *Wales* and *Ireland*, the Poſt goes only t
a Week ; *viz* on *Tueſdays* and *Saturdays* ; and co
from *Wales* every *Monday* and *Friday* : but from
land the Return is uncertain, becauſe it (as
other foreign Letters do) depends upon Winds

When the Court is in the Country, the Poſt
every Day to the place where it reſides. The l
is with *Kent*, and the uſual Stations of the R
Fleet, as the *Downs, Spithead,* and other Pla

which we may send every Day but *Sunday*; and
m whence we may also hear every Day but *Sun-*

For foreign Intelligence in Times of Peace, *Mon-*
s and *Thursdays* are the Posts for *France, Spain,*
d *Italy*, and *Tuesdays* and *Fridays* for *Holland, Ger-*
my, *Denmark*, and *Sweden.*
On *Mondays* and *Fridays*, the Post goes also for
nders, and from thence to *Germany, Denmark,* and
eden.
For the Transport of Letters and Pacquets over
, there are in Time of Peace,

ween *England* and
{ *France* 3
Spain 2
Flanders 2
Holland 3
Ireland 3 } Pacquet Boats.

he Pacquet Boats for *France*, go from *Dover* in
t for *Calais*, 7 Leagues over, on *Tuesdays* and
days in the Evening, if the Wind serves : For
in, one goes every Fortnight from *Falmouth* in
wal, to *Corunna*, or the *Groyn* : For *Flanders*,
Dover to *Newport*, 20 Leagues over, on *Tues-*
and *Saturdays* in the Evening · For *Holland*,
Harwich in *Essex* to the *Brill*, about 30 Leagues
, on *Wednesdays* and *Saturdays* in the Evening.
for *Ireland*, from *Holyhead* in *Anglesea*, (a *Welsh*
nty) to *Dublin*, about 20 Leagues over, on
days and *Thursdays.*
lso, for the farther Encouragement of Trade and
merce, the late Queen *Anne* appointed Boats,
arry Letters and Pacquets from *England* as far as
West Indies; which never was done before. One
ese Boats sets out from the *Thames* on the last
day of the Month, particularly for the Isles of
adoes, *Montferrat*, St. *Christopher, Antegoa,* and
ica. The Rate for every Letter is 9*d.* a Sheet,
uble Letter 18 *d.* a Pacquet weighing an Ounce
d. and so in proportion. And

And for the Conveniency of thofe who live
from the *Poft Office*, there are particular Pofthou
appointed to take in the Letters till 9 of the Clo
at Night, to be fent from thence in due Time
the General Poft Office ; which is done Gratis
Inland Letters , but if it is paft 9 of the Clo
Notice is given thereof by a Bellman every *Tuefi*
Thurfday and *Saturday* Night, who then has a Per
for every Letter he carries thither : But at all tu
the Office takes for each foreign Letter or Pacqu
one Penny.

Names and Places of the Six Offices, whe
Country Letters and Parcels are daily c
vey'd.

General Pennypoft office, is kept in St. Chriftoph
Churchyard in Threadneedle Street, *near Sto*
Market , *which collects, delivers and conveys Let*
and Parcels to the following and adjacent Places.

No.		No.	
1	ALdersbrook	2	Hackney
1	Avery Hatch	3	Hagerfton
1	Barking	1	Ham Eaft
1	Bednal Green	1	Hoxton
2	Bifhops hall	1	Jenkins
3	Bow	1	Ilford
3	Bromley *in Middlefex*	1	Kingfland
1	Bufh Hall	1	Laytonftone
2	Cambridge-Heath	1	Loughton hall
1	Chigwell *and* Row	1	Low Layton
1	Dalfton	1	Loxford
1	Edmington	1	Mile End
1	Green man	1	Newington Stoke
1	Green ftreet		Green

Oldfi

No.

		No.	
Oldford		1	Tottenham highCrofs
Palmer's Green		1	Valentines
Plaiftow *in* Effex		1	Upton
Riple Side		1	Walthamflow
Ruckolds		1	Wanfted
Southgate		1	Winchmore Hill
Stepney		1	Woodford
Stratford		1	Woodford Row *and*
Tottenham			Bridge

Paul's *Office, is kept* in Queen's Head Alley *in* Paternofter Row ; *which collects and delivers Letters and Parcels to and from the Places following and adjacent.*

		No.	
Black Mary's hole		1	Holloway Upper *and*
Boarded River			Lower
Cambray Houfe		3	Iflington
Cold Bath		3	Mount Mill
Copenhagen		3	Sir John Oldcaftles
Frog Lane		3	Tottington Lane
		3	Woods Clofe

Temple *Office, is kept* in Chichefter's Rents *in* Chancery Lane ; *which collects and delivers Letters and Parcels to and from the Places following and adjacent.*

		No.	
Battle Bridge		1	Hornfey
Bone Gate		2	Kentifh Town
Briil		1	Muffel hill
Coleharbour		2	Pancras
Coney Hatch		2	Pindar of Wakefield
Eaft Barnet		1	South Green
Finchly		1	Totteridge
Frog Lane		1	Whetftone
Hamftead		1	Wood Green
Highgate			

N   Weftmin-

Weſtminſter-*Office*, *is kept in* Pump Court *near C
ring Croſs; which collects, delivers and con
Letters and Parcels to and from the Places follow
and adjacent.*

No.
3 A Bery Farm
1   Acton Eaſt &
   Weſt
1 Acton Wells
1 Barrys Walk
1 Baſewatering
2 Blacklands
2 Bloody Bridge
2 Bluncot Lane
2 Bollow Lane
2 Boſton Houſe
2 Brentford Old *and*
   New
2 Brentford End
1 Brent's Cowhouſe
2 Brook Green
2 Broom Houſes
2 Brampton Park
2 Blindlane Houſe
1 Burrows
1 Caſtle Bear
1 Childs Hill
2 Corney Houſe
1 Cowhouſe Farm
2 Chelſea Great *and*
   Little
2 Chelſea College *and*
   Com. *and* Fields
2 Chiſwick
1 Counters Bridge
2 Crabtree Houſe

No.
1 Dowel Street
2 Daws Lane
1 Dollars Hill.
1 Ealing Great *a*
   Little
1 Ealing Lane
2 Earls Court
1 Ford Hook
2 Frog Lane
1 Fryers Place
2 Fulham
2 Fulham Fields
2 Gagglegooſe Gree
2 Great *and* Li
   Holland Houſe
2 Gibbs Green
2 Grain Houle
1 Greenman *in* U
   bridge Road
1 Gunnersberry
1 Gutters Hedge
2 Hammerſmith
1 Hanger Lane &
1 Haven
1 Hendon
1 Hide
2 Hog Lane
1 Holſdon Green
1 Hoywood hill
2 Hudicon Fields
1 Kilborn
      Kenſing

0.		N0.
Kensington	2	Parsons Green
Kensington Grav. Pits	2	Sandy End
Knightsbridge	1	Shepherds Bush
Laurence Street	1	Shevrick Green
Leasing Green	1	Shoot up hill
Lime Kilns	2	Sion Hill
London Stile	2	Sion House
Lord Mayor's Ban-	2	Sion Lane
quetting house	1	St. John's Wood
Maddox Lane	2	Stanford Brook
Marybone *and* Park	2	Starch Green
Masha Mapes *and*	2	Strand on the Green
Masha Brands	2	Sutton Court *and*
Millhill		Little Sutton
Neesdon	1	Tatnam Court
Neat Houses	2	Turnam Green
Nomands Lands	1	Tyburn Road *and*
North End		House
North Highway	2	Waltham Green
Notting Hills	1	Wemly *and* Green
Padington *and* Green	1	Westburn Green
Paddingwick Green	1	Westfield
Pimlico	1	West End
Pursers Cross	1	Willldon Green
Pages Street	1	Windmill Lane

Southwark *Office, is kept in* Green Dragon Court, *near St.* Mary Overy's *Church, which collects, deli-vers and conveys Letters and Parcels to and from the Places following and adjacent.*

B	Alam	2	Blackheath
	Barn Elms	2	Bristow Causeway
Barns Town		1	Brockly Upper *and*
Battersea, *and*			Lower
Battersea Ryes		1	Burnt Ash

Camberwell

No.

No.		No.	
2	Camberwell	2	Mortlack
1	Charlton	2	Morden
2	Clapham & Common	1	Motingham
3	Coleharbour	2	Newington Butts
2	Deptford Upper *and* Lower	2	New Cross
		2	Nine Elms
1	Dulwich & Common	1	Norwood
2	East *and* West Shene	2	Peckham Town Rey
1	Eltham		
1	Gammon Mill	2	Pigs Marsh
2	Garrets Green	1	Plumstead
2	Greenwich	2	Putney Heath Green
2	Grove Street		
1	Ireland Green	2	Redhouse
2	Kennington	1	Ricklemarsh
2	Kew *and* Green	2	Roehampton
1	Knights Hill	2	Rotherhith
3	Lambeth	1	Sidnam
3	Lambeth Marsh	2	South Lambeth
1	Lee	2	Stockwell
1	Lewisham	2	Stretham
2	Lime Kilns	1	Tooting Upper Lower
2	Long Barn		
2	Long Hedge	3	Vauxhall
2	Loughberry House	2	Wallworth
1	Martin Abby *and* Mills	2	Wandsworth *and* Common
2	Marsh Gate	1	Wimbleton
2	Mitcham	1	Woolwich

Hermitage *Office*, is *kept in* Queen Street on Little Towerhill, *which collects and delivers Letters* Parcels to and from the Places following and adjacent

3	Blackwall	3	Poplar
3	Isle of Dogs	3	Ratcliff
3	King David's Fort	3	Stepney Causeway
3	Limehouse *and* Hole		*No.*

Note, To the Places mark'd No. 1. Letters and Parcels are conveyed once a Day, No. 2. twice a Day, No. 3. three times a Day. And considering that several of these Places are remote, it is desired, That you put in your Letters and Parcels before 6 of the Clock over Night, at the Receiving Houses, from whence they will be collected and brought into the proper Offices, otherwise divers of the Country Messengers going on their Walks by 7 of the Clock next Morning, they may lose a Day's Time in the Delivery. But for those Places that are nearer, Letters are collected and delivered two or three times a Day, as above specified. All General post Letters, both Foreign and Domestick, directed to the Places abovementioned, not being post Towns, are conveyed from the aforesaid Offices every Day at 12 of the Clock: And Answers thereto being put into the Receiving Houses in the Country Towns, will next Night be safely carried to the General Post Office, an Officer being appointed for that purpose.

An exact Description of the great Roads from London *to all the considerable Cities and Towns in* England *and* Wales, *together with the Cross Roads from one City or eminent Town to another, in measured Miles.*

N.B. *E* signifies East, *W* West, *N* North, *S* South.

From Aberistwith *to* London 199 *Miles, thus reckon'd.* FROM Aberistwith to Riodergowy 28, to Ithon River 9, to Predain 13, to Leominster 13, to Bramyard 11, to Worcester 12, to Pershore 9, to Broadway 12, to Mortin in Marsh 7, to Easton 13,

N 3

to

to Iflip 12, to Wheatly Bridge 8, to Tetworth
to Wickham 12, to Beaconsfield 5, to Uxbridg
to Acton 10, to London 8, which is the Metrop
or principal City of Great Britain.

From Briftol to Banbury 74 Miles, thus reckoned
To Sudbury 12, to Tetbury 13, to Cirencester
to Burford 16, to South Newton 17, to Banbur
a Town in Oxfordfhire, having a fair and l.
Church, and noted for being the place where K
ris, King of the Weft Saxons, put the Britons
flight, for a Battle fought between the Houf
York and Lancafter, in which the Lancaftrians
the better, and took King Edward 4th Prifoner

From Briftol to Chefter 145 Miles, thus reckoned
To Auftferry 12, to Chepftow 6, to Monmo
14, to Hereford 18, to Leominfter 14, to Lud.
10, to Churchftretton 15, to Shrewsbury 14,
Whitchurch 20, to Chefter 20, a City in Chef
and Bifhoprick, fituated on the River Dee ;
under King Edgar was in good Efteem, when fe
Monarchs of the Scots and Britons paying him
mage, row'd his Barge from St. John's to his Pala
himfelf, as fupreme Lord, holding the Helm.

From Briftow to Exeter 78 Miles, thus reckoned.
To Bifhopschue 7, to Wells 12, to Glaffenb
5, to Grinton 6, to Lyng 8, to Taunton 8, to W
lington 7, to Welland 10, to Bradinch 5, to E
ter 8, a City and Bifhoprick in Devonfhire.

From Briftol to Weymouth 74 Miles, thus reckoned
To Bifhopschue 7, to Wells 12, to Glaffenbur
to Somerton 8, to Martlock 7, to Crookhorn 7,
Southparret 2, to Frampton 13, to Weymouth
which is fituated on the fouthermoft Point of
County of Dorfet, near the Ifle of Portland.

From Briftol to Worcefter 62 Miles, thus reckoned
To Acton 9, to Durfley 12, to Whitminfter 7
Glocefter 7, to Tewkesbury 10, to Severnftoke 8
Worcefter 7, a City in Worcefterfhire.

F

From Buckingham to Bridgnorth 81 *Miles, thus reckon'd.*

To Banbury 17, to Nether Pellerton 12, to Stratford 8, to Coughton 9, to Broomſgrove 11, to Kederminſter 9, to Quot 9, to Bridgnorth 4, a large and well built Town in Shropſhire, containing ſeveral good Inns.

From Cambridge to Coventry 80 *Miles, thus reckoned.*

To Elſley 11, to St. Neots 5, to Great Stoughton 5, to Highamſferries 12, to Northampton 15, to Watford 11 to Rugby 8, to Coventry 11, a City and Biſhoprick (with Lichfield) in Warwickſhire.

From Carliſle to Berwick 80 *Miles, thus reckoned.*

To Brakennill 9, to the Entring Scotland 9, to Caſtleton 5, to Jedburg 22, to Kelſo 10, to the Re-entring England 5, to Cornhill 4, to Weſſel 3, to Berwick 10, a Town in Northumberland, the Poſſeſſion of which, during the Diſcords between the two Kingdoms before the Union, was very vigorouſly ſtrove for by the oppoſite Parties. 'Twas taken by the King's Forces from the invading Scots, and 25000 of their numerous Army were ſlain, in the 25th Year of Edward 1ſt; but ſince the Reign of Edward 4th, it has been conſtantly poſſeſſed by the Engliſh.

From Cheſter to Cardiff 145 *Miles, thus reckoned.*

To Wrexham 11, to Sallaty 13, to Llanlylon 5, to Llanvelling 8, to Llantair 11, to Targunnon 6, to New Town 5, to Llanbeder-vunneth 9, to Llanbeder-vaur 10, to Bealth 10, to Brecknock 16, to Cardiff 37, a Corporation Town in Glamorganſhire, ſeated on Taff or Tave River.

From Dartmouth to Minehead 71 *Miles, thus reckoned.*

To Newton Buſhel 17, to Kenford 10, to Exeter 4, to Silverton 7, to Tiverton 7, to Bampton 7, to Bevry 4, to Embercomb 10, to Minehead 3, a Port Town in Somerſetſhire, whoſe convenient Harbour occaſions an indifferent Trade to Ireland.

From Davids to Holywell 156 *Miles, thus reckoned.*

To Fiftard 16, to Newport 6, to Cardigan 10, t
Llanarch 18, to Llanrifted 7, to Llanbader-vaur 8
to Talabont 6, to Machenleth 10, to Aberangel 10
to Llanam-mouthy 7, to Balla 13, to Bettus 10, t
Ruthyn 10, to Holywell 15, a fmall Town or Vil
lage in Flintfhire in Wales, fo called from St. Wi
nefied's Well, lyng fomewhat lower on the N E
fide of it, a Place ftill much reforted to, by thof
who to their Health's fake come to bath there, a
heretofore by Pilgrims paying their Devotions to th
Chriftian Virgin Winefred, whofe Name fignifies
Winner or Gainer of Peace. She was courted b
a certain young Prince, who meeting with a Re
pulfe at laft furprized and rav_fhed this beautifu
Maid, and afterwards, having killed her, cut o
her Head, which rolling down nither (as the Stoi
goes) from an adjacent Hill, gave Rife to the fai
Well. The Spring is cold, and has a fair Chap
built over it upon Pillars; on the Windows c
which is pourtrayed the Hiftory of St. Winefre
It gufhes forth in that Quantity, and with fo grea
Impetuofity, that it foon turns a Mill, and emptie
it felf into the Sea, about 1 Mile and a half below
The Mofs growing in the Well, of a fweet Scen
is taken for St. Winefred's Well.

From Exeter to Barnftable 38 *Miles, thus reckoned.*

To Crediton 8, to Chimleigh 13, to Barnftabl
17, otherwife called Barnftaple, a large Corporatio
Town in Devonfhire.

From Exeter to Truro 79 *Miles, thus reckoned*

To Dunsford 7, to Chegford 7, to Taviftock 10
to Lifcard 15, to Liftwithiel 8, to Grampound 1
to Truro 7, a Market Town in Cornwal.

From Paringdon to Oxford 21 *Miles, thus reckoned.*

To Abingdon 15, to Oxford 6, a City, Univerfit
and Bifhoprick in Oxfordfhire.

From Glocester to Coventry 58 *Miles, thus reckoned.*

To Cheltenham 9, Winchcomb 7, to Campden 1, to Stratford 11, to Warwick 8, to Coventry 0. a City seated near the middle of England, on Sherbourn River, whose Water is peculiar for the blue Dye. It hath 3 Parish Churches, and was enclosed with a strong Wall (demolished *anno* 1662) near 3 Miles in Compass, with 12 Gates and 26 Turrets.

From Glocester to Montgomery 70 *Miles, thus reckoned.*

To Huntley 6, to Rols 8, to Muchbirch 7, to Hereford 5, to Pembridge 12, to Prestain 6, to Knighton 4, to Cluna 5, to Montgomery 12, a Town in Montgomeryshire in North Wales, taking its Name from Roger de Montgomery, its first Founder, and formerly of more Note than now it is, having had a strong Wall and Castle, now ruinous. At present it scarce contains 100 Houses.

From Hereford to Leicester 86 *Miles, thus reckoned.*

To Frontshil 11, to Worcester 12, to Droitwich 6, to Broomsgrove 5, to Alchurch 4, to Solihul 5, to Merider 6, to Coventry 6, to Woolney 9, to Shamford 4, to Leicester 16, the Shire Town for Leicestershire, of more Antiquity than Beauty, said to be founded by King Leir, 844 Years before the Birth of Chirst, and called Cair Lerion; where he likewise built a Temple to Janus and placed therein a Flamen, or High Priest. However, it is certain that it was in Request under the Romans, and was made an Episcopal See *Anno Christi* 680, by Ethelred, King of the Mercians; re-edified, and encompassed with a Wall, by the Lady Edelfled, in the Year 914, which, with its Castle, are long since fallen to ruin

From Huntington to Ipswich 71 *Miles, thus reckoned.*

To St. Ives 5, to Erith 6, to Sutton 5, to Ely 6, to Soham 5, to Bury 18, to Walpit 8 to Needham 8, to Ipswich 9, an antient Corporation Town in Suffolk.

From

From Ipswich to Norwich 43 *Miles, thus reckoned.*

To Claydon 4, to Thwait 12, to Osmondston to Long Stretton 9, to Norwich 11, a City an Bishoprick in Norfolk.

From Kendal to Cockermouth 43 *Miles, thus reckone*

To Stanley 5, to Ambleside 8, to Keswick to Cockermouth 14, a Town of good Account Cumberland, seated on the Rivers Derwen and Coker ; and it is adorned with a fair Church an strong Castle.

From London to Arundel 55 *Miles, thus reckoned.*

To Towting 6, to Ewel 7, to Letherhead 5, Darking 4, to Stonestreet 5, to Billinghurst 11, Amberley 9, to Arundel 4, an antient Borou Town in Sussex, on the N W. of the Arun Riv over which it has a fair wooden Bridge, where Shi of 100 Tun may ride. The Castle, famous in t Saxon Times, having the Honour of an Earldo entailed upon the Possessors of it, is seated on t E. of the Tame River, and reputed a Mile in Com pass.

From London to Bath 108 *Miles, thus reckoned.*

To Brentford 10, to Hounsloe 2, to Colbrook to Maidenhead 8, to Twiford 7, to Reading to Theal 4, to Woolhampton 5, to Thatcham 3, Newberry 3, to Chilton 9, to Ramesbury 2, Marlborough 6, to Caln 12, to Chippenham 5, Bath 14, a City in Somersetshire, noted for its M dicinal Waters, and hot Baths.

From London to Berwick 339 *Miles, thus reckoned*

To Waltham 12, to Ware 9, to Royston 16, Huntington 19, to Stilton 12, to Stamford 13, Grantham 21, to Newark 14, to Tuxford 12, Doncaster 24, to Wentbridge 10, to Tadcaster to York 9, to Topcliff 23, to Northallerton 13, Darlington 14, to Durham 19, to Newcastle 14, Morpeth 14, to Alnwick 19, to Belford 13, Berwick 15, a Town in Northumberland, but not fo eminent for Antiquity, as for being a Place of great Strength, having the Sea on the E. and S. E. and the River Tweed on the S. W. encompaffed with a Wall, and fortified with a ftrong Caftle, 'tis large, populous, and well built, on the N. fide of the River Tweed, towards Scotland.

From London to Bofton 114 *Miles, thus reckoned.*

To Stilton (as you may fee in the Berwick Road from London) 69, to Peterborough 7, to Widrington 3, to Crowland 7, to Spalding 10, to Setherton 10, to Bofton 6, a Corporation Town in Lincolnfhire, commodioufly feated on both fides Witham River, near its Influx into the Sea, and on that account drives a confiderable Trade. 'Tis large, neat, and well inhabited, having a ftately Market Place and Church, whofe Tower is of a great Height, and ferves as a Landmark to Sailors.

From London to Briftol 115 *Miles, thus reckoned.*

To Chippenham (as in the Road from London to Bath) 93, to Marfhfield 9, to Briftol 12, a City and Bifhoprick on Avon River, (where it receives the Froom) over which it has a ftately Bridge. It contains 18 Parifh Churches, befides the Cathedral, founded by Robert Fitz Harding, Son to a Danifh King, dedicated to St. Auftin. It was made an epifcopal See by King *Henry* the Eighth, and had a Caftle in the N. E. part of it, demolifhed in the late Wars, and fince built into fair Streets. 'Tis encompaffed with a Wall, and 6 Gates; its principal Key is upon the Froom, (whither Ships of 150 Tun arrive) extending from Froom Bridge to the Marfh; the other called the Back, upon the W. fide of the Avon, begins at the great Bridge, alias Briftol Bridge, and extends likewife to the Marfh, the greater Veffels riding in Hung Road, about 3 Miles below.

From London to Buckingham 60 *Miles, thus reckoned.*

To Acton 8, to Uxbridge 10, to Amefham 11,

to

to Wendover 9, to Ailesbury 5, ro Eaſt Claydon(
to Buckingham 6, the Shire Town of the Count
of Buckingham, containing about 300 Houſes, t
the Owle River, over which it has a Stone Bridg
of 6 Arches.

From London to Chicheſter 63 Miles, thus reckoned.

To Guilford (as in the Road from London (
Portſmouth) 30, to Godalmin 4, to Chidingfold(
to Midhurſt 10, to Chicheſter 11, a City and B
ſhoprick in Suffex.

From London to Derby 122 Miles, thus reckoned.

To Stony Stratford (as in the Road from Londe
to Holyhead) 53, to Kings Grafton 4, to Northam
ton 8, to Brickſworth 7, to Haverborough 10,
Great Glenn 8, to Leiceſter 5, to Mountſorrel
to Loughborough 3, to Kegworth 5, to Derby 1
a large and well built Borough Town in Darb
ſhire, containing 5 Pariſh Churches, ſituated on t
Derwent River, and drives a conſiderable Trade.

From London to Dover 71 Miles, thus reckoned.

To Deptford 5, to Crayford 8, to Dartford 2,
Northfleet 5, to Chalkſtreet 3, to Rocheſter 5,
Sittingbourn 11, to Bocton Street 2, to Canterbu
5, to Dover 15, a Place in Kent, well fortifie
both by Art and Nature, and defended by a larg
and ſtrong Caſtle. It enjoys large Immunities,
one of the Cinque Ports, and yields a Proſpect (
Calais in France, to which it is the readieſt Pa
ſage, the Channel here being but 7 Leagues over

From London to Edmundsbury 75 Miles, thus reckone

To Newmarket 60, to Kenford 4, to St. Edmund
bury 9, a large well built Town in Suffolk, ſo call
from King Edmund the Martyr; and was former
famous for its Abby, which exceeded all others (
England, having 3 leſs Churches in its Church
yard, of which two remain fair and ſpacious, b
are too few for the numerous Inhabitants.

From *London to Flamborough* 212 *Miles, thus reckoned.*

To Stilton (as in the Road from London to Berwick) 69, to Peterborough 7, to Market Deeping 10, to Bourn 6, to Morton 2, to Sleaford 14, to Lincoln 18, to Redbourn 19, to Glamford Bridges 5, to Barton 10, to Hull 6, to Beverly 9, to Beleck 7, to Kilman 12, to Burlington 7, to Flamborough 5, a Village in Yorkshire, which at the distance of 3 Miles farther leads, by a Light House, to Flamborough Head, a Place well known by Seamen.

From *London to Gigglewick* 261 *Miles, thus reckoned.*

To York (as in the Road from London to Berwick) 192, to Allerton 13, to Knaresburg 4, to Ripley 5, to Boulton 15, to Skipton 6, to Comiston 7, to Settle 8, to Gigglewick 8, a Village in Lancashire, formerly noted for several small Springs, ebbing and flowing almost every quarter of an Hour.

From *London to Harwich* 71 *Miles, thus reckoned.*

To Rumford 11, to Burntwood 6, to Chelmsford 10, to Witham 8, to Keldon 3, to Colchester 9, to Maningtree 9, to Harwich 11, a small Town in Essex, but compact and well inhabited; it is a well fortified Garrison and Seaport, with a commodious Harbour, sometime the Station of the Royal Navy, whence is the readiest Passage for the Pacquet Boats to the Brill in Holland.

From *London to Holyhead* 269 *Miles, thus reckoned.*

To Barnet 11, to St. Albans 9, to Dunstable 12, to Brickhill 9, to Stony Stratford 9, to Tocester 7, to Daventry 12, to Dunchurch 8, to Coventry 11, to Coleshill 11, to Lichfield 15, to Rugely 7, to Haywood 4, to Stone 10, to Stableford Bridge 6, to Ware 6, to Namptwich 8, to Torperly 10, to Chester 9, to Harding 7, to Northop 5, to Denbigh 14, to Aberconway 20, to Beaumaris 12, to Boddedar 19, to Holyhead 8, a Town in Anglesey in North Wales, consisting chiefly of Houses for Entertainment of such Persons as are bound for Ireland,

O

or

or lately arrived thence ; 'tis seated directly opp
site to Dublin, being the shortest and safest Passa
over St. George's Channel.

From London to Ingerstone 20 Miles, thus reckoned
To Rumford 11, to Burntwood 6, to Ingersta
1, a large Village in Essex.

From London to Kingston 12 Miles, thus reckoned.
To Vauxhall 2, to Wandsworth 4, to Kingst
6, a Town in Surry, called also Kingston up
Thames, and Regioriunum, as having been the Se
of the Saxon Kings, of whom 3 were here crown'
and before known by the Name of Moreford.

From London to the Landsend 300 Miles, thus reckone
To Brentford 10, to Stones 8, to Bagshot 10,
Hartley Row 9, to Basingstoke 10, to Andover
to Salisbury 17, to Shaftsbury 19, to Sherbourn
to Crookhorn 14, to Axminster 13, to Honiton
to Rockbew 10, to Exeter 6, to Chudleigh 10,
Ashburton 8, to Brent 7, to Plympton 13, to Pl
mouth 4, to Lowe 16, to Foy 8, to Trewardre
3, to Tregony 12, to Phily 6, to Marketjew 4,
Penzance 3, to St. Burien 6, to Senan 4, a Villa
on the utmost Premontory or Cape, call'd the Land
end in Cornwal, washed with the West Sea.

From London to Lynn 98 Miles, thus reckoned.
To Enfield Wash 10, to Hoddesdon 7, to Wa
4, to Puckeridge 6, to Barkway 8, to Fowlmere
to Cambridge 9, to Stretham 12, to Ely 4, to L
tleport 5, to Soutbery 6, to Downham 6, to Seech
ing 7, to Lynn 5, an antient, large and well bu
Town in Norfolk, containing 3 Parish Churche
encompassed with a Wall and deep Trench ; a
otherwise called Lyn Regis, also Bishops Lyn, a
Llyn by the Welsh, signifying a Lake, seated ne
the Mouth of Owse River.

From London to Montgomery 158 Miles, thus reckone
To Campden 87, to Evesham 7, to Worcester 1
to the Hundred house 9, to Tenbury 10, to Ludlo

, to Bishops Castle 14, to Montgomery 8, the Shire Town of the County of Montgomery in North Wales.

From London to Newhaven 56 Miles, thus reckoned.

To Streham 6, to Croyden 4, to East Grinsted 9, to Lewes 20, to Newhaven 6, a small Town in Sussex, inhabited chiefly by Maritim People, having a Key on the E. side of it, where Ships may ride secure in foul Weather; it is situated at the Mouth of Owse River, but the Name of the River is now obsolete.

From London to Norwich 108 Miles, thus reckoned.

To Puckeridge 27, to Barkway 8, to Whittleford Bridge 10, to Newmarket 14, to Berton Mills 8, to Thetford 10, to Larlingford 8, to Attleborough, to Windham 6, to Norwich 9, a City and Bishoprick in the County of Norfolk, encompassed with a Wall, giving Entrance by 12 Gates, and contains Parish Churches besides the Cathedral.

From London to Oakham 94 Miles, thus reckoned.

To St. Albans 21, to Luton 8, to Selsoe 9, to Bedford 8, to Chillington 9, to Wellingborough, to Kettering 7, to Rockingham 10, to Uppington 4, to Oakham 6, the Shire Town of the County of Rutland, indifferently well built, in the Vale of Catmus, having a good Church, Free School, and Hospital.

From London to Portsmouth 73 Miles, thus reckoned.

To Wandsworth 6, to Kingston 6, to Cobham 7, to Guilford 10, to Godalmin 4, to Lippock 12, to Petersfield 8, to Harnden 5, to Portley Bridge 6, to Portsmouth 4, a large well built Town in Hampshire, defended by 2 strong Castles, and other Works to secure the Haven, and into this well fortified Garrison and Seaport, which is the usual Station of the Royal Navy, you must enter over 4 Draw Bridges.

From

From London to Queenborough 44 *Miles, thus reckoned*

To Rochester (as in the Road from London to
Dover) 30, to Milton 5, to Kings Ferry 3, to
Queenborough 5, a Town in the Isle of of Sheppey
in Kent, where is a Castle built by King Edward
3d, who so named it in Honour of his Queen.

From London to Rye 64 *Miles, thus reckoned.*

To Lewisham 6, to Bromley 3, to Farnborow 4,
to Sevenoke 9, to Tunbridge 6, to Lamberhurst 10,
to Newenden 14, to Rye 10, a fair and well built
Town, which is one of the Cinque Ports, with a
commodious Haven, fortified and walled in the
Time of King Edward 3d.

From London to Shrewsbury 157 *Miles, thus reckoned*

To Meriden 98, to Bermingham 11, to Dudley
10, to Bridgnorth 6, to Wenlock 8, to Shrewsbury
13, a large Corporation, Market and Shire Town in
Shropshire, called Scrobesbirig by the Saxons, and
Pengovern and Yonwithig by the Britons.

From London to Southampton 78 *Miles, thus reckoned.*

To Bagshot 29, to Farnham 11, to Alton 9, to
Alresford 9, to Twiford 8, to Southampton 9, a
Town in Hantshire, having a Key, where Ships of
a considerable Burthen may arrive, which makes it
a Place of good Trade. 'Tis large, and well built,
containing 6 Churches, fenc'd with a double Ditch
and strong Walls, besides having 7 Gates, and several Watch Towers.

From London to Swanzy 202 *Miles, thus reckoned.*

To Brentford 10, to Hounslow 2, to Colebrook 6,
to Maidenhead 8, to Henly 8, to Dorchester 13, to
Abingdon 6, to Faringdon 13, to Lechlade 6, to
Barnesley 5, to Glocester 18, to Michael Dean 11, to
Coverd 5, to Monmouth 5, to Newchurch 12, to
Carr's Ash 7, to Newport 10, to Cardiff 11, to St.
Nicholas 6, to Cowbridge 6, to Corntwon 5, to
Aberavon 13, to Burton Ferry 3, to Swanzey 5, a
large and well built Town on Tawy River, near

its Influx into the Sea, and therefore called Aber-
taw by the Welsh, driving the greatest Trade of any
in the County of Glamorgan, especially for Coal,
and hath a great Correspondence with Bristol.

From London to Truro 196 Miles, thus reckoned.

To Andover (as in the Road from London to the
Landsend) 66, to Amesbury 14, to Shrawton 5,
to Warminster 13, to Maiden Brackly 6, to Burton
9, to Weston Regis 10, to Ascot 7, to Bridgwater
9, to Hartrow House 13, to Dulverton 13 to Southmoulton 13, to Barnstable 10, to Torrington 11, to
Hatherly 10, to Ivy 10, to Newport 8, to Hall
Drunkard 9, to Camelford 5, to St. Endulion 8, to
Padstow 6, to St. Columb 8, to St. Michael 7, to
Truro 7, a large and well built Seaport on Foy River in Cornwal.

From London to Wells 120 Miles, thus reckoned.

To Marlborough (as in the Road from London
to Bristol) 95, to Devizes 13, to Troubridge 9, to
Philipsnorton 5, to Chilcompton 8, to Wells 7, a
City, which, with Bath, is a Bishoprick, and hath
a very stately Cathedral.

From London to Weymouth 132 Miles, thus reckoned.

To Basingstoke (as in the Road from London to
the Landsend) 48, to Sutton 13, to Stockbridge 7,
to Broughton 5, to Dounton 11, to Cranbourn 11,
to Blandford 11, to Dorchester 16, to Weymouth 8,
a Seaport Town in Dorsetshire, in which the Chapel
stands on a Rock so steep, that 'tis ascended to by
60 Steps.

From London to Yarmouth 122 Miles, thus reckoned.

To Colchester (as in the Road from London to
Harwich) 50, to Stratford 7, to Ipswich 11, to
Woodbridge 7, to Saxmundham 11, to Blyborough
10, to Beckles 10, to Hadsho 5, to Yarmouth 9, a
large, strong and well built Seaport Town in Norfolk, enjoying several Privileges and Immunities, it
has a great Fishing Trade, and yields a ready Passage
to Holland.　　　　O 5　　　　*From*

From Lynn to Harwich 76 Miles, thus reckoned.

To Swatham 15, to Stanford 9, to Thetford 7, to Ickſworth 9, to Stow Market 11, to Ipſwich 12 to Harwich 12.

From Monmouth to Llanbeder 68 Miles, thus reckoned

To Llandelo Cruſſeny 8, to Abergavenny 7, to Crecowel 5, to Brecknock 12, to Redbrue 8, to Lla mindefoy 10, to Llanbeder 15, a ſmall Town, other wiſe called Llanbedor Pont ſteffan, in Cardigan ſhire in South Wales ; 'tis meanly built, conſiſting in about 50 Houſes, yet affords one very good Inn

From Nottingham to Grimsby 67 Miles, thus reckoned

To Newark 17, to Lincoln 14, to Walton 6, to Market Raiſing 9, to Stanion 5, to Briggeſly 7, to Grimsby 5, a Port Town in Lincolnſhire, near the Sea, where it formerly had a Caſtle, to ſecure it now almoſt choak'd up Harbour.

From Oxford to Briſtol 68 Miles, thus reckoned.

To Fiefield 8, to Faringdon 9, to Hyworth 6, to Purton 8, to Malmesbury 10, to Lockington 7, to Pucklechurch 10, to Briſtol 8.

From Oxford to Cambridge 80 Miles, thus reckoned.

To Burceſter 13, to Buckingham 11, to Newpor Parnel 13, to Bedford 13, to Gamlinghay 13, to Cambridge 15, a Corporation, Market and Shir Town, and an antient Univerſity.

From Preſtain to Carmarthen 61 Miles, thus reckoned.

To New Radnor 5, to Bealth 10, to Ludlowvaugh 12, to Llanimodoſry 7, to Abermarles 6, to Ru Radnor 8, to Carmarthen 12, the Shire Town of the County of Carmarthen, large and well built on Towy River, over which it has a large Stone Bridge and Key, where ſmall Veſſels do arrive to unload their Goods. 'Tis ſaid to have given Birth to Merlin, the Britiſh Prophet or Soothſayer, ſaid to be begot on his Mother by an Incubus ; and was once fortified with a Wall, and ſtrong Caſtle now ruinous.

From

From Queenborough to Chelmsford 42 Miles, thus reckoned.

To Kings Ferry 5, to Milon 3, to Rochester 5, to Gravesend 8, to Billericay 14, to Chelmsford 8, a Town in Essex, where the Assizes are commonly held for that County.

From Rochester to London 29 Miles, thus reckoned.

Take the Reverse of the Road from London to Dover, where it mentions Rochester ; and the like is to be observed of the Dimensuration of any other Place herein set down.

From Shrewsbury to Holywell 52 Miles, thus reckoned.

To Ellesmere 16, to Wrexham 13, to Mould 13, to Holywell in Flintshire 11.

From Tinmouth to Durham 22 Miles, thus reckoned.

To Sunderland 9, to Durham 13, a City and Bishoprick, seated on the River Ware, in the County of Durham.

From Uxbridge to Oxford 35 Miles, thus reckoned.

To Beaconsfield 8, to Wickham 5, to Testworth 12, to Wheatly 5, to Oxford 5, a City, Bishoprick, and most famous University, in Oxfordshire.

From Whitby to Tinmouth 92 Miles, thus reckoned.

To Skelingdam 11, to Gisbrough 10, to Marton 6, to Norton 8, to Sedgfield 8, to Durham 11, to Sunderland 13, to Tinmouth 9, an indifferent large Town, of some Note in Northumberland, fortified with a Castle.

From York to Scarborough 43 Miles, thus reckoned.

To New Malton 19, to Rollington 5, to Sherborn 6, to Seamor 7, to Scarborough 4, a strong well built Town in Yorkshire, almost surrounded with the Sea : It was called Scearburgh by the Saxons, and drives a good Trade ; being much resorted to, for its famous Spaw.

A List

A List of all the Market Towns in England and Wales ; with the Days of the Week whereon kept.

Note, m. signifies *Monday* ; t. *Tuesday* ; w. *Wednesday* ; th. *Thursday* , f. *Friday* , and f. *Saturday*.
Those Places printed with *English* Letters, are Cities , those with *Italick* Letters, Shire Towns.

A Bbotsbury *in Dorsetshire*, th
Aberforth, *Yorksh.* w.
Abergavenny, *Monm.* t.
Aberistwith, *Cardig.* m.
Abingdon, *Berks*, m. f.
Ailesbury, *Bucks*, f.
Aldborough, *Suff.* f.
Alesham, *Norf.* f.
Alford, *Linc.* t.
Alfreten, *Derbysh.* m.
Alnwick, *Northumb.* f.
Alresford, *Hantsh.* th.
Alstonmore, *Cumberl.* f.
Altrincham, *Chesh.* t.
Ambleside, *Westmorl.* w.
Amersham, *Bucks*, t.
Ampthill, *Bedf.* th.
Andover, *Huntsh.* f.
Apulby, *Westmorl.* f.
Arundel, *Suss.* w. f.
Ashbourn, *Derbysh* f.
Ashburton, *Devon.* f.
Ashby de la Zouch, *Leic.* f.
Ashford, *Kent*, f.
Atherston, *Warwic.* t.

Attleborough, *Norf.* th.
Aubourn, *Wilts.* t.
Aukland, *Durh.* th.
Aulcester *Warwic.* t.
Autrey, *Devon.* t.
Axbridge, *Somerset.* th.
Axminster, *Devon.* f.
Aye, *Suff.* f.
Bakewell, *Derbysh.* m.
Bala, *Merionethsh.* f.
Baldock, *Hertf.* th.
Bampton, *Oxon* w.
Banbury, *Oxon*, th.
Bangor, *Carnarv.* w.
Barking, *Ess* w.
Barnet, *Hertf.* m.
Barnard Castle, *Durh.* w.
Barnsly, *Yorksh.* w.
Barnstable, *Devon.* f.
Barton, *Lincol.* m.
Barwick, *Northumb.* f.
Basingstoke, *Hant.* w.
Bath, *Somerset.* w. f.
Battle, *Suss.* th.
Bautry, *Yorksh.* f.
Beaconsfield, *Bucks*, th.
Beaumar

Beaumaris, *Anglesey*, w.	Breewood, *Stafford* t.
Beccles, *Suff.* f.	Bridgend, *Glamorg.* f.
Bedes, *Yorksh.* t.	Bridgnorth, *Salop*, f.
Bedford, *Bedf.* t. f.	Bridgwater, *Somerset* th.
Bediford, *Devon.* t.	Bridlington, *Yorksh.* f.
Bemister, *Dorset.* t.	Bridport, *Dorset.* f.
Berkhamstead, *Hertf* m.	Brigs, *Lincoln.* th.
Beverly, *Yorksh.* w. f.	Bristol, *Somerset.* w. f.
Bewdly, *Worcest.* f.	Bromley, *Kent*, th.
Bicester, *Oxon*, f.	Bromley, *Staff.* t.
Biggleswade, *Bedf.* t.	Broomsgrove, *Worcest.* t.
Bildeston, *Suff* w.	Bruton, *Somerset.* f.
Billericay, *Eff.* t.	Buckenham, *Norf.* f.
Bilsdon, *Leicest.* f.	Buckingham, *Bucks*, f.
Binbrook, *Lincol.* w.	Buddeldaie, *Suff.* th.
Bingham, *Nottingh.* th.	Built, *Brecon*, m. f.
Birmingham, *Warwic.* th.	Bullingbrock, *Linc.* t.
Bishops Castle, *Salop*, f.	Bungey, *Suff.* th.
Blackbourn, *Lancash.* m.	Buntingford, *Hertf.* m.
Blandford, *Dorset.* f.	Burford, *Oxon*, f.
Bodwin, *Cornw.* l.	Burgh, *Linc.* t.
Bolsover, *Derbysh.* f.	Burnham, *Norf.* f.
Bolton, *Lancash.* m.	Burton, *Linc.* th.
Boston, *Lincolnsh.* w. f.	Burton, *Westmorl.* t.
Bosworth, *Leicest.* w.	Caersilly, *Glamorg.* th.
Bourn, *Lincolnsh.* f.	Caerlion, *Monm.* th.
Bow, *Devon.* th.	Caerwis, *Flintsh.* t.
Brackley, *Northamp.* w.	Cain, *Wilts*, t.
Bradfield, *Eff.* th.	Cambridge, *Camb.* f.
Bradford *Wilts*, m.	Camelford, *Cornw.* f.
Bradforth, *Yorksh.* th.	Campden, *Gloc.* w.
Brading, *Hant.* t.	Canterbury, *Kent*, w. f.
Braintree, *Eff.* w.	Cardiff, *Glamorg.* w. f.
Brampton, *Cumberl.* t.	Cardigan, *Cardig.* f.
Bramyard, *Herefordsh* m.	Carlisle, *Cumberl.* f.
Brecknock, *Brecon*, w. f.	Carmarthen, *Carm.* w. f.
Brentford, *Midd.* t.	Carnarvon, *Carnar* f.
Brentwood, *Eff.* w.	Cartmel, *Lancash.* m.
	Castle-

Caftlecurry, *Somerf.* t.
Cafton, *Norf.* t.
Caftor, *Lincol.* m.
Cawood, *Yorkf.* w.
Caxton, *Camb.* t.
Cerne, *Dorfetf.* w.
Chard, *Somerfet.* t.
Charley, *Lancafh* t.
Cheadle, *Staff.* f.
Chelmsford, *Eff.* f.
Cheltenham, *Gloc.* th.
Chepftow, *Monm.* f.
Chefham, *Bucks,* w.
𝕮𝖍𝖊𝖘𝖙𝖊𝖗, *Chef.* w. f.
Chefterfield, *Derbyf.* f.
𝕮𝖍𝖎𝖈𝖍𝖊𝖘𝖙𝖊𝖗, *Suf* w. f.
Chimligh, *Devon.* th.
Chippenham, *Wilts,* f
Chippingnorton, *Oxon,* w.
Chudleigh, *Devon.* f.
Churchftretton, *Salop,* th.
Cirenceffer, *Gloc.* m. t.
Clare, *Suff* f.
Clebury, *Salop,* w.
Cliffe, *Northampt.* t.
Clitnero, *Lancafh.* f.
Cockermouth *Cumberl.* m.
Cogfhal, *Eff.* f.
Colchefter, *Eff.* f.
Colebroke, *Bucks,* w.
Colefhil, *Warwic.* w.
Calne, *Lancaf.* w.
Columpton, *Devon.* f.
Congleton, *Chef.* l
Conwey, *Carnarvon.* f.
Corfe, *Drfet.* t.
𝕮𝖔𝖛𝖊𝖓𝖙𝖗𝖕, *Warwic.* f.
Cambridge, *Glamorg.* t.

Cranborn, *Dorfet.* w.
Cranbrook, *Kent,* f.
Cray, *Kent,* W.
Crediton, *Devon* f.
Creeklade, *Wilts,* f.
Crickhowel, *Brecon,* th.
Cromer, *Norf.* f.
Crookhorn, *Somerfet.* f.
Croyden, *Surry,* f.
Cuckfield, *Suff* t.
Culliton, *Devon.* th.
Dalton, *Lancafh.* f.
Darly, *Darbyfh.*
Daraing, *Surry,* th.
Darlington, *Durh.* m.
Dartford, *Kent,* f.
Dartmouth, *Devon.* f.
Daventry, *Northampt.* w.
Dean, *Gloc.* m.
Debenham, *Suff.* f.
Deddington, *Oxon,* f.
Denbigh, *Denbigf.* w.
Dereham, *Norf.* f.
Devizes, *Wilts,* th.
Dieping, *Lincolnfh.* th.
Dinas-mouthwye, *Meriof*
Dis, *Norf.* f.
Dodbrook, *Devon.* w.
Doluelle, *Merronethf.* w.
Doncafter, *Yorkfh.* f.
Dorchefter *Dorfet.* f.
Dover, *Kent,* w. f.
Downham, *Norf.* f.
Drayton, *Salop,* w.
Droitwich, *Worcef.* f.
Dronfield, *Darbyf.* t.
Dudley, *Worcef.* f.
Dulverton, *Somerfet.* f.
　　　　　　　　Dunckton,

Duncktôn, *Wilts*, f.
Dunnington, *Lincolnſ.* f.
Dunmore, *Eſſ.* f.
Dunſtable, *Bedfordſ.* w.
Dunſter, *Somerſet.* t.
Dunwich, *Suff.* f.
Durham, *Durh.* f.
Durſley, *Gloc.* th.
Eccleſhal, *Staff.* t.
Eadgworth, *Midd.* th.
Egremond, *Cumberl.* f.
Eleham, *Kent*, m.
Elliſmere, *Salop*, t.
Ely, *Cambridgſh.* f.
Enfield, *Midd.* f.
Epping, *Eſſ.* tn. f.
Everſhot, *Dorſet.* t.
Eveſham, *Worceſt.* m.
Ewel, *Surry*, th.
Exeter, w. f.
Fairford, *Gloc.* th.
Fakenham, *Norf.* th.
Falmouth, *Cornw.* th.
Foreham, *Hant.* th.
Faringdon, *Becks*, t.
Feverſham, *Kent*, w. f.
Fiſhgard, *Pembrokeſ.* f.
Flint, *Flintſh.* tho' a Shire Town, hath no Market.
Fokingham, *Lincolnſ.* th.
Folkeſton, *Kent*, th.
Fowey, *Cornw.* f.
Framlingham, *Suff.* f.
Frampton, *Dorſet.* th.
Frodeſham, *Cheſh.* w.
Froom, *Somerſet.* w.
Gainsborough, *Lincolnſ.* t.

Garſtand, *Lancaſh.* th.
Gisborough, *Yorkſ.* m.
Glaſſenbury, *Somerſet.* t.
Gloceſter, *Gloc.* w. f.
Godalmin, *Surry*, f.
Grampound, *Cornw.* f.
Grantham, *Lincolnſ.* f.
Gravelend, *Kent*, w. f.
Grimsby, *Lincolnſ.* w.
Grinſtead, *Suff.* th.
Guilford, *Surry*, f.
Hadley, *Suff.* m.
Haleſworth, *Suff.* t.
Halifax, *Yorkſ.* th.
Hallaton, *Leic.* th.
Hampton, *Gloc.* t.
Harborough, *Leic.* t.
Harlech, *Merionethſ.* f.
Harleſton, *Norf.* w.
Hartford, Hartf. f.
Harwich, *Eſſ.* t.
Haſlingden, *Lanc.* w.
Haſtings, *Suff.* w. f.
Hatfield, *Hartf.* f.
Hatherly, *Devon.* f.
Haverfordweſt, *Pemb.* t. f.
Haveril, *Eſſ.* w.
Hawkſhead, *Lancaſ.* m.
Hay, *Brecon*, m.
Helmeſly, *Yorkſ.* f.
Helmeſton *Suff.* th.
Helſton, *Cornw.* f.
Henly, *Oxon*, th.
Henly, *Warwic.* m.
Hereford, *Heref.* w. f. f.
Herling, *Norf.* t.
Hexham, *Northumb.* t.
Heydon, *Yorkſ.* f.

Higham-

Highamferries, *North.* f.
H.ndon, *Wilts,* th.
Hinkley, *Leicef.* m.
Hitcling. *Hertf.* t.
Hoddefdon, *Hertfordf* th.
Holbeck, *Lincolnf.* th.
Holt, *Norf.* f.
Honiton, *Devon.* f.
Horncaftle, *Linc.* f.
Hornden, *Eff.* f.
Horfham, *Suff.* f.
Houlfworth, *Devon.* f.
Howden *Yorkf.* f.
Hull, *Yorkf.* t. f
Hungerford, *Berks,* w.
Huntington, Hunt. f.
Hyth, *Kent,* f.
Hyworth, *Wilts,* w.
Ilchefter, *Somerfet.* w.
Illfey, *Berks,* w.
Ilminfter, *Somerfet.* f.
Ipfwich, *Suff.* w. f. f.
Ireby, *Cumberl.* t.
Irworth, *Suff.* f.
Ivingo, *Bucks,* f.
Kederminfter,*Worcef.* th.
Kendel, *Weftmorl.* f.
Kefwick, *Cumberl.* f.
Kettering, *Northampt.* f.
Keynfham, *Somerfet.* th.
Kidwelly, *Carmarth.* t.
Kilgarren, *Pembrokef.* w.
Kilha.n, *Yorkf.* th.
Kinbolton, *Huntingt.* f.
Kingsbridge, *Devon.* f.
Kingfclere, *Hant.* t.
Kingfton upon Thames, *Surry,* f.

Kingfton, *Heref.* w.
Kirbymoorfide, *Yorkf* w.
Kirby-Stephen, *Weftm.* f
Kirkham, *Lancafh.* t.
Kirk Ofwald,*Cumberl.*th
Kirton, *Lancafh.* f.
Knighton, *Radnorf.* th.
Knottesford, *Chefh.* f.
Keekyth, *Carnarvonf.* w.
Kyneton, *Warwic* t.
Lanbeden, *Cardiganf.* t.
Lancafter, Lancafh. f.
Lanceflon, Cornw. f. It i an antient Market Town ; and the Mar ket, in King *John* Days, was kept on *Sun days* ; but for a Fine (5 Marks, was altere to *Thurfday,* and finc is remov'd to*Saturday* as it now remains.
Landaff, *Glamorg.* tho' City and Bifhopricl has no Market.
Landelghawe, *Carmart.*
Lanelly, *Carmarth.* t.
Langadock,*Carmarth.* th
Langport, *Somerfet.* f.
Lanindovery,*Carmar.*w
Lanroft, *Denbighfh.* t.
Lantriffent, *Glamorg.* f.
Lanvilling, *Montgom.* t;
Lavenham, *Suff* t.
Laughern, *Carmarth.* f.
Lavington, *Wilts,* w.
Lechlade, *Gloc.* t.
Leeds, *Yorkf.* t. f.

Lee

Leek, *Staffordfh.* w.
Leicester, *Leiceft.* f.
Leighton, *Bedfords.* t.
Lenham, *Kent,* t.
Leominster, *Heref.* f.
Leskard, *Cornw.* l.
Leftoff, *Suff.* w
Leftwithiel, *Cornw.* f.
Leverpool, *Lancafh* f.
Lewes, *Suff.* l.
Lichfield, *Staff.* t. f.
Lidbury, *Heref.* t.
Lincoln, *Lincolnf.* f.
Linton, *Camb.* th.
London, every Weekday
  at one place or other.
Longtown, *Cumberl.* th.
Lonfdale, *Weftmorl.* th.
Loughborough, *Leiceft.* th
Lowe, *Cornw.* f.
Ludlow, *Salop,* m.
Luton, *Bedfordf.* m.
Lutterworth, *Leiceft.* th.
Lyme, *Dorfet.* t.
Lymington, *Hant.* f.
Lynn, *Norf.* t. f.
Macclesfield, *Chefh.* m.
Machynleth, *Montgom* m.
Maidenhead, *Berks,* w.
Maidftone, *Kent,* th.
Maldon, *Eff.* f.
Malling, *Kent,* f.
Malmsbury, *Wilts,* l.
Malpas, *Chefh.* m.
Malton, *Yorkfh.* l.
Manchefter, *Lancafh.* f.
Maningtree, *Eff.* t.
Mansfield, *Nottingh.* th.
Marketjew, *Cornw.* th.

Marlborough, *Wilts,* f.
Marlow, *Bucks,* l.
Marfhfield, *Gluc.* t.
Mafham, *Yorkf.* t.
Melcomb, *Dorfet.* t. f.
Melton, *Leiceft.* t.
Mendlefham, *Suff.* t.
Mercle *Camb.* f.
Mere, *Wilts,* t.
Midhurft, *Suff.* th.
Middlewich, *Chefh.* t.
Milbrook, *partly in Devon,*
  partly in Cornwal, f.
Mildenhall, *Suff.* f.
Milton, *Dorfet* m.
Milton, *Kent,* f.
Modbury, *Dorfet.* th.
Monmouth, *Monmouth's.* f.
Montgomery, *Mongom.* th.
Montforrel, *Leiceft.* m.
Moreton, *Devon.* l.
Morpeth, *Northumb.* w.
Namptwich, *Chefh.* f.
Narbarth, *Pembrokes.* w.
Neath, *Glamorg.* f.
Needham, *Suff.* w.
Nevon, *Carmarth.* f.
Newark, *Nottingh.* w.
Newborough, *Anglefey,* t.
Newbury, *Berks,* th.
Newcaftle, *Northumb.* t. f.
Newcaftle, *Staff.* m.
Newent, *G'oc.* t.
Newmarket, *Suff.* th.
Newnham, *Gloc.* f.
Newport, *Hant.* w. f.
Newport, *Monm.* f.
Newport, *Pembrokes.* f.
Newport, *Salop,* f.

P   Newport-

Newport pagnel, *Bucks*, f.
Newton, *Devon*. w.
Newton, *Montgom*. t.
Neyland, *Suff*. f.
Northallerton, *Yorkf*. w.
Northampton Northampt. f.
Northcurry, *Somerfet*. t. f.
Northfleet, *Kent*, where a Market is only kept every *Tuesday* after *Easter Tuesday* till *Whitsun Tuesday*.
Northwich, *Chefb*. f
𝕹𝖔𝖗𝖜𝖎𝖈𝖍, *Norf*. w. t. f.
Nottingham Notting. w. f. f.
Nuneaton, *Warwic*. f.
Oakham, *Rutland*. f.
Oaknampton, *Devon*. f.
Ockingham, *Berks*, t.
Odiam, *Hant*. f.
Onger, *Eff*. f.
Orford, *Suff*. m.
Ormskirk, *Lancafb*. t.
Orton, *Weftmorl*. w.
Ofweftry, *Salop*, m.
Otley, *Yorkf*. t.
Oulney, *Bucks*, m.
Oundle, *Northampt*. f.
𝕺𝖗𝖋𝖔𝖗𝖉, *Oxon*, w. f.
Packlington, *Yorkf*. f.
Padftow, *Cornw*. f.
Panfwick, *Gloc*. t.
Patrington, *Yorkf*. f.
Pembridge, *Heref*. t.
Pembroke, *Pembrok*. f.
Penkridge, *Staff*. t.
Penreth, *Cumb*. t.
Pentife, *Glamorg*. th.
Penryn, *Cornw*. w. f. f.

Pensford, *Somerfet*. t.
Penzance, *Cornw*. th.
Pershore, *Worcef*. t.
𝕻𝖊𝖙𝖊𝖗𝖇𝖔𝖗𝖔𝖚𝖌𝖍, *North*. f.
Petersfield, *Hant*. f.
Petworth, *Suff*. f.
Philipfnorton, *Somerfet*.th
Plymouth, *Devon*. m. th.
Plympton, *Devon*. f.
Pontefract, *Yorkf*. f.
Pontypole, *Monm*. f.
Pool, *Dorfet*. m. th.
Portfmouth, *Hant*. th. f.
Potton, *Bedfordf*. t.
Poulton, *Lanc*. m.
Prefcot, *Lanc*. t.
Preftain, *Radnorf*. f.
Prefton, *Lanc*. w. f. f.
Pulhely, *Carnarvonf*. w.
Queenborough, *Kent*, th.
Radnor, *Radnorf*. th.
Ramfey, *Hantf*. w.
Rafen, *Lincolnf*. t.
Ravenglas, *Cumb*. f.
Rayleigh, *Eff*. f.
Reading, *Berks*, f.
Repeham, *Norf* f.
Retford, *Notting*. f.
Rhiradergwy, *Radnorf*.w
Richmond, *Yorkf*. f.
Ringwood, *Hunt*. w.
Ripley, *Yorkf* f.
Rippon, *Yorkf*.th.
Risborough, *Bucks*, f.
Rochlade, *Lanc*. t.
𝕽𝖔𝖈𝖍𝖊𝖘𝖙𝖊𝖗, *Kent*, f.
Rockingham, *Northam*.th
Rofs, *Heref*. th.
Rotherham, *Yorkf*. m.
Rothwell

Rothwell, *Northamp.* m.
Rugby, *Warwic.* f.
Rugeby, *Staff.* t.
Rumford, *Eff.* w.
Rumney, *Kent,* th.
Rumfey, *Hant* f.
Ruthyn, *Denbighfh.* m.
Rye, *Suff.* w. t.
Rygate, *Surry,* t.
𝕾alisburp, *Wilts,* t. f.
Saltafh, *Cornw.* f.
Sandbach, *Chefh.* th.
Sandway *Kent,* where a
   Market is kept for
   Bullocks, upon every
   Tuefday after *Alhallows*
   Day till *Chriftmas.*
Sandwich, *Kent,* w. f.
Saxmundham, *Suff* th.
Scarborough, *Yorkf.* th.
Seechy, *Norf.* m.
Selby, *Yorkf.* m.
Settle, *Yorkf* t.
Sevenoke, *Kent,* f.
Shaftsbury, *Dorfet.* f.
Sneffield, *Yorkf.* t.
Shefford, *Bedfordf.* f.
Sherbourn, *Dorfet.* f.
Shipfton, *Worcefl* f.
Shiptonmallet *Somerfet.*f.
Shoreham, *Suff.* f.
Shrewsbury, *Salop,* w.th.f.
Shipton, *Yorkf.* f.
Slatford, *Linc.* m.
Snathe, *Yorkf.* t.
Snelfham, f.
Somerton, *Somerfet.* m.
Southampton, *Hamp.* t. f.
Southmoulton, *Devon* f.

South-Petherton,*Som.* th.
Southwark, f.
Southwell, *Notting.* f.
Southwold, *Suff.* th.
Spalding, *Linc.* t.
Spilsby, *Linc.* m.
St. Albans, *Hertf.* f.
St. 𝕬faph, *Flintfh.* f.
St. Columb, *Cornw.* th.
St. 𝕯abid's, *Pemb* but
   tho' a Bifhoprick,hath
   no Market.
St.Edmundsbury,*Suff.* w.
St. Ives, *Huntingt.* w. f.
St. Neots, *Huntingt.* th.
Stafford, Staff. l.
Stamford, *Linc.* m. f.
Stanes, *Midd.* f.
Stanhope, *Durh.* t.
Stanton, *Lanc.* m.
Steyning, *Suff.* w.
Stevenage, *Hertf.* f.
Stockport, *Chefh.* f.
Stokefly, *Yorkf.* f.
Stone, *Staff.* t.
Stony-Stratford, *Bucks,* f.
Storeford, *Hertf.* t.
Stow, *Gloc.* th.
Stow, *Suff.* th.
Stowey, *Somerfet.* t.
Stratford, *Warwic.* th.
Stratton, *Cornw.* t.
Stroud, *Gloc.* t.
Sturbridge, *Worcefl.* f.
Sturminiter, *Dorfet* th.
Sudbury, *Gloc.* th.
Sudbury, *Suff.* f.
Sunderland, *Durh.* f.
Sutton-Colcfield,*Warw.*m

Swanzey,

Swanzey, *Glamorg.* w. f.
Swasham, *Norf.* f.
Swindon, *Wilts,* m.
Tadcaster, *Yorkf.* th.
Tame. *Oxf* t.
Tamworth, *Staff.* f.
Tapershal, *Linc.* f.
Tavestock, *Devon.* f.
Taunton, *Somerset.* w. f.
Tenbury, *Worcest.* t.
Tenby, *Pemb* w. f.
Tenterden, *Kent,* f.
Terring, *Suff.* f.
Tetbury, *Gloc.* w.
Tewkesbury, *Gloc.* f.
Thaxted, *Eff.* f.
Thetford, *Norf.* f.
Thornbury, *Gloc.* f.
Thrapston, *Northampt.* t.
Thursk, *Yorkf.* m.
Tickhal, *Yorkf.* f.
Tiddeswal, *Derbyf.* w.
Tiverton, *Devon.* t.
Toceiter, *Northampt.* t.
Torrington, *Devon.* f.
Totnes, *Devon.* f.
Tregaron, *Cardiganf.* th.
Tregony, *Cornw.* f.
Tring, *Hert.* f.
Troubridge, *Wilts,* f.
Truro, *Cornw.* w. f.
Tunbridge, *Kent,* f.
Turbury, *Staff.* t.
Tuxford, *Nott.* m.
Ulversian, *Rutlandf.* th.
Uppingham, *Rutland.* w.
Upton, *Worcest.* th.
Usk, *Monm* m.
Utoxeter, *Staff.* w.

Uxbridge, *Midd.* th.
Wainfleet, *Linc.* f.
Wakefield, *Yorkf.* th. f.
Walden, *Eff.* f.
Wallingford, *Berks,* t. f.
Walsal, *Staff.* t.
Walsham, *Norf* t.
Walsingham, *Norf.* f.
Waltham, *Eff.* t.
Waltham, *Leicest.* th.
Wantage, *Berks,* f.
Ware, *Hertf.* t.
Wareham, *Dorset.* f.
Warrington, *Lanc.* f.
Warminster, *Wilts,* f.
Warwick, f.
Watchet, *Glamorg.* f.
Watford, *Hertf.* t.
Watlington, *Oxon,* f.
Watton, *Norf.* w.
Welshpool, *Montg.* m.
Wellingborough, *North.* w
Werington, *Somerset.* th
Wells, *Somerset.* w. f.
Wem, *Salop,* th.
Wendover, *Bucks,* th.
Wenlock, *Salop,* m.
Weobly, *Heref.* th.
Westbury, *Wilts,* f.
Westminster, *Midd.* every
    Day but *Sunday.*
Westcam, *Kent,* w.
Wetherby, *Yorkf.* th.
Weymouth, *Dorset.* t. f
Whitby, *Yorkf.* t.
Whitchurch, *Salop,* f.
Whitehaven, *Cumberl.* th
Wicomb, *Bucks,* t.
Wickware, *Gloc.* m.
            Wigan

Wigan, *Lanc.* m. f. Woodbridge, *Suff.* w.
Wighton, *Yorks.* w. t. Woodstock, *Oxf.* t.
Wigton, *Cumberl.* t. Woolwich, *Kent,* f.
Wilton, *Wilts,* w. **Worcester,** *Worc.* w. f. f.
Winbourn, *Dorset.* t. Workfop, *Notting.* w.
Wincaunton, *Somerset.* w. Worfted, *Norf.* t.
Winchcomb, *Gloc.* f. Wotton, *Gloc.* f.
Winchefter, *Hant.* w. f. Wotton-baffet, *Wilts,* th.
Windham, *Norf.* t. Wrexham, *Denbigs* m. th.
Winflow, *Bucks,* th. Wrinton, *Somerset.* t.
Windfor, *Berks,* f. Wrotham, *Kent,* t.
Wickfworth, *Derbys.* t. Wuller, *Northumb.* th.
Wisbich, *Camb.* l. Wye, *Kent,* th.
Wifton, *Pemb.* f. Yarmouth, *Norf.* f.
Witham, *Eff.* f. Yarum, *Yorks.* th.
Witney, *Oxf.* th. Yexley, *Huntingt.* t.
Wivelfcomb, *Som.* t. Yeovil, *Somerset.* f.
Wobourn, *Bedf.* t. **York,** *Yorks.* th. f.
Wolverhampton, *Staff.* w.

---

*A Lift of all the Shires, Cities, Towns, and Bo-
roughs, in* England, Wales, *and* Scotland,
which fend Members to Parliament.

E N G L A N D.
Bedfordshire 4.
Bedford 2
Berkshire 9.
New Windfor 2
Reading 2
Wallingford 2
Abingdon 1
Buckinghamshire 14.
Buckingham 2
Chipping Wicomb 2
Aylesbury 2
Agmondefham 2

Wendover 2
Great Marlow 2
Cambridgshire 6.
University 2
Cambridge 2
Cheshire 4.
Chefter 2
Cornwall 44.
Launcefton 2
Lefkard 2
Lestwithiel 2
Truro 2
Bodman 2
I 3   Helfton

Heſſion 2
Saltaſh 2
Camelford 2
Wenlow 2
Grompound 2
Eaſtlow 2
Penryn 2
Tregony 2
Boſſivy 2
St. Ives 2
Foway 2
St. Germain 2
St. Michael 2
Newport 2
St. Maws 2
Kellington 2
    Cumberland 6.
Carliſle 2
Cockermouth 2
    Derbyſhire 4.
Derby 2
    Devonſhire 26.
Exeter 2
Totneſs 2
Plymouth 2
Oakhampton 2
Barnſtable 2
Plympton 2
Honiton 2
Taviſtock 2
Aſhburton 2
Clifton Dartmouth-
   Hardneſs 2
Boralſton 2
Tiverton 2
    Dorſetſhire 20.
Pool 2
Dorcheſter 2
Lyme Regis 2

Weymouth 2
Melcolm-Regis 2
Bridport 2
Shattsbury 2
Warnham 2
Corf Caſtle 2
    Durham 4.
Durham 2
    Eſſex 8.
Colcheſter 2
Maldon 2
Harwich 2
    Gloceſterſhire 8.
Gloceſter 2
Cirenceſter 2
Tewkesbury 2
    Herefordſhire 8.
Hereford 2
Leominſter 2
Weobly 2
    Hertfordſhire 6.
St. Albans 2
Hertford 2
    Huntingtonſhire 4.
Huntington 2
    Kent 10.
Canterbury 2
Rocheſter 2
Maidſtone 2
Queenborough 2
    Lancaſhire 14.
Preſton 2
Lancaſter 2
Newton 2
Wigan 2
Clithero 2
Liverpool 2
    Leiceſterſhire 4.
Leiceſter 2
       Lincoln-

Lincolnshire 12.
Lincoln 2
Boston 2
Great Grimsby 2
Stamford 2
Grantham 2
    Middlesex 8.
Westminster 2
London 4
    Monmouthshire 3.
Monmouth 1
    Norfolk 12.
Norwich 2
Lyn Regis 2
Yarmouth 2
Thetford 2
Castlerising 2
    Northamptonshire 9.
Peterborough 2
Northampton 2
Brackley 2
Highamferries 1
    Northumberland 8.
Newcastle upon Tine 2
Morperh 2
Berwick upon Tweed 2
    Nottinghamshire 8.
Nottingham 2
East Retford 2
Newark upon Trent 2
    Oxon 9.
University 2
Oxford 2
New Woodstock 2
Banbury 1
    Rutlandshire 2.
    Salop 12.
Shrewsbury 2
Bridgnorth 2

Ludlow 2
Great Wenlock 2
Bishops Castle 2
    Somersetshire 18.
Bristol 2
Bath 2
Wells 2
Taunton 2
Bridgwater 2
Mirehead 2
Ilcester 2
Milbournport 2
    Southampton 26.
Winchester 2
Southampton 2
Portsmouth 2
Yarmouth 2
Petersfield 2
Newport 2
Stockbridge 2
Newton 2
Christchurch 2
Lymington 2
Whitchurch 2
Andover 2
    Staffordshire 10.
Lichfield 2
Stafford 2
Newcastle under Line 2
Tamworth 2
    Suffolk 16.
Ipswich 2
Dunwich 2
Orford 2
Aldborough 2
Sudbury 2
Eye 2
Edmundsbury 2

Sur

Surry 14.
Southwark 2
Blechingly 2
Rygate 2
Guilford 2
Gatton 2
Haslemere 2
    Sussex 20.
Chichester 2
Horsham 2
Midhurst 2
Lewis 2
Shoreham 2
Cramber 2
Steyning 2
East Grinstead 2
Arundel 2
   Warwickshire 6.
Coventry 2
Warwick 2
   Westmorland 4.
Apulby 2
   Wiltshire 34.
New Sarum 2
Wilton 2
Downton 2
Hinder 2
Heytesbury 2
Westbury 2
Calne 2
Devizes 2
Chippenham 2
Malmsbury 2
Cricklade 2
Great Bedwin 2
Luggershall 2
Old Sarum 2
Wootten-baffet 2.
Marlborough 2

Worcestershire 10.
Worcester 2
Droitwich 2
Evesham 2
Bewdley 2
   Yorkshire 30.
York 2
Kingston upon Hull 2
Knaresborough 2
Scarborough 2
Rippon 2
Richmond 2
Heydon 2
Boroughbrig 2
Malton 2
Thirsk 2
Alborough 2
Beverly 2
Northallerton 2
Pontefract 2

Cinque-Ports 16.
Hastings 2
Dover 2
Sandwich 2
Hyeth 2
New Rumney 2
Rye 2
Winchester 2
Seaford 2

W A L E S.
Anglesey 1
Beaumaris 1
Brecon 1
Brecknock 1
Cardiganshire 1
Cardigan 1

Carn.

Carmarthenshire 1
Carmarthen 1
Carnarvonshire 1
Carnarvon 1
Denbighshire 1
Denbigh 1
Flintshire 1
Flint 1
Glamorganshire 1
Cardiffe 1
Merionethshire 1
Montgomeryshire 1
Montgomery 1
Pembrokeshire 3
Pembroke 1
Haverford West 1
Radnorshire 1
New Radnor 1

SCOTLAND.
Shire *Aberdeen* 1
Aberdeen 1
Shire *Ayre* 1
Ayre 1
Shire *Argyle* 1
Shire *Bamf* 1
Shire *Berwick* 1
Shires *Bull* and *Cathness* 1
Shires *Clackaman* and *Kinross* 1
Shire *Dunbarton* 1
Shire *Dumfries* 1
Dumfreis 1
Shire *Edinburgh* 1
Edinburgh 1
Elgin 1

Shire *Fyfe* 1
Dysert 1
Anstruther East 1
Shire *Forfar* 1
Shire *Hadington* 1
Hadington 1
Shire *Inverness* 1
Inverness 1
Shire *Kinkarden* 1
Kirkubright 1
Shire *Lanerk* 1
Glasgow 1
Shire *Linlithgow* 1
Linlithgow 1
Shires *Nairn* & *Cromarty* 1
Shires *Orkney* & *Zetland* 1
Shire *Peelles* 1
Shire *Perth* 1
Perth 1
Shire *Renfrew* 1
Shire *Ross* 1
Tain 1
Shire *Roxburgh* 1
Shire *Selkirk* 1
Shire *Sterling* 1
Sterling 1
Shire *Sutherland* 1
Shire *Wigtoun* 1
Wigtoun 1
Weik, Dornock, *and* Dingwell 1

Commons in all 553

A List of all the Towns in England and Wales to which the General Post-Office duly send Letters.

Note, Those Places in Italick Letters, are Archbishopricks, and Bishopricks.

ABingdon, *Berks*
  Ailesbury, *Bucks*
Alnwick, *Northumb.*
Andover, *Hantf.*
Arundel, *Suff.*
Ashburton, *Devon.*
Attleborough, *Norf.*
Axminster, *Devon.*
Banbury, *Oxon*
Bangor, *Carmarth.* tho' a
  Bishoprick, is no Post-
  Town.
Barnet, *Hertf.*
Barnstaple, *Devon.*
Barwick, *Northumb.*
Basingstoke, *Hant.*
Bath, Somerfet. is a Bisho-
  prick, with Wells.
Bautry, *Yorkf.*
Beaumaries, *Anglefea*
Beaford, *Bedf.*
Bedfford, *Devon.*
Bolton *Lincolnf.*
Braintree, *Eff.*
Brecknock, *Breccon*
Brentwood, *Eff.*
Bridgwater, *Somerfet.*
Bath, *Somerfet.*
Bromley, *Staff.*
Bromfgrove, *Worcest.*

Buckingham, *Bucks*
Burford, *Oxon*
Cambridge, *Camb.*
Canterbury, Kent
Cardiff, *Glamorg.*
Cardigan, *Cardig.*
Carlisle, Cumb.
Carmarthen, *Carmarth.*
Carnarvon, *Carnarv.*
Caxton, *Cambridg.*
Chelmsford, *Eff.*
Chepstow, *Monm.*
Chester, Chesh.
Chichester, Suff.
Chippenham, *Wilts*
Cirencester, *Gloc.*
Colchester, *Eff.*
Convey, *Carnarvon.*
Coventry, Warwickf. is
  Bishoprick with Lich
  field.
Crookhorn, *Somerfet.*
Derby *Derbyf.*
Darlington *Durh.*
Dartford, *Kent*
Dartmouth, *Devon.*
Daventry, *Northampt.*
Denbigh, *Denbighf.*
Devizes, *Wilts*
Dorchester, *Dorfet.*
                    Dover

Dover, *Kent*
Dunstable, *Bedfordf.*
Durham, *Durh.*
Ely, *Camb.*
Exeter, *Devon.*
Falmouth, *Corn.*
Faringdon, *Berks*
Fowey, *Cornw.*
Glocester, *Gloc.*
Godalmin, *Surry*
Grantham, *Linc.*
Guilford, *Surry*
Harwich, *Eff.*
Haverfordweft, *Pemb.*
Hereford, *Heref.*
Hertford, *Hertf.*
Honiton, *Devon.*
Hounsloe *Midd.*
Hull, *Yorkf.*
Hay, *Brecon*
Huntington, *Huntingt.*
Ipfwich, *Suff.*
Kederminfter, *Worcest.*
Kendal, *Weftmorl.*
Kidwelly, *Carmarth.*
Lancafter, *Lanc.*
Landaff, *Glamorg.* tho' a
   Bifhoprick, is no Post-
   Town.
Lavenham, *Suff.*
Launcefton, *Cornw.*
Lechlade, *Gloc.*
Leicefter, *Leic.*
Leominfter, *Heref.*
Leverpool, *Lanc.*
Lichfield, *Staff.*
Lincoln, *Linc.*
London, *Midd.*
Loughborough, **Leic.**

Ludlow, *Salop*
Lyme, *Dorfet.*
Lynn, *Norf.*
Maidftone, *Kent*
Mancheffer, *Lanc.*
Maningtree, *Eff.*
Monmouth, *Monm.*
Morpeth, *Northumb.*
Namptwich, *Chefh.*
Newark, *Notting.*
Newborough, *Anglefea*
Newcaftle, *Northumb.*
Newmarket, *Suff.*
Northallerton, *Yorkf.*
Northampton, *North.*
Norwich, *Norf.*
Nottingham, *Notting.*
Oakham, *Rutlandfh.*
Oxford, *Oxon*
Padftow, *Cornw.*
Penreth, *Cumberl.*
Peterborough, Northampt.
Petersfield, *Hampf.*
Plymouth, *Devon.*
Pool, *Dorfet.*
Portfmouth, *Hampf.*
Reading, *Berks*
Rochefter, *Kent*
Rumford, *Eff.*
Rye, *Suff.*
Salisbury, *Wilts*
Sandwich, *Kent*
Saxmundham, *Suff.*
Shaftsbury, *Dorfet.*
Sherbourn, *Dorfet.*
Shrewsbury, *Salop*
Somerton, *Somerfet.*
Southampton, *Hampf.*
St. Alban's, *Hertf.*
                  St. *Afaph,*

St. *Afaph, Flintfh.*	Troubridge, *Wilts*
St. David's, *Pemb.*	Truro, *Cornw.*
St. Edmundsbury, *Suff.*	Tuxford, *Notting.*
Stafford, *Staff.*	Waringdon, *Lanc.*
Stamford, *Linc.*	Warwick *Warwic.*
Stanes, *Midd.*	Wells, *Somerfet.*
Stratford. *Warnic.*	Weymouth, *Dorfet.*
Swauzey, *Glamorg.*	Whitchurch, *Hampf.*
Tadcafter, *Yorkf.*	Whitehaven, *Cumb.*
Tamworth, *Staff.*	Winchefter, *Hamp.*
Taunton, *Somerfet.*	Worcefter, *Worceft.*
Thaxted, *Eff.*	Yarmouth, *Norf.*
Thetford, *Norf.*	York, *Yorkf.*
Tocefter, *Northampt.*	

TABLES,

With plain Directions for the Ufe of them.

A perpetual Tide-Table for the Port of London.

The Ufe of the Tide Table.

D's Age.		H.	M.
1	16	3	0
2	17	3	48
3	18	4	36
4	19	5	24
5	20	6	12
6	21	7	0
7	22	7	48
8	23	8	36
9	24	9	24
10	25	10	12
11	26	11	0
12	27	11	48
13	28	12	36
14	29	1	24
15	30	2	12

Enter this Table in the Left hand Columns, with the Day after the Change or New Moon and againft it to the Right hand you have the Time of High Water at *London.* For Example, The 6th of *May* 172 the Moon was two Days ol ard againft it I find it is Hig Water at *London* Bridge at 4 Minutes paft 3 of the Cock.

A perpetual Almanack.

G	F	E	D	C	B	A
Sun.	Mon.	Tuef	Wed.	Thur	Frid.	Sat.
April	Sept.	June	Febr.	Aug.	May	Jan.
July	Dec.	June	March Novem	Aug.	May	Oct.
1	2	3	4	5	6	7
8	9	10	11	12	13	14
15	16	17	18	19	20	21
22	23	24	25	26	27	28
29	30	31	0	0	0	0

1722	G
1723	F
1724	E D
1725	C
1726	B
1727	A
1728	G F
1729	E
1730	D
1731	C
1732	B A
1733	G
1734	F
1735	E
1736	D C
1737	B
1738	A
1739	G
1740	F E
1741	D
1742	C

Ufe of the perpetual Almanack.

First knowing the Dominical Letter for the Year, find it in the uppermoft Line, and underneath it is the Day of the Week ; then look for your Month in the third Line, and the Figure under it fhews that Day of the Week to be fuch a Day of the Month ; and fo proceed to the next, and fo forwards. As for Example ; A is the Dominical Letter for the Year 1721, which I find in the uppermoft Line, and under it *Saturday*, the Day of the Week for the faid Year ; then look for my Month in the third Line, and fuppofe it to be *May*; underneath it I find the Figure 6, that the firft *Saturday* in *May* is the 6th Day of the Month : And if I know what Day of the Month any of the firft Week is, I cannot mifs any other Day.   *Note*, In *Leap-Year* are two dominical Letters ; the firft of which ferves for *January* and *February*, and the other for all the Year after.

Q

A

A Table of Rates for Hackny Coaches in London, *settled by Parliament, by Stat.* 5. *and* 6. Will. *and* Mary.

	s.	d.
FOR ore Day of 12 Hours	10	0
For one Hour	1	6
For every Hour after the firft	1	0
From any of the Inns of Court to any part of St. *James's*, or City of *Weftminfter*, except beyond *Tuttle ftreet*	1	0
From the Inns of Court, or thereabouts, to the *Royal Exchange*	1	0
From any of the Inns of Court to the *Towei, Aldgate, Bifhopfgate*, or thereabouts	1	6

And the fame Rates back again, or to any Place of the like Diftance.

And if any Coachman fhall refufe to go at, or exact more Hire than the Rates hereby limited, he fhall for every fuch Offence forfeit 40 Shillings, if you give Information againft him at the Othce for Licenfing Hackney Coaches, in *Surry ftreet* in the Strand.

What is related about Coachmen, will ferve for Directions in the Affairs of Chairmen : Let the Weather be Wet or dry, or the Time be Day o Night, it's the fame ; get into the Chair, and orde the Chairmen to carry you as you defign ; and i they behave themfelves unmannerly, take the Num ber of the Chair, as you do of a Hackney Coach and complaining at the Office abovementioned, th Comuffioners will correct their Infolence.

A Table of Rates for Watermen, as they are fet fortht the Lord Mayoi and Aldermen of London.

	Oars		Scu
	s.	d.	s.
FRom *London Bridge* to *Limehoufe, New Crane, Shadwell Dock, Bell Wharf, Ratcliff Crofs*	1	0	0

	Oars	Scul:
	s. d.	s. d.
To *Wapping Dock, Wapping* New & Old Stairs, the *Hermitage, Rotherhith* Church Stairs	0 6	0 3
From St. *Olave's* to *Rotherhith* Church Stairs, and *Rotherhith* Stairs	0 6	0 3
From *Billingsgate* and St. *Olave's* to St. *Saviour's* Mill	0 6	0 3
All the Stairs between *London* Bridge and *Westminster*	0 6	0 3
From either side above Bridge to *Lambeth* and *Vauxhall*	1 0	0 6
From *Whitehall* to *Lambeth* & *Vauxhall*	0 6	0 3
From the *Temple, Dorset, Blackfryers* Stairs, and *Paul's Wharf,* to *Lambeth*	0 8	0 4
Over the Water directly betwixt *Vauxhall* and *Limehouse*	0 4	0 2

The Rates of Oars down the River.

	Whole Fair.	Company.
	s. d.	s. d.
From Lond. to Gravesend	4 6	1 0
Greys, or Greenhith	4 0	0 9
Purfleet, or Erith	3 0	0 8
Woolwich	2 6	0 6
Black Wall	2 0	0 4
Greenwich, Deptford	1 6	0 3

The Rates of Oars up the River.

	Whole Fair.	Company.
From London to Battersea, Chelsea, Wandsworth	1 6	0 3
Barn-Elms, Fulham, Putney	2 0	0 4
Chiswick, Hammersmith, Mortlack	2 6	0 6
Brentford, Isleworth, Richmond	3 0	0 6
Twittenham	4 0	0 6
Kingston	5 0	0 9
Hampton Court	6 0	1 0
Hampton Town, Sunbury, Walton	7 0	1 0
Chertley, Weybridge	10 0	1 0
Stains	12 0	1 0
Windsor	24 0	1 0

Rates

Rates for carrying of Goods in the Tilt-Boat between Gravesend *and* London.

	s.	d.
A half Firkin ————————	0	1
Whole Firkin———————————	0	2
Hogshead ————————————	2	0
One hundred Weight of Cheese, Iron, or any heavy Goods ———————————	0	4
Sack of Salt, Corn, an ordinary Chest, Trunk, or Hamper —————————————	0	6
Every single Person in the ordinary Passage—	0	6
The Hire of the whole Tilt Boat————————	22	6

What Waterman takes and demands more than these Rates, lies liable to pay 40 *s.* and suffer half a Year's Imprisonment. And if they refuse to carry any Passenger, or Goods, at these Rates, upon Complaint made to the Lord Mayor and Court of Aldermen, he shall be suspended from his Employment for 12 Months. Farthermore observe That if a Waterman makes you pay more than the abovesaid Rates, get his Name, or else take the Number of his Boat, then go to Watermen's Hall, which is at *Cold Harbour,* near the *Old Swan* in *Thames Street,* and relate your Business to the Clerk, giving him the Number of the Boat, or the Waterman's Name, and he (paying him 6 *d.*) will summon him to attend at the Hall, and answer the Complaint you have against him, where you will be sure to have Justice done you, and the Person punished as the Fault deserve.

Directions for passing & repassing on Water about London.

Observe, that below Bridge, the Water ebbs 7 Hours, and flows 5; above Bridge it ebbs 8 Hours and flows 4, according to the Watermen's Observations; who, in their way of Business, use these Terms: When the Water is at lowest, then it is call'd Flood, if rising, the young or old Flood when at highest, and begins to fall, Ebb-water.

High Water is the Time at *Billingsgate* for all

Passen-

Paſſengers that are bound for *Gravesend, Tilbury, Greys,* and other Places below Bridge ; if bound to *Woolwich, Blackwall, Greenwich,* or *Deptford,* any time till 1, 2 or 3 hours after High Water, will ſerve ; if you are to paſs far up the River, as to *Kingston, Hampton Court, Windsor,* and other Places Weſtward, then take Water at Flood, that is, 4 hours before High Water ; to *Brentford, Putney, Richmond,* or the like Diſtance, 3 hours before High water will do ; and to *Battersea, Chelſea,* or *Mortlack,* at 1 or 2 hours before the Time of High water.

An exact and compleat Liſt of the Flying Coaches, Stage Coaches, Waggons, and Carriers, with the Inns they come to, and Days of the Week they go out of London, collated this preſent Year 1721.

Note, m. ſignifies *Monday,* t. *Tueſday,* w. *Wedneſday,* th. *Thurſday,* f *Friday,* ſ. *Saturday ;* Fl. Co. Flying Coach, Co. Stage Coach, Wag. Waggon, and Car. Carrier.

A*Bingdon,* Co. Sarazen's Head in Breadſtreet, th. ſ. Car. ditto, th.

Aborn, Wag. White Swan, Holbourn hill, t.

Acton, Co. Talbot in the Strand, every day, Summer and Winter.

Ailesbury, Co. Crown in Holbourn, m. w. f. Black Swan ditto, t th. ſ. Car. Saracen's Head, Snow-hill, w. Crown, Warwick Lane, w.

Aldenham, Car. White Horſe, Holbourn Bridge, w.

Amerſham, Car. White Swan, Holbourn Bridge, f.

Ampthill, Car. Roſe and Crown, St. John ſtreet, w.

Andover, Car. King's Arms, Holbourn Bridge, th.

Arundel, Car. Queen's Head, Southwark, m. w.

Aſhbourn, Car. Caſtle, Woodſtreet, m.

Aſhby de la Zouch, Car. Axe in Aldermanbury, m.

Aſhdon, Car. Two Swans without Biſhopſgate, t.

Aſhford, Car. Star, Fiſhſtreet Hill, th.

Aſhwell, Car. Catherine Wheel, Biſhopſgateſtreet, t. Cock in Old ſtreet, t.

Baldock, Car. Red Lion, Redcroſs Street, t. f.

Banbury, Co. Bell, Holbourn, t th. ſ. Car. Ram, Weſt Smithfield, th.   Q 3   Bark-

Barklamſtead, Co. Bell, Mid Holbourn, t. th. ſ.
Barking, Co. Three Nuns, Whitechapel, every Day.
　Py'd Bull ditto, every Day.
Barnet, Co. Croſs Keys, Sr. John Street, twice a day.
Barnſtable, Car. Bull & Mouth within Alderſgate, ſ.
Baſingſtoke, Wag. Bellſavage, Ludgate Hill, ſ.
Bath, Fl. Co. Bell in Bellſavage Yard, Ludgate Hill,
　m. w. ſ. from Ladyday to Michaelmas ; St. Co.
　ditto, m. th. from Michaelmas to Ladyday. Wag.
　King's Arms, Snowhill, m. th. Ditto, Roſe, Hol-
　bourn Bridge, m. th. Co. Checquer Inn, Charing
　Croſs, m. w. ſ. Bell in the Strand, m. w. f. Co.
　Talbot in the Strand, m. th. Wag. White Swan,
　Holbourn Bride, m.
Battle, Car. Spur, Southwark, th.
Beaconsfield, Car. Bell, Warwick Lane, t.
Beardfield, C. Ram's Head, Fenchurch ſtreet, th.
Bedford, Co. Red Lion, Alderſgateſtreet, t. f. Wag.
　ditto, w. Car. Roſe and Crown, St. John ſtreet, w.
Berwick, Co. Black Swan, Holbourn, m.
Billericay, Car. Blue Boar without Aldgate, th.
Bingham, Wag. Black Bull, Mid Holbourn, ſ.
Birmingham, Wag. Caſtle, Alderſgateſtreet, ſ. Car. dit. m
Biſciter, Car. Bull, Holbourn, w. ſ. Oxford Arms,
　Warwick Lane, w.
Biſhop ſtafford, Co. Three Nuns, Whitechapel, t. th. ſ.
　Wag. ditto, m. th. Py'd Bull ditto, m. th.
Blanford, Wag. Sarazen's Head, Friday ſtreet, m.
　Car ditto, ſ. Co. Bell in the Strand,
Bleckingly, Car. Halfmoon, Southwark, w.
Bocking, Wag. Pewter pot, Leadenhall Street, t. th.
　Black Bull ditto, m. w.
Boſton, Co. Horſeſhoe, Goſwell Street, th.
Brainford, Co. White Horſe, Fleetſtreet, every Day
　but *Sundays*.
Braintree, Wag. Pewter pot, Leadenhall Street, f
　Black Bull ditto, f.
Brentwood, Co. Blue Boar without Aldgate, t. th. ſ.
　Car. ditto, w. l.
Brickhill, Car. Saracen's Head, Carter Lane, w.

Bridgnorth, **Co.** Blue Boar, Holbourn, m.

Bristol, **Co.** Checquer, Charing Crofs, m. th. Fl.Co. Bell ditto, m. w. f. St. Co. m. th. Co. Coach and Horfes, Swan Yard in the Strand, m. th. Wag. King's Arms, Snowhill, t. th. Ditto, Rofe by Holbourn Bridge, m. th. Co. Bell in Bellfavage Yard, Ludgate Hill, m. th. Fl.Co. ditto, m.w.f. Wag. White Swan, Holbourn Bridge, m. th.

Bromingham, Car. Caftle & Falcon, Alderfgateftreet, m.

Broxbourn, Car. Catherine Wheel without Alderf- gate, m. w. f.

Buckingham, Car. Saracen's Head, Carter Lane, w.

Buntingford, Car. Catherine Wheel without Bifhopf- gate, t.

Burford, Car. Bell, Friday ftreet, th.

Caerlion, Car. Bell, Friday ftreet, f.

Cadicoat, Car. Horfefhoe, Gofwell Street, f.

Caln, White Swan, Holbourn Bridge, t. th.

Cambridge, Co. Vine, Bifhopfgateftreet, m. w. f. Wag. th. Co. Four Swans ditto, w. f. Wag. Green Dragon ditto, t. w. th. f. Wag. Black Bull ditto, t. w. th. f. Co. Pewter pot in Leadenhal Street, m. th. Wag. ditto, t. th.

Canterbury, Co. Spread Eagle, Gracechurch Street, t. th. f. in Summer, m. th. Winter, Coach and Horfes, Charing Crofs, the fame Days ; Bell in Bellfavage Yard, Ludgate Hill, m. th. Car. Checquer, Charing Crofs, t. th. f. Star by the Monument, the fame Days.

Carlifle, Car. Caftle, Woodftreet, f.

Carmarthen, Car. Bell, Friday Street, f.

Chelmsford, Wag. Py'd Bull, Whitechapel, w. f.

Chefhunt, Co. Vine, Bifhopfgateftreet, every Day. Four Swans ditto, daily. Black Bull ditto, every Day, from Ladyday to Michaelmas, afterwards till Candlemas, t. th. f.

Chefter, Wag. Caftle & Falcon, Alderfgateftreet, m.th.

Chichefter, Car. Queen's Head, Southwark, th. White Hart ditto, m. w. th. f.

Chippenham, Wag. White Swan, Holbourn Bridge, m. w.

Clippingnorton, Co. King's Arms, Leadenhall Street, t. th. f. Bear in Weft Smithfield, t. th.

Cirencefter, Co. Bellfavage, Ludgate Hill, t. th. f. Wag. Sarazen's Head, Great Carter Lane, f.

Clapham, Co. Crofs Keys, Gracechurch ftreet, every day.

Colchefter, Co. Spread Eagle, Gracechurch Street, m. f. Car. ditto, f.

Co umpton, Car. Bear, Bafinghall Street, f.

Conwey, Car. Bell, Friday Street, f.

Coventry, Co. George, Weft Smithfield, th. f. Wag. Caftle in Alderfgateftreet, f.

Coxhall, Car. Spread Eagle, Gracechurch Street, f.

Croyden, Co. Crofs Keys, Gracechurch ftreet, every day.

Culworth, Car. Ra n, Smithfield, th.

Darking, Car. Greyhound, Southwark, w. f.

Dartford, Co. Spur, Southwark, every Day.

Daventry, Car. Rofe and Crown St. John Street, f.

Deal, Co. Bell in Bellfavage Yard, Ludgate hill, m. w. f.

Denbigh, Car. Bloffoms Inn, Laurence Lane, m. f.

Derby, Co. Ram, Weft Smithfield, m. th. Wag. Caftle in St. John Street, m.

Devizes, Car. White Swan, Holbourn Bridge, t. f.

Doncafter, Car. Red Lion, Alderfgateftreet, m.

Dorchefter, Wag. Sarazen's Head, Friday Street, m. Car. ditto, f.

Dover, Co. Bell in Bellfavage Yard, Ludgate hill, m. th. Checquer, Charing Crofs, t f.

Downham, Wag. Green Dragon, Bifhopfgate Street, t. w. th. f. Black Bull ditto, the fame Days.

Drayton, Car. Bloffoms Inn, Laurence Lane, f.

Dulwich, Co. Crown, Southwark, every day in Summer.

Dunftable, Car. Three Cups, Alderfgateftreet, t. f. Co. ditto, th. f.

Durham, Car. White Horfe, Cripplegate, m.

Edgworth, Co. Black Bull, Mid Holbourn, every Day. Bell ditto, every Day but Sunday.

Edinburgh, Co. Black Swan, Holbourn, m. once a Fortnight.

Edmonton, Co. Green Dragon, Bifhopfgateftreet, every day.

Egham

Egham, Co. Black Lion, Water Lane, t. th. s.

Eltham, Crofs Keys, Gracechurch Street, and Saracen's Head in Camomile Street within Bishopsgate, every Day.

Ely, Wag Green Dragon, Bishopsgateftreet, t. w. th. f. Black Bull ditto, t. w. th. f.

Enfield, Co. Vine, Bishopsgateftreet, every Day.

Epping, Wag. Three Nuns, Whitechapel, t. th s.

Efom, Co. Checquer, Charing Crofs, every day. Wag. Bellfavage, Ludgate Hill, every day in Summer.

Evefham, Car. Caftle, Woodftreet, f.

Exeter, Wag. Sarazen's Head, Friday Street, m. Car. ditto, f. Wag. Bell in Breadftreet, comes in on Saturdays, goes out on Mondays.

Falmouth, Wag. Sarazen's Head in Friday Street, m. Car. ditto, f.

Faringdon, Co. Sarazen's Head, Friday Street, w. Car. ditto Bell, f.

Farminghain, Car. Spur, Southwark, w. f.

Fennyftratford, Car. Cock, Alderfgateftreet, th.

Finchly, Co. Swan in St. John Street, every Day.

Froom, Car. White Swan, Holbourn Bridge, f.

Gainsborough, Car. Red Lion, Alderfgateftreet, m.

Glocefter, Co. White Horfe, Fleetftreet, m. w. f. Co. Bell and Tun, Fleetftreet, m. t. f. Car. Saracen's Head, Great Carter Lane, f.

Godalmin, Car. King's Head, Southwark, th.

Gofport, Wag. Bellfavage, Ludgate Hill, th.

Grantham, Co. Red Lion, Alderfgateftreet, m. White Hart in Drury Lane, m. w.

Guilford, Co Talbot, Southwark, t. f.

Halifax, Car. White Horfe, Cripplegate, th.

Hammerfmith, Co. Bell in the Strand, every Day

Hampftead, Co. Greyhound, Holbourn, every Day.

Hampton Court, Co. Checquer, Charing Crofs, every Day.

Harborough, Co Red Lion, Alderfgateftreet, m th Wag ditto, t.

Harrow on the Hill, Co George, Snowhill, every day Wag ditto, m w. f

Harwich, Co Saracen's Head, Aldgate, t. f.

Hendon, Co Bell, Holbourn, every Day

Henly upon Thames, Co White Horfe, Fleetftreet, t. th. f.

Hereford, Crofs Keys, Woodftreet, f. Co. Bolt and Tun, Fleetftreet, Pl Co m w. f in Summer, m th in Winter.

Hertford, Co Four Swans, Bishopfgateftreet, every day Black Bull ditto, t. th f.

Highgate, Co. in Hobourn, every day, and at Alderſgate.

Hitching, Car. White Hart, St. John ſtreet, m. w.

Headeſdon, Co Four Swans, Biſhopſgateſtreet, t. f.   Black Bull
    ditto, t th f.

Holt, Wag. Black Bull in Mid Holbourn, t.

Horſham, Car White Horſe, Southwark, th.

Hill, Co Three Cups, Alderſgateſtreet, m. Car. Red Lion ditto, m.

Hungerford, Wag White Swan, Holbourn Bridge, t.

Huntington, Co Red Lion, Alderſgateſtreet, w f. Wag. ditto, m.

Highworth, Car. George, Holbourn Bridge , Oxford Arms, War-
    wick Lane, m

Ilham, Co Three Nuns, Whitechapel, m. w. f.

Ipſwich, Co Spread Eagle, Gracechurch ſtreet, m. w. f

Kederminſter, Car Saracen's Head, Snowhill, f. Roſe, Smithfield, th.

Kendal, Car Caſtle, Woodſtreet, f

Kingſclere, Wag Bellſavage, Ludgate Hill, th.

Layton buzzard, Car. Saracen's Head, Carter Lane, th.

Leiceſter, Co Ram, Weſt Smithfield, m. th. George ditto, m. th.
    Wag Caſtle, St. John ſtreet, m

Leominſter, Wag Bull and Mouth within Alderſgate, f. White
    Swan, Ho'bourn Bridge, f

Leverpool, Wag. Caſtle, Alderſgateſtreet, th. Car. ditto, f.

Lichfield, Wag Caſtle, Alderſgateſtreet, m. th

Longfield, Co. Saracen's Head, Great Carter Lane, t. f.

Loughborough, Co Ram, Weſt Smithfield, t

Low Layton, Co. Three Nuns, Whitechapel, every Day.

Lynn, Wag Green Dragon, Biſhopſgateſtreet, t. w. th. f. Pewter
    pot, Leadenhall Street, w.

Maidenhead, Co. Black Lion, Water Lane, Fleetſtreet, t. th. f.

Maidſtone, Co. Spread Eagle, Gracechurch ſtreet, t. th. Car.
    King's Head, Southwark, th.

Malden, Co Blue Boar, Whitechapel, w. f.

Malmeſbury, Car White Swan, Holbourn Bridge, w.

Mancheſter, Wag Caſtle, Alderſgateſtreet, th. Car. ditto, f.

Mansfield, Car Swan with two Necks, Lad Lane, f.

Marlborough, Co Angel, the Backſide of St. Clement's, th. Car
    White Swan, Ho'bourn Bridge, w.

Melton moſbray, Car Ram, Weſt Smithfield, m.

Midhurſt, Car. White Hart, Southwark, w

Mountſier, Wag Pewter pot, Leadenhall Street, w.

Newbury, Co Bellſavage, Ludgate Hill, t th f

Newcaſtle under Line, Car Swan with 2 Necks, Lad Lane, m.

Newcaſtle upon Tyne, Co Black Swan, Holbourn, m. Wag. Ca
    ſtle, Alderſgateſtreet, t

Newmarket, Co. Four Swans, Biſhopſgateſtreet, m. th. Green
    Dragon ditto, t f

Newport pannel, Car Bull and Mouth by Alderſgateſtreet, m.

Newton, Wag Saracen's Head, Great Carter Lane, t.

Northampton, Co George, Weſt Smithfield, m. th. Black Bull
    Mid Holbourn, m. th.   *Norwich*

Norwich, **Co.** **Four Swans**, Bishopsgatestreet, w. **Green Dragon** ditto, th. Wag. Black Bull ditto, f.

Nottingham, **Co.** Ram, West Smithfield, m. t.

Ockingham, **Co.** George in Drury Lane, t. th. f.

Odiam, **Car.** King's Arms, Holbourn Bridge, f.

Onger, **Co** Three Nuns, Whitechapel, t. Wag ditto, w. Co Py'd Bull ditto, w. Wag th. Wag Pewter pot, Leadenhall street, w.

Oundle, **Wag.** Castle, St. John Street, th. f.

Oxford, **Fl. Co** White Horse, Fleetstreet, m. w. f in Summer , St. Co. m. th Winter. Fl Co Black Swan, Holbourn, m. w. t. **Co.** Bull, Mid Holbourn, t. th. f. **Car.** Saracen's Head, Great Carter Lane, th.

Peckham, **Co** Gracechurch Street, twice every Day.

Peterborough, **Co.** Horseshoe, Goswell Street, th.

Petworth, **Car.** King's Head, Southwark, w

Plymouth, **Wag** Sarazen's, Friday Street, m **Car** f.

Pool, **Car.** Rose, Holbourn Bridge, th.

Portsmouth, **Wag.** Bellsavage, Ludgate Hill, th. **White Hart**, Southwark, th. Queen's Head ditto, m.

Preston, **Car.** Castle, Woodstreet, f.

Puckeridge, **Car.** Swan without Bishopsgate, f.

Pulborough, **Car.** Queen's Head, Southwark, f.

Ramsbury, **Car.** White Swan, Holbourn Bridge, th.

Reading, **Co** White Horse, Fleetstreet, t. th. f. Coach and Horses, Swan Yard against Somerset House, m. w. f. Bolt and Tun, Fleet-street, every day.

Redbourn, **Car.** Windmill, St John Street, w.

Richmond, **Car** White Horse, Cripplegate, m.

Rochester, **Co.** Star, Fishstreet Hill, w. t.

Rotheram, **Car.** Axe in Aldermanbury, f.

Royston, **Wag.** Vine, Bishopsgatestreet, f.

Rumford, **Co** Pewter pot, Leadenhall Street, every Day.

Rye, **Co** Bell in Bellsavage Yard, Ludgate Hill, m. w. f.

Rygate, **Co.** Catherine Wheel, Southwark, w **Car.** Greyhound ditto f.

Saffron-Walden, Vine, Bishopsgatestreet, th.

Salisbury, **Co.** Angel on the Backside of St. Clement's, m. w. f. **Car.** King's Arms, Holbourn Bridge, f.

Sevenoke, **Car.** Spur, Southwark, t f.

Sherbourn, **Wag** Sarazen's Head, Breadstreet, m.

Shipton, **Car.** Rose, West Smithfield, th.

Shrewsbury, **Wag.** Castle, Aldersgatestreet, th.

Southampton, **Co.** Swan, Holbourn Bridge, m. w. f.

Spalding, **Co** Horseshoe, Goswell Street, th.

Stafford, **Car** Castle and Falcon, Aldersgatestreet, m.

Stamford, *Grantham*, and *Newark*, **Car.** Bell, Woodstreet, m.

Stanmoor, **Co** Black Bull, Mid Holbourn, t. f.

Stanstead, **Wag.** Pewter pot, Leadenhall Street, t. th.

Stony-Stratford, **Wag.** Castle, St. John Street, t. f.

Stow, **Wag** Castle, Aldersgatestreet, t.

Stroudwater, **Car.** Bell, Friday Street, f.

St. Al-

St. Albans, Co. Bell, Alderfgateftreet, t. th. f. Car. ditto, m. w.
St. Afaph, Car Caftle and Falcon, Alderfgateftreet, m. th.
St. Edmundsbury, Co Vine, Bifhopfgateftreet, m t. Four Swan
   ditto w. Green Dragon ditto, m t.
St. Ives, Car. Bell, Warwick Lane, m f. Dolphin, Bifhopfgateftr. t
St. Neets, Car Three Cups Alderfgateftreet, m.
Swasham, Wag Black Bull, Mid Holbourn, m. th.
Swindon, Wag White Swan, Holbourn Bridge, w.
Tamworth, Wag Caftle, St. John Street, m.
Taunton, Wag Sarazen's Head Breadftreet, m.
Theobalds, Co. Black Bull, Bifhopfgateftreet, t th. f. from Michael
   mas to Candlemas, afterwards every Day to Michaelmas again.
Tocefter, Car Rofe and Crown, St John Street, f.
Tunbridge, Co Bell, Bellfavage Yard, Ludgate Hill, from Michael
   mas to Decem m w f from thence to Candlemas, m. f. to th
   Wells every Day in Summer. Checquer, Charing Crofs, every day
Turbury, Wag. White Swan, Holbourn Bridge, t
Twittinham, Co. White Horfe, Fleetftreet, every day but Sunda
Uppingham, Co Ram, Weft Smithfield, th.
Utoxeter, Wag. Caftle, St John Street, m.
Uxbridge, Car. Bell, Warwick Lane, t.
Wakefield, Co Black Swan, Holbourn, m w.
Waltham Abby, Co Three Nuns without Bifhopfgate, t. w. f.
Walfingham, Wag Black Bull, Mid Holbourn, t.
Walthamftow, Co. Three Nuns, Whitechapel, every Day. Py
   Bull ditto, every Day.
Walton, Car. Vine without Bifhopfgate, th.
Hare, Co. Dolphin without Bifhopfgate, t th f. Car. ditto.
Harington, Wag. Caftle, Alderfgateftreet, th. Car f.
Warwick, Wag Saracen's Head, Snowhill, f Bell, Smithfield th
Harringbury, Wag. George, Southw. m.w.f. in Summer, t. t Winte
Watford, Co Black Bull, Mid Holbourn, every Day in Summer
   Bell ditto.
Welford, Wag Caftle, St John Street, m f.
Wellingborough, Co. Ram, Weft Smithfield, t.
Wells, Car Caftle, Woodftreet, f.
Wickham, Wag. Bellfavage, Ludgate Hill, th.
Winchefter, Co. Angel, Backfide St. Clement's, t. Car. Rofe, Hol
   bourn Bridge, m th.
Windfor, Co Bellfavage, Ludgate Hill, every Day. White Horf
   Fleetftreet, every Day. Cnecquer, Charing Crofs, every Day.
Wifbich Wag Green Dragon, Bifhopfgateftreet, t w. th. f. Blac
   Bull ditto, t w. th f.
Witham, Wag Pewter pot, Leadenhall Street, m. w.
Worcefter, Fl Co. Blue Boar, High Holbourn, m w. f. in Summer
   m. th. in Winter. Wag. & Car. Caftle and Bell, Woodftreet,
Wotton baffet, Wag. White Swan, Holbourn Bridge, w.
Yarmouth, Co Four Swans, Bifhopfgateftreet, w.f. Green Drago
   ditto, th. f.
York, Co. Black Swan, Holbourn, t th. f Car. Bear, Bafinghall lane,

F I N I S.

9 781140 858737